The film music of Malcolm Arnold

Compiled by Alan Poulton and David Dunstan

With contributions from Malcolm Arnold, Mervyn Cooke, James Cox, David Huckvale, John Huntley, James Brooks Kuykendall, Philip Lane, Craig Lysy, Alan Poulton, Christopher Ritchie and Jan G Swynnoe

Foreword by Neil Brand

Malcolm Arnold Society

The Film Music of Malcolm Arnold

Compiled by Alan Poulton and David Dunstan

Published by The Malcolm Arnold Society,
15 Birch Close, Sonning Common, Reading, RG4 9LE, UK
E-mail: david@malcolmarnoldsociety.co.uk
Website: www. malcolmarnoldsociety.co.uk

ISBN: 9798781218080

Cover image by Gerd Altmann from Pixabay

Contents

Foreword by Neil Brand

When we cast our minds back to the sound of British Cinema in the late 1940s and 1950s, the chances are that what we are hearing are the ideas and textures of Malcolm Arnold's music.

He seems to embody an attitude, if not an idiom, of post-war Britain – witty, tuneful, soulful when necessary, and able to turn from noble heroism to broad slapstick in the blink of an eye. Whilst able to sum up human suffering and endeavour with his work with David Lean or Carol Reed, he could equally provide the devilish machinations of the St Trinian's girls for Launder and Gilliat and conjure up a childish fantasy around a murderer on the run for Bryan Forbes in *Whistle Down the Wind*. In a vast number of partly-forgotten dramas and thrillers of the 1950s and 1960s he never failed to raise the quality of the film with the beautifully contextualised and deftly composed addition of his scores.

That he was capable of such a broad range of styles and subjects whilst creating a prodigious output of concert works, commissions, ballets and symphonies is remarkable; that it took its toll on him as a man is to be expected. His music very much embodies himself – outwardly affable, mischievous and warm, but with depths of abysmal self-doubt, suffering and deep remorse.

Arnold was more complex than anybody at the time entirely understood, and his mood swings and addictions were terrible. He should have been vastly more lauded than he was, but he was never one to compromise with establishments, national or musical, and he paid the price. And all the heights of his elation and depths of his dreadful despair are right there in his music – above all in his film scores.

With this book we come closer than ever before to a definitive overview of all Malcolm's work in cinema, a field which he influenced in so many ways and which, for me, produced his greatest work. His personality is never far away from these pages, whether through interviews and reminiscences of his own and those he worked with, or the authors' meticulous sharing of cues, musical decisions and well-informed notes.

And as we trace here his vast output from the earliest scores to his final works of the late-1960s, including his documentaries, TV works and personal appearances, we get a true picture of this most multi-faceted of British artists, and probably the one he would be most happy for us to have.

Neil Brand
7 December 2021

An introduction to the feature films

Malcolm Arnold wrote the music for 70 feature films between 1948 and 1969 averaging a steady three films a year. He was easily the most prolific of post-war British composers, not only in films but in the concert hall as well. Arnold's astonishing creativity covered not only films but radio, television, ballet, theatre, concert and stage work as well as arrangements of music by other composers. The downside to all this was virtual burnout by the end of the 1970s, both physically and mentally. The 1980s provided a temporary return but in 1991 Arnold retired from composition at the age of seventy.

Somehow one associates Arnold with scoring comedies and war films. However out of seventy feature films Arnold scored, only eight are war films in the true sense and about twelve could be described as comedies. Although several of the films originated in Hollywood, Arnold never worked there. Most of his writing would appear to have been done wherever he was living at the time, whether Richmond in Surrey or St Merryn in Cornwall. His working method was to write straight on to manuscript paper in ink and very often into the early hours. A typical example of this was the 'Sunset' cue from his score to *The Bridge on the River Kwai* which was written at around four in the morning and took just twenty minutes of inspiration. There was none of the hi-tech equipment that today is seen as an essential part of a composer's workplace. Arnold, like many an author, worked chronologically from the main to the end titles using the natural development and structure of the film to indicate the right road to take.

While many of Arnold's contemporaries also worked in films with varying degrees of success, he had distinct advantages over them. First, he already loved the world of film from childhood. He had also been a trumpeter with the London Philharmonic Orchestra during much of the 1940s and could see what worked and what did not in the work of other composers. He possessed a great dramatic sense, essential for any composer working in the medium of film, and above all he had a supreme natural gift for melody and therefore had no problem in communicating with any audience.

The most famous and celebrated of Arnold's film scores was the one for David Lean's *The Bridge on the River Kwai* which won Arnold the Oscar for Best Score in 1957. The irony here is that most people who have seen the film, if they were asked about the music, would think of 'Colonel Bogey', which Arnold did not write. However, there is far more to the score than just 'Colonel Bogey', as a close examination of the film soundtrack would reveal. Arnold's score is a veritable feast of good things in its 34 minutes and forms a major constituent of what is arguably David Lean's greatest film.

Of the other 69 films the next one to really stand out on its own is the magical and very melodic score that he wrote for *The Inn of the Sixth Happiness*. Perhaps the American Academy just could not bring themselves to nominate Arnold, a British composer, for a second year running. A nomination would have been no more than he deserved. His music is the very soul of the film. To some extent Arnold suffered from coming along before the introduction of hi-fi stereo soundtrack LPs. If he had worked in Hollywood, his scores would have had a better chance of showcased promotion by studios and record companies. This was not to be, for the world of Hollywood as a work place never appealed to Arnold's nature. During the 1950s in Britain work for him was plentiful. The fully booked studios supplied a steady stream of product.

The films of the 1950s that Arnold worked on were a mixed bunch. One cannot blame him for that. Much depended on being available at just the right moment when a producer or director needed a composer for their latest film. In this way, the process of getting new film commissions was very much hit and miss. If Arnold did a good job for one particular director then it was likely that he would get the chance to do the score for that same director's next picture. Hence certain names crop up more than once in Arnold's filmography such as Terence Fisher (four films), Frank Launder (four films), Cyril Frankel (three films), Mark Robson (three films) and David Lean (three films).

During the late 1950s and early 1960s Arnold benefited from working on several 20th Century Fox productions where the cast, stars and budget were on a larger scale, with more variety for scoring, such as *Island in the Sun* (West Indies), *The Roots of Heaven* (Africa), *The Inspector* (Europe), *The Lion* (Africa) and *Nine Hours to Rama* (India). Yet on many an occasion when a particular subject appealed to him on a personal level, such as *Whistle Down the Wind*, Arnold found that extra helping of inspiration.

Arnold's scoring was always so individual. Like all the great composers who have worked in the medium of film he never compromised himself. His own personal and highly identifiable style imprinted itself on every film he worked on. His music seemed ready-made for the British films of the 1950s, the busiest decade in a long career of composition. It sounded an integral part of not just the films but the very life and times of the 1950s. Listen even to one of his symphonies from these years and you can almost imagine it as part of some British film of the day. Arnold's music seemed born to be a vital part of British post-war cinema.

During the 1960s the product became more international and the number of films that he worked on became less. Finally in 1969, sensing the downward spiral of the British film industry, he bade farewell promising never to return. His absence was cinema's loss and I think maybe something in Arnold's life was lost as well. His legacy in film-scoring terms is large and one that he could be rightly proud of. Maybe in years to come the true value of his work on the sound stages of Shepperton and Pinewood will be fully appreciated. His Oscar-winning score for *The Bridge on the River Kwai*, written in under two weeks, was a towering achievement at a time when British composers were not expected to break into the stronghold of the Hollywood community. Sir Malcolm Arnold is one of the very best British composers ever to work in the medium of film and his contribution from 1948 to 1969 was a major factor in the development of British cinema in the post-war years.

Christopher Ritchie

from 'Malcolm Arnold: A 75th birthday tribute' in 'Music from the Movies' Nos. 15 & 17 (1997)

The music notes in the film descriptions are also by Christopher Ritchie from the same source

Muir Mathieson talks to Malcolm Arnold

Muir Mathieson (MM): In this programme 'Music from the Films' coming to you from the studios of the British Broadcasting Corporation in London, this is Muir Mathieson speaking and my guest today is one of our most brilliant young composers, Malcolm Arnold. In spite of his enormous output Malcolm is not long-haired – but rather large, benign and beaming, and has just taken time off lately from writing music to learn to drive a car – much to the public danger! His works so far include two symphonies, a string quartet, an overture and six orchestral suites, seven sonatas and five concertos, the Coronation Ballet 'Homage to the Queen' and, of course, music for the films! Well, Malcolm, how do you reconcile those two kinds of music?

Malcolm Arnold (MA): That's a tough question to start off with. Let me see, now in the first place I don't really believe they need reconciling. They're not two different sorts of thing. You just write what you think is appropriate and hope the director likes it! You wouldn't in any case write the same sort of music for a singer as you would for a violinist, nor would you write the same sort of music for films as for ballet, it's as simple as that, I think.

MM: Let's hear how you actually tackle a film score.

MA: Well, I'm glad to say that in this country, because of your work in this field, a composer is given a great deal of freedom by the film makers. A lot of confidence is put in us and we are not just asked to do this or that to order but allowed to interpret a scene as we think best.

MM: Interpret or *counterpoint* it with a different sort of theme.

MA: Or that, of course. You don't just have to turn out synthetic emotion according to a set of rules.

MM: You've heard, of course, the story of the studio which had a Music Director's room, lined with little cubby holes marked love music, hurry music, scurry music, storm music and so on, with a composer inside each one?

MA: Yes. Well, thank goodness we don't have to work like that – film music is actually composed, not laid on to a recipe. There's another point. People often ask how one is able to work in such a restricted medium, but in fact I find there is less restriction in writing for films than there is, for instance, in writing for the ballet.

MM: Now that's an interesting statement, Malcolm. Would you like to amplify it?

MA: Well, in writing for the ballet you're confined to an almost continuous rhythmic pattern because of the needs of the dancers, whereas in films there is complete freedom of rhythm.

MM: And how do you feel about what is commonly called the time bogey – the necessity of making each bit of music fit into just 15 seconds or 50 seconds or whatever is called for by the length of the scene?

MA: Well, you know I find that stimulating, because you are given a form which you can interpret always different and which stimulates you to find exactly the right musical form to illustrate it with.

MM: It's as though instead of always buying ordinary oblong postcards to send to your friends you could choose round ones or square or triangular ones.

MA: Yes, that's it. It's a sort of artistic challenge.

MM: Can you give us a specific instance of what you mean by this artistic challenge?

MA: Well, what about the opening scene of the 'Sound Barrier'?

MM: Oh yes, that got an Oscar, didn't it, not just for the actual music score but for the entire sound track. The opening sequence was a very striking one – what was your problem there?

MA: Well, it is a very good example of one of the basic problems of music in films: how to combine the use of music with the use of sound effect.

MM: How did that all work out?

MA: The director here gave the general idea – the opening chimes of Big Ben, part of the trademark, so to speak, then the lonely crying of seagulls, the noise of an approaching plane, the exuberance in the pilot's mind as he makes his Spitfire dance in the sky, the onlooker playing his mouth organ on the cliff top, and finally, as the pilot musters his plane in a great dive, the grandiose idea of the triumph of man over nature. In this picture it became clear that sound effects and music ought not to come together but to blend into each other. When people watch this scene they are not conscious of where the music and the sound effects begin and end.

Excerpt from 'The Sound Barrier'

MM: That's certainly an interesting example of the use of sounds and music. But let's take something quite different. Broad comedy, for instance like the film 'You Know What Sailors Are'.

MA: Oh yes, that gave me a wonderful opportunity to fit in the national anthem of Agraria.

MM: By the way, Malcolm, where *is* Agraria?

MA: It's where they play my national anthem.

MM: Well, I shall avoid it this summer. I remember the tune. But what about that exotic dance in the Sultan's Palace? I know you've never quite forgiven the censor for taking out your best bit of music, well, not so much the music but the bit of film that went with it – but how did you think up all that nonsense?

MA: There was a wonderful troupe of girl dancers as English as could be but all dressed up as Sultan's daughters who did a very colourful harem dance. This called for something half Eastern, half Western, and when I got it finished it turned out to be a mixture of an Oriental snake dance and a rumba.

Excerpt from 'You Know What Sailors Are'

MA: I quite agree, that's enough of that nonsense.

MM: What about the question of speed? Don't you sometimes find that a difficulty? When there is a highly topical film, for instance, like the film of the Queen's New Zealand tour. I know you only had one day and what remained of the night after you and I had finished dinner to write the music for that! How on earth did you manage? What would have happened if the inspiration had not come in time or had dried up before you'd finished the last sequence?

MA: One can only keep one's fingers crossed – as a matter of fact, I usually find that when the occasion presents itself the idea comes too, almost by reflex actions, and in this case the film itself was a natural source of inspiration. Of course, it would probably have come out better if I had had two days instead of one to do it in – but I don't know, one always thinks it could have been better, but actually having so little time is a stimulus in itself.

MM: I liked the march from that score.

Excerpt from 'Queen's Tour'

MA: Of course, there was a totally different problem in 'Hobson's Choice'.

MM: I know, it was a totally different picture, but expounded your problem

Malcolm Arnold (left) and Muir Mathieson (right) with the leader of the orchestra take a break while recording the soundtrack. Photo from the Mathieson archive at the British Library with thanks to the Curator, Sandra Tuppen.

without getting too highbrow about it.

MA: That film, as you know, was based on an old play about the North of England, and it had Charles Laughton, John Mills and Brenda de Banzie in it with David Lean directing. The problem there was to recreate the atmosphere of Victorian music halls and ballads within the framework of a film score.

MM: How did you tackle that one?

MA: Well, instead of looking just for themes and motives I went bald-headed for the atmosphere. I wrote a sort of old-time soft shoe dance as a music hall overture and a Victorian ballad for the love scene.

MM: And then when those were safely done, you built the score around them.

MA: That's right. All the scenes with music seemed to fit together without any difficulty then.

MM: Let's have the first one – the old time soft shoe dance.

MA: The Victorian music hall idea is first stated in the opening title music like this – before old Hobson the boot maker comes home tipsy.

Excerpt from 'Hobson's Choice'

MM: And then there was the love scene between Maggie and the boot hand Will, which takes place in the park on a Sunday morning. Tell us how you planned the music there, Malcolm.

MA: Well, it starts with the ballad tune in polka time, as though it were played by a military band in the park. Then you can hear it following Maggie as she walks down the steps, as she meets Will Mossop and as other people see them together. At the bottom of the park steps I made the tune into a real sentimental Victorian ballad and used a purely orchestral background for the rest of the scene.

Excerpt from 'Hobson's Choice'

MM: And then finally the whole thing is summed up at the end of the film where the two main tunes – the ballad and the soft shoe dance – come together in a sort of reconciliation.

MA: There was another interesting point, Muir, in that final sequence, remember, about the special way dialogue can be used over music in a film score.

MM: Yes, I remember, it was used just like recitative in an opera with the music commenting and colouring between the words but leaving the words themselves free to make their own impact.

Excerpt from 'Hobson's Choice'

MM: Well, thank you very much, Malcolm.

MA: Thank *you*, Muir.

MM: Your guest in today's 'Music from the Films' was Malcolm Arnold, and you have heard extracts from the sound track of the 'Queen's Tour' – Associated British Pathe, 'You Know What Sailors Are' – Rank Organisation, and 'The Sound Barrier' and 'Hobson's Choice' – British Lion. This is Muir Mathieson saying goodbye to you from the studios of the British Broadcasting Corporation in London, England.

Recorded 21 May 1954

published with the kind permission of the Mathieson family and BBC Written Archives Caversham

Writing music for films

In 1961, Malcolm Arnold wrote and presented two half-hour programmes about Film Music for the BBC's long-defunct Transcription Service, which primarily existed to supply programmes on tape direct to overseas radio stations,. He also conducted the London Symphony Orchestra in various specially-recorded excerpts. The following is a transcript of his commentary. It has been slightly edited for the sake of continuity.

Music has always played an important part in the theatre, from Greek Drama to the present day, so it always surprises me that musicians should have come into the cinema purely by chance. They were introduced first of all only to drown out the projector, and a pianist was engaged to play any music, whether it was in the mood of the film or not. The only stipulation was that it had to be loud. The pianists who were engaged to perform this awful task gradually began to introduce music that would fit the mood – and sometimes even the action – of the film they were accompanying. This added such a great deal to the film that it became general practice to have orchestras playing suitable music, even when the projector had been silenced. Very little of this music was specially composed for the purpose; it consisted mostly of selections from the well-known classics.

The first film music

The first music specially composed by a reputable composer for film was for *The Assassination of the Duke of Guise*. This was a French film, with music composed by Saint-Saëns for the Paris performance in 1908. It is written for a small body of strings, five wind instruments, piano and harmonium. Its general form, springing from the incidental music to the old melodrama, is still in use today. The music to the final scene, after the assassination of the Duke, begins with the main theme from the film, leading to a tender section when a crucifix is placed on the body of the Duke.

Saint-Saëns was commissioned to write film music in 1908, but it was not until sound films came along that specially-composed music became the rule and not the exception. The first serious composer in Britain to write for

The Assassination of the Duke of Guise (1908) had music composed by Saint-Saëns

the film was Arthur Bliss, and in 1935 he composed some of his finest music for the film *Things to Come*. A year before that, Prokofiev had written the music for a Russian film called *Lieutenant Kijé*. I think the Russians were more conscious of the value of good music in films: there were a few specially-composed scores for some of the silent film classics, and it was no exceptional thing when Prokofiev composed this score in 1934, as against when Arthur Bliss composed his in England in 1935.

It is an interesting point that Russian serious composers nowadays are inclined to compose less for the cinema than their Western counterparts. This is because of the way composers are paid in Russia. Their system is unique, and it makes it just as lucrative to compose for the opera, ballet or concert hall as it is for the cinema. In Britain, many serious composers rely on film commissions to subsidise their more serious work, which brings in next to nothing. *Lieutenant Kijé* inspired Prokofiev to write some of his most delightful and characteristic music; and incidentally it was used for a more recent film *The Horse's Mouth*, with Alec Guinness.

In America it is exceptional for serious composers to write for films. This is partly because Hollywood film companies like to have their composers on contract for several years, giving them exclusive rights over their services. This means that a serious composer would have to live in California, and so might he forgotten by his own musical circle. The most notable exception to this rule is Aaron Copland, who I think is the most American of American composers. All his distinguished film scores bring out the most characteristic Copland music, such as the score he wrote in 1948 for the John Steinbeck film *The Red Pony*.

In my opinion, though, the finest music ever written for films is by William Walton. His lyrical and heroic qualities can he heard at their best in the music he wrote for the Shakespeare productions of Laurence Olivier, in particular, *Henry the Fifth*.

For the flavour of film music today, I would mention a piece of my own: the overture specially written for the New York performance of the Darryl Zanuck production *Roots of Heaven*, which despite its star-studded cast was mainly about elephants. When the film unit went to East Africa, they recorded a number of traditional songs. One of them, an elephant herder's song, I used as the main theme of the film. A fragment of this theme is played by the trumpets at the very beginning of the overture, and at the end it is played in full. It is an overture in the sense of the old operatic overture and features all the themes heard in the film.

It is important to avoid the obvious and hackneyed. The Wait Disney production *Greyfriars Bobby* is the true story of a dog and is set in Scotland. You might expect to hear bagpipes and folk tunes; but Francis Chagrin managed to evoke the Scottish flavour with great charm and simplicity, again without sacrificing his own personal style. By way of contrast, consider a very different type of music indeed, that for the Hammer production of *The Curse of the Werewolf*. As one would expect, the music conjures up an atmosphere of horror. The composer Benjamin Frankel used the twelve-note technique in this score, at times very strictly, more freely at others.

To demonstrate the way in which a composer writing for a film changes the mood of his music to fit the actual picture, let me describe the music I wrote for the Rank production *No Love for Johnnie*. It begins on a sunny summer's day on the Serpentine in Hyde Park,

The Red Pony (1949): Aaron Copland was one of the few serious American composers to write film music

where the central figure, a Member of Parliament, and a girl he has recently met are boating. Then this dissolves back to the girl's flat, which, as you might have guessed, develops into an extremely passionate love scene. The Member of Parliament, Johnnie, should be in the House of Commons to put a question on which a great deal depends, and the tension caused by his refusal to leave the girl, and the time slipping on to his question time, is created by the time-worn convention of cutting from the girl's bedroom to the House of Commons and back. On the first cut to the House of Commons the music is meant to be ironically grand, but on all the subsequent cuts to the House of Commons the music attempts to create the impression of time running out. The section ends in the girl's flat, in a more tranquil mood – though with some doubts present – when Johnnic has asked the girl to marry him, I am glad to say.

Commercial pressures

Seeing films being made, it always surprises me that they are ever finished; there are so many commercial pressures and conflicting opinions that a solution often seems impossible. This applies very much to the music. So many attempts are made to fit pop theme songs into film scores, that they have reached a lower standard than at almost any time in the past. Even the choice of pop tunes is dominated by commercial pressures. A tune is sometimes forced into a film merely because one publisher offers a larger percentage of publishing profits to the film company than another. Needless to say, these very bad quality tunes never become popular, and the scores do not help the films either. Although in America this phase has reached its peak and is dying, in England it is at its height. and will remain so for some time yet.

Of course, it is an ideal thing if a theme from a film becomes a popular success in its own right. But it is only likely to do so if used with skill and subtlety as part of a score that helps to tell the story the film maker is trying to tell. In so many films it is not possible to use a theme which is likely to become popular. The range of emotions and ideas acceptable to the pop music public are far too limited. The ridiculous situation can arise when a film producer asks a composer to write a pop theme to be used in a score for a Tennessee Williams film! This strange contradiction is one of the major problems for film composers today all over the world. It is only very rarely you get a satisfactory solution.

When a composer sees a film for the first time it is in a fairly rough stage, and many of the sound effects are missing. These are recorded later, usually without reference to the composer, so that when the film is completed, quite often music and sound effects are both trying to create the same atmosphere, and cancel each other out. A composer for films thinks of the score as a complete whole. He thinks of its effect over the entire length of the picture, and not merely in so many sections. Unless you are lucky enough to work with a director who has a very sensitive ear, sound effects are introduced quite haphazardly into music sections, without any overall conception of the sound throughout the film. And that of course is disastrous for the music score.

The problem of the loudness or softness of the music is one of the greatest importance; and I do not mean just preventing the music from drowning the dialogue. The composer is often surprised to find that a section where the whole dramatic point is made by a long *diminuendo* has been turned into *crescendo* during the dubbing – or re-recording, as it is known in America. Most of the big names among American film composers have their own music editor, whose job is to see that this sort of thing does not happen.

Henry V (1944): Malcolm Arnold rates William Walton's film music highly

More time and money are spent on recording film music in America than anywhere else in the world. But this does not lead to ideal conditions for film composers in America. They are usually full-time contract employees of a film studio, not allowed to do any work other than film work. It is better for the composer to be engaged to compose for a film on a freelance basis so that he can write other types of music. The stimulating effect of working continuously in different media should help him to evolve a fresh language from the sum total of his experience. It seems to me that this is the only way for a composer who believes he has something to say to survive, and not, as so many people do, try to use two separate languages, one for concert music (the respectable language) and one for films (the commercial one). It is high time this quite artificial attitude towards serious and popular music disappeared. I think there are some scores around which show that there are composers writing in a personal style which is also good film music.

Malcolm Arnold
BBC Transcription Service, 1961

Malcolm Arnold recalls his career in film music

I became involved in film-scoring through John Swain who was a very, very close friend. Dear John got me *Avalanche Patrol*, a film made by one man – a photographer who did his own editing. There's music all the way through – no dialogue. All it used to say on the posters was 'A Film by Jack Swain and Malcolm Arnold'. I thought I was made. I used to take my whole family and in-laws to see this film. It played to packed houses and has to be about the only documentary that made money apart from Auden's *Night Mail*.

The technique of writing film music is absolutely easy. Something like doing a jigsaw puzzle. But you won't know how to conduct it. All the best film composers conduct their own music.

Making The Bridge on the River Kwai. Photo: BFI

Working with David Lean

The Sound Barrier was the first one I wrote with David Lean. One thing about David Lean was that he was very particular about sound. I once said to him, "You're a frustrated musician," and he said, "Yes, I am. I should much rather have done music." The sound department got an Oscar – just the sound department – and I said, "Well, that includes me." David Lean said, "Well, yes, of course." I said, "Well, where's the Oscar go – your studio?" "No, it stays in the sound department in Shepperton." As far as I know, it's still there. I did a rhapsody and conducted it with the Royal Philharmonic in the Festival Hall and I put on the back, for want of space, 'a grand, grand overture by Arnold'.

While *The Bridge on the River Kwai* was a big-budget picture, there was no more time than the average film. We required ten days for the complete scoring. (It has a counter-melody, which was called 'Brothers All' and became a very great hit in Europe and America and made a considerable amount of money for Columbia Pictures Music Corporation – not me, I'm sorry to say.) David Lean said, "I don't care a damn what you're going to use. I used Colonel Bogey because it was on a disc and they whistled with it." I said, "Yes, but the picture changes; you've got to give me a version where the picture's the same, the right footsteps and things." So the footsteps were added by 16 members of the Coldstream Guards with one piccolo, a friend of mine called Richard Adeney. He said, "What the hell am I doing up here playing this silly tune?" I said, "Look. You're making money and the whole thing's driving me mad. I shall stop making films after this." And after *The Bridge on the River Kwai* I was asked to do every bloody war film that was written! I turned down far more than I ever made. I got to the stage where I wouldn't read all the scripts.

I turned *Lawrence of Arabia* down. Sir William Walton was asked to do a march and my friend Adam Khachaturian was asked to do the Arabian music. We saw it in a place in Soho and I said to Sir William, "No music, unless you're going to write it." He said, "What can I do for a lot of camels going in the sand?" I suggested, "You have silence except for the sound of camels hooves." He then confessed, "Well, but I don't know as much about the technique of scoring." But Khachaturian wasn't allowed to do it by the Soviet government at the time and he actually didn't want to come out of the country anyway. We didn't do *Lawrence of Arabia*. Maurice Jarre did and Maurice Jarre did every David Lean film until he died. But he only made one every twelve years!

Of course, the oldest joke in history is that they used to call me 'Master of the Lean's music' because I did three: *The Sound Barrier*, *Hobson's Choice* and *Bridge on the River Kwai*. I was very privileged to work with David Lean – very, very privileged indeed.

Heroes of Telemark

A war film I didn't turn down was *The Heroes of Telemark* for Tony Mann. He was strange. He was very American and an inveterate gambler. The last time I saw him he came to my club to thank me for the score and I said, "Well, I've been very well paid and I like you, Tony." I offered to take him for a meal at the White Elephant Club but he said, "I won't stay long, because I've just gotta have a gamble." I said, "Well, you work for your money," and he went up into the casino room. I didn't wait for him. I don't like to gamble. He died a day after.

The Sleeping Tiger

I worked with Joseph Losey on *The Sleeping Tiger* in 1954 – one of the greatest directors of the world cinema. Our introduction was unusual. He said, "I can't be seen in daytime." I said, "Why not? Am I so disreputable?" "No, because I'm an un-American." I asked, "That means you can't ever return to the United States?" and he said "I don't particularly want to." We had to meet at the dead of night to record, which made it very difficult to get my usual musicians at that time, but they would always do anything for me. For the jazz, I got my favourite jazz trumpeter Kenny Baker and we went on until one in the morning in the studios at Beaconsfield. Everything was locked up and there was red hot jazz coming out. I said "Is this all right, Joe?" He said "I'm enjoying it. I'm recording the whole lot." I said, "You're paying these men, you're paying me, we're all enjoying it, so we're not complaining, feeling no pain at all."

I conducted the music for *Blind Date* five years later and I introduced a young composer to Joe Losey – a very shy young man of seventeen called Richard Rodney Bennett. I said, "This is the man to do that film. I would do it, but he'll do it far better." And he did it with a string quartet, a bass guitar, Roy Preiro on the bass trumpet, a good jazz player – and it was brilliant. It was hell to fit because he had no idea of fitting, but *Blind Date* is a good score.

Whistle Down the Wind

My own favourite is *Whistle Down the Wind*. I think it's a very good one. Do you know who did the whistling? Sir Richard Attenborough, who produced it. He came to the Decca Studios off Edgware Road and said, "I've only come to listen. I'm not going to criticise." I said, "I know you're not, but you're going to whistle and you're going to get the same as my musicians." He sat, very embarrassed, and said, "You'll have to give me a lead," and I gave him a lead.

In *Whistle Down the Wind*, when Hayley Mills sees those men dancing, I brought in 'We Three Kings of Orient are' with the tiny orchestra, because that is what they were actually singing. It was Hayley Mills singing and I said, "Now take her voice out and the children, and I will do a very nice accompaniment." I pointed it; it was difficult to do but I thought it was worthwhile.

The Key

The best score I ever wrote was *The Key*, a film by Sir Carol Reed, who wanted it to be a love story. I wrote a jolly good tune for that but the film was cut around. It's very sad, it had two endings, one for the American market, one for Europe. I was so sad that I never went to see it. I didn't go to the premiere because I felt that Carol Reed had been badly let down. But he was pleased with the music and so was I.

Director Anthony Mann on the set of The Heroes of Telemark

St Trinian's

Leslie Gilliat said to me, "I've got something to interest you. The *St Trinian's* films. I'm going over to Paris to introduce you to Ronald Searle." I said, "That'll be nice." So we went and what was meant to be the weekend turned out to be three weeks with Sidney Gilliat and I showed him some of Paris he didn't know! The *St Trinian's* films were the most difficult to do because they required a lot of pointing. I used a small orchestra, and in a small orchestra it's very exposed and you have to conduct it properly.

While I was recording one of them, Jerry Goldsmith appeared and said, "I've just come over to watch you scoring because you've turned down *The Blue Max* and I've got to do it and I hope it'll be as good as your score." I said, "Why come to sit in on a St Trinian's film when I use an orchestra of ten?" I didn't bother to see *The Blue Max*. I'd already seen it and turned it down. Again another bloody war film!

Battle of Britain

Battle of Britain was the only film I ever collaborated on – with William Walton – to write practically the whole score and conduct it. I orchestrated it. The part where the Spitfire dives into the sea is entirely by me. Walton gave me two bars of indecipherable music for twelve minutes of it. He said, "Continue any way you like." "You mean you want me to write it?" I asked. "Yes, here's the transcript, it's all barred for you." And so I wrote that beat and, of course, it sounds like Shostakovich!

Afterwards I took my family, their girlfriends and boyfriends, to Ischia, and the telephone rang. It was for Walton and he said, "How dare the British press ring me on Sunday. Do you know what they told me? They're not using any of that delicious music you wrote for the *Battle of Britain*." I asked "Who's doing it?" "They asked John Addison for it and he refused; he said the music was excellent" – as it is. It was Ron Goodwin.

Walton didn't do many films. He didn't want to, that was the reason. But he was very jealous of other people's royalties. He was very jealous of Ravel's royalties and Gershwin's. I said, "Well, don't look at me. I haven't got talent. I may have more money but I haven't got the talent." I only had money that I've earned. I never had any private income.

With modern scores the orchestras are far too large and you can make a bad tune sound even worse by having more strings. Composers are brought in last. They always have to save bad films. You try to find a tune – not necessarily a pop tune but a tune original. There's a good friend of mine Adolph Deutsch who said, "A movie composer can make the corpse look awful pretty, but he can't bring it to life."

Malcolm Arnold
from 'Movie Collector Magazine', Vol.1, Issue 5, April 1994

Malcolm Arnold and the war film

In 1958, the year in which Malcolm Arnold won the 'Best Music' Academy Award for his score to David Lean's *The Bridge on the River Kwai*, a noted British film critic lamented the war film's popularity as a genre: "A dozen years after World War II we find ourselves in the really quite desperate situation of being not sick of war, but hideously in love with it." As recently as 2011, Germany's first federal culture minister controversially declared that the United Kingdom remained obsessed with the Second World War, and was the only country to have made this conflict the "spiritual core of its national self, understanding and pride". Particularly during the 1950s, this characteristic attitude had often been inescapably reflected in the upbeat style of the music written for British films concerned with the conflict, and it is fascinating to see how Arnold – who made a prolific and varied musical contribution to the genre – negotiated the challenge of simultaneously capturing the horrors of modern warfare and the often heroic resilience of those entangled in it.

In his 2014 book *Projecting Britain at War*, Jeremy Havardi identifies four aspects of the national character which have been constantly promoted in British war films: chivalrous stoicism (the 'stiff upper lip'), understated humour in adversity, amateurish improvisation, and pride in the indomitability of the underdog. Connoisseurs of Arnold's various creative personalities, whether manifested in the film studio or the concert hall, will have no difficulty in identifying the equivalent musical idioms that were part of his formidable general armoury of film-scoring techniques.

The 'chivalrous stoicism' is reflected in Arnold's continuation of the post-Elgar march idiom which Walton had modernised in his coronation marches, the latter characterised by William McNaught as "regulation strut and swagger, plenty of plain diatonics, and a *nobilmente* tune in the middle". This overtly patriotic style, first attached to the war film by Walton in *The First of the Few* (1942), became prominent once more in British film scoring following the accession of Elizabeth II to the throne in 1953 – and not just in war films: Walton (reluctantly) agreed to plaster it rather heavily on to Laurence Olivier's *Richard III* (1955) too. In many British war films of the era, this rousing style (with its 'big theme' mentality making such films something of a counterpart to the American western) is applied uncritically – though a few composers, notably Alan Rawsthorne and Brian Easdale, managed largely to avoid it in search of subtler, more modern soundscapes. There are several instances, however, where film-makers seemed distinctly uncomfortable with the tub-thumping implications of the coronation-march style. In *The Dam Busters* (1955), for example, Eric Coates' famous Elgarian march (which was not written for the film) is eventually drowned out by the homecoming bombers' engine noise and briefly sneaked back in at low volume beneath a radio announcer's report of the mission, before being faded out into solemn silence when it emerges that eight of the aircraft failed to return. By the time of *A Bridge Too Far* (1977), John Addison's cheerful military march seemed woefully inappropriate for the images of carnage, dejected troops, devastation, and displaced civilians with which the movie ends: during the end credits the tune had to be faded in after an appreciable pause.

The 1950s: Arnold's first war films

Arnold's score to his first war film, the real-life prisoner-of-war story *Albert R.N.* (1953), also resorts to the patriotic march idiom for the end credits, but the rest of the score is both sparse and (on occasion) typically witty. For example, it prophetically includes a crude quotation of Kenneth Alford's 'Colonel Bogey' march as an insult to the Germans; here, as in the melody's more famous starring role in *The Bridge on the River Kwai*, the offensive nature of the gesture is rather lost on those who aren't aware that the tune was sung during the war by British troops with the addition of scurrilous lyrics alleging that various Nazi luminaries had either missing or misshapen gonads. It's a pity Lean fought shy of including those lyrics in *The Bridge on the River Kwai*, as it would have helped to explain to the uninitiated why such a cheerful tune keeps cropping up in an otherwise grim context. In that film, in spite of the dominance of both 'Colonel Bogey' and the original march Arnold wrote as a counterpoint to it (his own tune also jauntily resilient rather than patriotic), he nevertheless incorporated an unmistakable nod towards the Waltonian idiom in a broad melodic strain half-way through his

otherwise turbulent and grittily dissonant main-title overture. The closing recapitulation of Arnold's cheerful march comes surprisingly quickly after the final catastrophe, but its almost *St Trinian's*-like jollity might be taken to suggest how ludicrous (albeit fatal) the closing situation is.

After *Albert R.N.* came *A Hill in Korea* (1956), the first British war film to depict a more recent conflict in South East Asia rather than the Second World War. Again, shades of ceremonial Elgar and Walton dominate the opening music, which is briefly recapitulated at the end of the film. But elsewhere the scoring is grimmer, though still influenced by march- and fanfare-like rhetoric, and in this instance juxtaposed with contrasting flashes of ethnic colour to suggest the locale. Arnold's commission to score *Dunkirk* (1958) followed hard on the heels of the international success of *The Bridge on the River Kwai*, which meant he was instantly typecast as a composer for the war genre: "Afterwards I was sold every bloody war movie that there was!" he once moaned. Although the subject of *Dunkirk* (as with the portrayal of the Arnhem disaster in *A Bridge Too Far*) was a notorious large-scale military defeat, Arnold's score still subscribed to the current fashion by commencing with a lush Waltonian main-title march. This is recapitulated for the triumphant arrival, cavalry-like, of the Royal Navy, but – in a similar strategy to that in *The Dam Busters* – it's then quickly replaced by sombre underscoring as a voice-over reminds us of the appalling human cost of the defeat. *Dunkirk* was a success at the box office and received a Royal Command performance, but critic William Whitebait wrote a scathing review of it, which reflected on the genre's changing cultural and political context as Britain increasingly lost its influence on global politics: "So while we 'adventure' at Suez, in the cinemas we are still thrashing Rommel – and discovering that he was a gentleman! … It is less a spur to morale than a salvo to wounded pride; and as art or entertainment dreadfully dull." Arnold's later scores for war films show a variety of responses to changing audience tastes in the 1960s as traditional combat films were on the verge of being replaced by more horrifyingly realistic war films reflecting public consciousness of the ongoing Vietnam War.

The 1960s: changing audience tastes

The Heroes of Telemark (1965) is a good illustration of how the 1960s British war movie and its music were not solely about stiff-upper-lip patriotism: indeed, the coronation-march idiom (which again appears fleetingly in Arnold's score) began to dwindle markedly as British approaches to the genre became more concerned with cultivating a heroic sense of adventure. Here the excitement of the chase, the ingenuity of the escapades, and the ability to overcome seemingly impossible odds were the order of the day – and, of course, cinematically thrilling rather than 'dreadfully dull'. At times, the adventures portrayed on screen in 1960s British war movies become so implausibly entertaining – and so far removed from the grim and bloody reality of modern combat – that they seem more akin to schoolboy yarns or sporting fixtures than historical accounts. Yet the trend was a surprisingly accurate reflection of the tone of the first-hand wartime accounts on which several films of this type were based, albeit now exaggerated for the silver screen under the influence of the popular fictional adventure stories (and movies based on them) by bestselling authors Ian Fleming and Alistair Maclean. Ron Goodwin's rousingly memorable war-movie scores, which included *633 Squadron* (1964) and *Where Eagles Dare* (1968) – the latter based on a story by Maclean – were perfectly attuned to the new mood, and he became the acknowledged leader in the genre just as Arnold was becoming less engaged with it.

Not surprisingly, it was Goodwin who ended up scoring *Battle of Britain* (1969) when Walton's score for this American-funded RAF blockbuster was summarily rejected. The sorry story is well known, and need not be recounted in full here – other than to note that Walton seemed overridingly obsessed with writing yet another memorable quasi-coronation march. The latter no longer came easily, however. "No sign of a tune!" he informed Arnold (who once claimed he had helped his friend compose *Orb and Sceptre*, and who had agreed to conduct the new film score), and continued: "Every time I think of one I find I've written it before." The undoubted high point of what turned out to be a somewhat meagre score was a dog-fighting scherzo which had to be heavily arranged by Arnold, who supplied transitional material in order to patch together repeats of identical passages: a substantial part of the manuscript for this cue is in Arnold's hand, but his creative contribution is in any case clearly audible to anyone who knows his style. Thankfully this 'Battle in the Air' cue was reinstated in the soundtrack thanks to Olivier's bullish intervention after the score had been rejected in its entirety, and this unique moment of collaborative scoring by two of the most pre-eminent of all British film composers is pleasingly foregrounded, with all potentially competing sound effects suppressed during the entire aerial sequence.

Comparison with modern remakes

The difference between modern approaches to scoring war films and the methods used by Arnold is strikingly shown by a comparison between two of his films in this genre and their later remakes. *The Thin Red Line* (1964), perhaps because it was an American production, finally saw Arnold avoiding the Elgar-Walton style altogether. Instead, his march-style music here, subjected to various transformations in the course of the film, is far more grimly defiant, and its overtly melodic basis complements the use elsewhere of subdued but threatening percussion effects intended to create a subliminal mood of ominous expectancy. The soundtrack as a whole treads an unpredictable line between allowing battle scenes to speak for themselves – albeit with the aid of loud sound effects – and enhancing them with sometimes hyperbolically dissonant orchestral music. Some music cues feature stock scoring techniques such as stinger chords and isomorphic mickey-mousing (e.g. descending music as small rocks tumble down a slope, and even when a sniper falls out of a tree), which – being so readily associated with cartoon scoring – do not

fit comfortably with today's tastes.

By contrast, Hans Zimmer's music for Terrence Malick's *The Thin Red Line* (1998) is replete with drones and pedals, basic ostinato patterns, simple modal writing, a few moments of elegiac commentary from the strings, and a strictly limited use of percussion effects. The concept of the 'big theme' had long since evaporated, and this is even more the case in Zimmer's almost wall-to-wall contribution to Christopher Nolan's *Dunkirk* (2017). It is hard to think of the music track here as a 'score' in the traditional sense: as usual with Zimmer, the music is a team effort involving several credited composers, all very much aware of the benefits of subliminally blurring the distinction between music and sound effects.

Christopher Palmer, who arranged a substantial orchestral suite from the score to *The Bridge on the River Kwai* in 1991, had a general knowledge of – and experience of working in – film music that was second to none. Comparing Arnold with the very greatest film composers, he summarised his strengths in working for the medium of film: sheer efficiency, an ability to capture 'dramatic undercurrents', the vividness of his orchestrations, his being endowed with arguably the most impressive gift of melodic invention possessed by any post-war British composer, and the ability (very necessary in mainstream commercial cinema) to make an instant emotional impact on his audience. All these virtues are in abundance in Arnold's war-film scores – though opinion will perhaps remain divided (in this specific genre at least!) about the truth of his assertion that "if a film score comes out uninfluenced by Berlioz, it's no damn good!".

Mervyn Cooke

The horrors of Malcolm Arnold's film music

In 1971, Decca released a compilation LP entitled *Danse macabre*, complete with a plastic skeleton dancing against a lurid background on the cover. I discovered these marvellously performed and engineered recordings about three years later, and, always having had a penchant for musical spookiness, it was a godsend to 15-year-old me: Alexander Gibson presided over the New Symphony Orchestra of London with Liszt's *Mephisto Waltz* in its orchestral Sunday best, Humperdinck's Witch's Ride from *Hansel and Gretel*, Mussorgsky's *Night on a Bare Mountain*, and Ravel's orchestral version of his 'The Gnome', plus Ernst Ansermet conducting Dukas's *Sorcerer's Apprentice*. The seventh track, back with Gibson, was, however, new to me.

This was Malcolm Arnold's *Tam O'Shanter Overture*, and it fascinated me because it was at once quite terrifying and absurdly grotesque. Based on the Robert Burns poem of the same name, the frightening passages, particularly towards the end, when drunken Tam is pursued by ghouls, seemed like the music I was beginning to hear on the BBC's late-night horror film double bills; but these passages alternated with jaunty Scottish folk tunes on piccolos, orchestral imitations of bagpipes, and tipsy trombones. Later, I compared it to that moment in Wagner's *Siegfried*, when Mime the dwarf is absolutely terrified by the flickering lights and hair-raising noises of the dark forest, and convinces himself that Fafner the dragon is out to get him. This scene drew forth archetypal musical shudders from Wagner, full of chromatic terror; but then Siegfried turns up and the music completely changes character into boisterous comedy. It struck me, even then, that both Arnold and Wagner were doing much the same thing here, and though Wagner lived before the invention of the movies, he would, like Arnold, have made a fantastic film composer.

I later discovered, that the first person to record the *Tam O'Shanter Overture* was John Hollingsworth. That recording was made in 1955, the same year that he conducted James Bernard's first score for Hammer films, *The Quatermass Experiment* (director Val Guest). Hollingsworth went on to conduct scores for Hammer's horror films before his untimely death and replacement first,

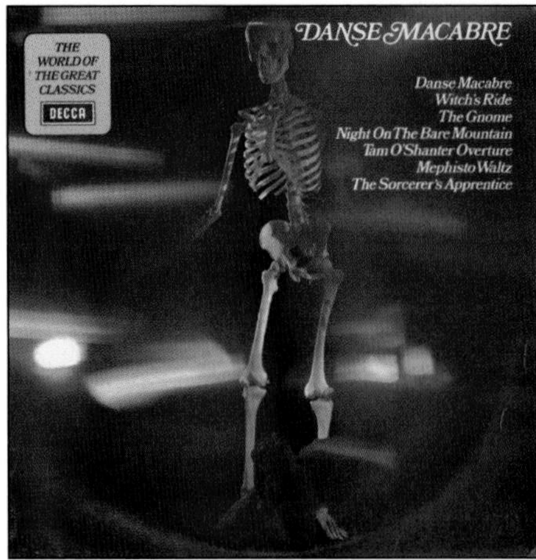

The Tam O'Shanter Overture, composed in 1955, was included on Decca SPA 175 (1971); it was a reissue of a recording made by Alexander Gibson in 1958.

briefly, by Marcus Dods, and then by the great Philip Martell, who, like James Bernard, I later got to know well. In fact, Hollingsworth had been instrumental in securing Arnold's first job writing music for a documentary. When I looked into the matter, I discovered that Arnold had scored quite a few films for Hammer before that company became famous as a House of Horror. He also worked on two films directed by Terence Fisher before Fisher became famous as the great 'auteur' of Hammer Gothic; but though he followed Fisher and Hammer as far as the science fiction thriller *Four Sided Triangle* in 1953 – a film that presaged the Hammer's Frankenstein series – Arnold afterwards followed a different path.

Hobson's Choice

With *Tam O'Shanter* still ringing in my ears from my early exposure to it on disc,

John Hollingsworth (1916-1963) did much to encourage Arnold to write for film, and conducted many of his film scores

it intrigued me to consider what might have happened had Arnold remained with Hammer. His style was perhaps better suited to the genres in which he later worked, but he was definitely quite capable of being a master of terror. Even in a comedy film like David Lean's *Hobson's Choice* (1954), the famous scene, in which Charles Laughton pursues reflections of the moon in several puddles late at night, blended that same mixture of spookiness with comedy that had so impressed me in the *Tam O'Shanter Overture*. To convey the ghostly reflection of the moon, Arnold used the weird timbre of the musical saw, which sounds rather like the electronic ondes Martenot, but isn't quite so 'sci-fi' in its effect. The music perfectly complements Laughton's confused glimpses of the eerie moon, while brilliantly 'Mickey-Mousing' the action, catching all of Laughton's movements and gestures.

David Lean was the height of film respectability at the time. Indeed, Arnold became known as 'Master of the Lean's Music'; but Hammer was far from being respectable in the late 1950s, and if Arnold had stayed with them, it might have curtailed further possibilities in the film industry. James Bernard always suspected that Rank (for whom he scored three non-horror films) dropped him after his sensational association with Hammer's Dracula and Frankenstein films, which one critic of the time described as being fit 'for Sadists only'. Having said that, Hammer had always been keen to employ leading composers of the day for its films, such as Benjamin Frankel, Malcolm Williamson, Humphrey Searle and Elisabeth Lutyens, and they never suffered from the association.

The Astonished Heart

Arnold's first involvement with Terence Fisher was for the Gainsborough Pictures drama, *The Astonished Heart* in 1949, but this was not to supply original music. Noel Coward, who starred in film and had written the original play on which it is based, had also composed the music, but this needed to be arranged for orchestra. The deadline being so tight, Arnold lent his (uncredited) services to assist William Blezard in the task.

Home to Danger

The following year Arnold worked for

Fisher once more, this time gaining a much-deserved credit for the score of *Home to Danger*. This was an Eros rather than a Hammer film, though the action was shot at Riverside Studios in Hammersmith, a district of London that curiously lent its name to the stage names ('Hammer and Smith') of Enrique Carreras and Will Hinds who had originally founded the Hammer company. Arnold accompanies the Eros logo with a typically strident, though unofficial, brass fanfare, which, following Max Steiner's approach for Warner Brothers, leads into the main theme. Appropriately for a film with 'Danger' in the title, Arnold employs the sinister interval of the augmented fourth, or tritone, also known as 'diabolus in musica' – the devil in music – which would soon become an indispensable part of the musical vocabulary of James Bernard's horror scores. Arnold makes sure to expose one of these tritones to coincide with his title card.

Home to Danger is an engaging, though fairly standard whodunit. A young woman (Rona Anderson) inherits a large mansion, and her father's drug-dealing partner, Hughes (Alan Wheatley), tries to kill her to gain the estate for himself. Music of differing moods was required, however, and Arnold obliged with pastoral oboes playing the main theme for the journey to the idyllically named Greensleeves mansion. String tremolos and bass clarinets appear for suspense scenes; galloping triplets accompany scenes on horseback, while celeste and wind neatly convey the atmosphere of the misty morning of the shooting party when the assassination is planned to take place. Added tension is created by a sustained suspended cymbal; and during the shoot, when Peter Jones as the hired assassin aims his shotgun at the girl, rising scalic passages for brass anticipate the ghoulish climax of *Tam O'Shanter* three years later. Unfortunately for him, the assassin is shot by Willie (Stanley Baker), the girl's faithful, if somewhat 'touched' servant, who knows what's afoot. The assassin drowns in the lake before firing the fatal shot, and Arnold accompanies his hat floating on the water with three deft and well-placed chords on the celeste.

Arnold also had an opportunity for some solo stride piano in a short scene set in a night club, but tritones soon return as a muted piano ostinato during the hero's pursuit of Mick O'Ryan – or 'Mick the Dope' (Philo Hauser) – who will lead our protagonists to the dealer, Hughes, himself. The main theme is intoned by

desolate lower strings over this ostinato, followed by a lonely flute, all of which are resonant of Mick's hopeless addiction (again, a mood with which Arnold was so unfortunately familiar).

During the final struggle, after several more chromatic foreshadowings of *Tam O'Shanter*, Arnold uses a rapid four-note scalic ostinato on strings, which is very similar to a figuration James Bernard often used for bat attacks in his Dracula scores. Ultimately, Hughes is sucked under the marshland like the villain, Stapleton, in *The Hound of the Baskervilles* (a colour adaptation of which was directed for Hammer by Fisher eight years later, with another James Bernard score).

Wings of Danger

More danger awaited in Arnold's first Hammer film proper the following year. This was a crime drama concerning a smuggling airline pilot, also directed by Fisher, called *Wings of Danger*. Accordingly, Arnold dusts off yet another tritone for the main theme, which is preceded by a gusty flurry of strings, which is highly appropriate for a story featuring aeroplanes; but this time, he has rather more opportunities to have fun with jazzy diegetic or 'source' music. Arnold always took great care with this kind of music, which the characters can also hear, as opposed to the non-diegetic soundtrack score, which only the audience is aware of. A splendid example of this kind of 'radio' music, as it is also known, occurs in Carol Reed's *Trapeze* (1956). 'Lola's theme' in that film can hardly be heard on the soundtrack due to there being so much dialogue over it, but soundtrack recordings reveal what a charming example of Arnold's jazz idiom it is. Around 20 minutes into the action of *Wings of Danger*, we hear the first example of this kind of music during a scene set in a stylish art deco apartment between Zachary Scott's Richard Van Ness, and Kay Kendall's Alexia LaRoche. Strings plays a blues theme with the piano quietly vamping below, which is later joined by flute. This is followed by an up-tempo rumba to accompany a scene set in a nightclub featuring a wildly exuberant maraca player in the background.

Suspense obviously plays an important role in the picture as well. For the scene in which Van Ness locates a toolkit that is actually made out of solid gold (part of the smuggling operation), Arnold accordingly provides string tremolos and more 'bat attack' motifs; but it's not long before we are able to enjoy more jazzy background music in Alexia's flat. We actually see her put on a record, and Van Ness comments what a 'nice record' it is, as he walks in. It is too. Later, more string tremolos, low clarinets and spooky flutes add to the tension as Van Ness searches for clues in his employer's office by torchlight, unaware that he is being watched by an as yet unidentified figure, who's presence is suggested by sinister timpani rolls, like distant thunder. A chase sequence follows, which, again, has quite a few of the effects that Arnold would rework in *Tam O'Shanter*. Van Ness crashes his car, and wakes up looking at the face of the man he was chasing – his former colleague Nick Talbot (Robert Beatty), whom he believed dead. Van Ness then delivers the film's best line: "This can't be heaven with you in it."

The action reaches its climax in a deserted windmill, the sets of which are curiously reminiscent of the laboratory in James Whale's *Frankenstein* (1931). Here, Van Ness discovers the printing press for forged notes, which his employer has been smuggling out of the country.

Stolen Face

Arnold also worked for Fisher on *Stolen Face*, made almost simultaneously with *Wings of Danger* (they were both released in May 1952). *Stolen Face* is a reworking of the Pygmalion legend, but it also strongly anticipates the kind of stories Hammer would use in their Frankenstein series, concerned as they are with swapped identities and advanced surgery. A plastic surgeon called Philip Ritter (Paul Henreid) falls in love with Alice Brent, a concert pianist (Lisabeth Scott), but Alice is already engaged to be married, and leaves him. Unable to live without her, the surgeon remodels the face of a disfigured female convict called Lily to mirror exactly the features of the woman he loved. They marry, but Ritter soon learns that looks aren't everything, and living with an ex-convict of low morals proves too much for him. Ultimately, Alice breaks off her engagement and returns to Ritter. During an argument on a train, Lily falls out of the carriage and is killed, leaving Ritter free to marry Alice.

Obviously, with a concert pianist in a leading role, Arnold had to write his own kind of 'Warsaw Concerto'. Richard Addinsell had unwittingly started a craze for 'film concertos' when composing his famous 'Warsaw Concerto' for Brian Desmond Hurst's *Dangerous Moonlight* in 1941, and Arnold's piece follows in this tradition, though the idiom is not so obviously inspired by Rachmaninov, as Addinsell's piece was. The piano part was performed by Bronwyn Jones, and the orchestra was conducted by Muir Mathieson, who had also presided over the original recording of the 'Warsaw Concerto' with Louis Kentner at the keyboard. Eleven years later, James Bernard would compose a Gothic film 'concerto' – his tritone-fuelled homage to Liszt that became known as the 'Vampire Rhapsody' – for Hammer's *The Kiss of the Vampire* (director Don Sharp).

There are no tritones in Arnold's 'concerto' as this is primarily a romantic love story, so there are far fewer cues

requiring musical tension, but there is an appoggiatura in the second bar of the main theme, which emphasises the story's yearning mood. An operation scene early on uses a low flute and string tremolos to create an undertow of anxiety, but this doesn't last for long. Ritter, who has been working too hard, very nearly has a fatal accident when he nods off at the wheel of his car, and Arnold responds with yet another foretaste of *Tam O'Shanter*; but the mood lightens considerably in the next scene when he takes himself off to a remote inn for a holiday. The weather is appalling, and in the adjacent room, Ritter can hear a woman sneezing. Here, a delightfully rising and falling theme, mostly played on the clarinet and accompanied with pizzicato strings, punctuates the action, the sneezes being accurately accommodated into the phrasing. There's even a musical 'sigh' on the strings as Ritter turns over and pulls the bed sheets over his head in a foiled attempt to get some sleep. In the end he gives up and decides to confront his noisy neighbour, who turns out to be Alice, while fragments of the main theme, later accompanied by gentle 'heavenly' harps, support their meeting.

They decide to extend their stay at the inn and experience a fox hunt (a brief opportunity for hunting horns), go fishing (watery harp glissandi) and then take a ride on a pony trap, which gives Arnold a chance to respond to Benjamin Frankel's most popular piece of film music, 'Carriage and Pair', from the 1950 Dirk Bogarde feature, *So Long at the Fair*, which had also been directed by Fisher.

Later, in the bar of the inn, Alice entertains the locals and then strums out Arnold's 'concerto' theme on the somewhat out-of-tune upright in the bar; but the idyll cannot last. Alice runs away and returns to her fiancée, David (André Morell). Of course, we all know she is now in love with Ritter, as does David, but nonetheless they drink to their forthcoming marriage, and Arnold very subtly picks up on the underlying discord in their relationship by shifting the tonality with a string tremolo and a chime bar, which provides an ironic reference to the wedding bells that aren't going to ring. It is these small but psychologically revealing details in the score that mark Arnold out as such a master of film music technique.

When Ritter measures up Lily's face for her transformation, Arnold transforms the 'bedroom' theme to suggest that the new Alice is not going to be the real thing: the new theme is reminiscent of the happiness conveyed by the old theme, but it's not quite the same. The cue then ends in textbook style when a telephone rings.

A concert montage follows, informing us of Alice's tour and David's growing realisation that she no longer loves him. It also gives Arnold another opportunity to reprise his theme on the piano and orchestra, building up to a virtuoso 'coda', which gives the impression of an entire concerto in one and a half minutes.

Hindsight, and the fact that this is a Hammer film directed by Terence Fisher, cannot help one comparing the unveiling of Lily's new face with Fisher's *Frankenstein Created Woman* (1967), which contains a very similar scene, but Arnold's music is very different from Bernard's. We have already had a minute-and-a-half 'concerto'; now we have a half-a-minute waltz to accompany Lily's clothes shopping trip with Ritter. Later, bored by the opera, Lily takes Ritter to a night club, where Jack Parnell provides the jazz dance numbers. This is much more Lily's type of music, and, as she reverts to type, she starts stealing again. Her theme (that transformed 'bedroom' tune) returns when she steals a mink coat, and we hurtle towards the inevitable dénouement. Rising chromatically sequence phrases, again predicting *Tam O'Shanter*, raise the tension on the final train journey, and another four-note string ostinato accentuates her final struggle with Alice before she falls to her death from the carriage door.

For all this film's foreshadowings, Terence Fisher of course had no idea he was destined to become famous as a director of horror films. He always regarded himself as a jobbing director, and, while no doubt flattered to be called an auteur by French film critics, he never really believed it. Indeed, he was quite happy to leave the various departments to get on with the job, leaving him free to concentrate on the final 'arranging', as Christopher Lee once put it. He certainly left the music to the music department. James Bernard told me that he once asked Fisher if he'd like to attend a recording session and find out what they were doing, but Fisher replied with a smile, "Oh no. I know nothing about music. I'm happy to leave that to you boys, and I trust you to do what's needed."

Four Sided Triangle

Arnold's final collaboration with Fisher and Hammer was a film that further pointed in the direction the company was soon to take. This was *Four Sided Triangle* in 1953. It begins with a typical Arnold fanfare for brass leading into a main theme that refrains from signalling too much. Then, a taste of the Biblical epic accompanies a quotation from Ecclesiastes: "God hath made man upright, but they have sought out many inventions." The particular invention to which this refers is a 'replicator', which does exactly that. It can replicate anything down to the smallest detail, including human beings. So, when John van Eyssen's Robin marries Lena (Barbara Peyton), a woman also loved his friend Bill (Stephen Murray), Bill decides to use the machine he and Robin have invented to make a replica of Lena for himself. The new Lena is called Helen, who while not launching a thousand ships nonetheless leads to disaster, for Helen is the *exact* replica of Lena, which means that she has the same emotions, and is still therefore in love with Robin, rather than Bill. An attempt to wipe her memory clean and start afresh leads to a fire in the lab, and Helen is destroyed.

The main idea of creating a woman of course foreshadows Fisher's later *Frankenstein Created Woman*, and Frankenstein would have been very much at home in the laboratory scenes of *Four Sided Triangle*. Fisher was

unwittingly warming up for his celebrated Frankenstein films later on, but the film also looks back to Fritz Lang's *Metropolis* (1927) and the creation of its female robot. This is especially the case when Lena lies back in her chair with electrodes pressed against her temples.

However, the first thing Bill and Robin try to replicate is a pocket watch, and for this impressive lab scene no music is used, the aural drama being provided by the noise of the machinery alone. The second replication (of a bank cheque) employs ethereal strings, and these do somewhat foreshadow the sound world of Bernard's Frankenstein scores. Robin then marries Lena to the accompaniment of Mendelssohn's 'Wedding March', which segues into the darker timbre of horns as Bill sadly waves them off on their honeymoon. Left to his own devices, Bill now starts to experiment with the replication of living creatures, and attempts to duplicate a guinea pig. Sadly, the duplicate dies. (In *The Curse of Frankenstein* (1957), Peter Cushing's Baron has more success with a puppy.) During Bill's revelation of his plans to try a different approach, Arnold supplies horror music consisting of oscillating tremolo strings, a style he would no doubt have been required to develop had he continued with the genre.

The next replication again uses no music, but after the experiment, Arnold brings back the oscillating strings with a low clarinet appropriately playing a tritone. (Bernard would create a similar music mood during the scene in which Noel Willman's Dr Ravna wills the return of Jennifer Daniel's Marianne to the chateau towards the end of *The Kiss of the Vampire*.) Bill's second attempt is successful: the guinea pig survives, and the time is now right for Lena herself to be reproduced. She is willing to subject herself to this ordeal, having been assured that no harm will come to her, but she is obviously nervous as she enters the lab. Arnold walks in with her with a sequence for rising brass, which will later inform *Tam O'Shanter*. For the replication process, music (featuring an underlying pulse of a drum to suggest a heartbeat) is blended with the sound of a ticking clock. The high-pitched, ethereal string textures here curiously anticipate the effect Barry Gray would use to accompany Gerry Anderson's 21st-Century Television logo.

Arnold now surrounds the new Helen with mysterious harp glissandi and a vibraphone, timbres that Bernard would use so often for Hammer. An ostinato for tremolo strings is joined, for added menace, by flutter-tongue flutes and a low clarinet. Altogether, this creation sequence was one of Arnold's longest film cues to date, and demonstrates what a marvellous composer for Hammer's Frankenstein films he would have made, had not James Bernard been available.

But he also had another opportunity for a jazz interlude when Helen and Bill go on holiday and enjoy a nightclub. The film ends, however, with a fiery finale.

The Sleeping Tiger

Four Sided Triangle proved to be one of the foundation stones of the future Hammer House of Horror, with Fisher and much of the crew poised for gory glory. Though van Eyssen would appear as Jonathan Harker in *Dracula*, Stephen Murray did not become Hammer's Frankenstein. Neither did Arnold continue with this particular kind of fantasy, though he did score Joseph Losey's 1954 psychological thriller *The Sleeping Tiger* with Dirk Bogarde as a violent criminal, who begins an affair with the infatuated wife of the psychotherapist who is treating him. Losey would go on to make *The Damned* for Hammer in 1963, with a score by James Bernard. *The Damned* was science fiction, but *The Sleeping Tiger* looked forward to the type of psychological thrillers with which Hammer were to balance their Gothic fare. Arnold employs a jazz idiom featuring a desolate saxophone for *The Sleeping Tiger*, which also uses a vibraphone ostinato to create an atmosphere of anticipation on several occasions. There's also a somewhat arbitrary concertante piece for piano and orchestra, reminiscent of the *Stolen Face* concerto, which underscores an early conversation between Bogarde and Alexis Smith; and when they go out to a nightclub together, there are some marvellous blues numbers featuring Arnold's beloved trumpet. The critic Virginia Graham remarked that neither Losey's 'intelligent directing, nor Malcolm Arnold's nerve-scraping music, helps to dispel the illusion that under a cloak of psychoanalytical claptrap everybody is being very silly'[1]; but it's certainly worth putting up with the silliness to experience the nerve-scraping music.

1984

Arnold also scored Michael Anderson's 1956 film adaptation of George Orwell's *1984*, which capitalised on the immense popularity of the BBC's television adaptation two years earlier, starring Peter Cushing. Cushing's success in that production as Winston Smith ultimately led him to be cast in the title role of Hammer's *The Curse of Frankenstein*, and in many ways, Anderson's *1984* could be a Hammer production, featuring, as it does, many actors who later became associated with the company, such as Michael Ripper, Patrick Allen, Patrick Troughton and David Kossoff.

Arnold's score is interesting principally because of the way in which he uses 'radio' or source music as a kind of deliberately depressing 'musak', designed to placate those over whom Big Brother forever watches. The effect of false, indeed enforced, cheer is suitably alienating. There is a fast waltz while Smith (Edmund O'Brien) writes in his forbidden diary, a four-square piece for small ensemble in 'The Chestnut Tree' bar, another fast waltz in a canteen (music-while-you-eat), and later even some circus style radio music, reminiscent of Arnold's St Trinian's theme, during which Smith again writes in his diary. Most of the other cues for this film are unexpectedly romantic in character, accompanying, as they do, the love scenes between Smith and Julia (Jan Sterling). Significantly, there is no music at all for the famous horror scene in which Smith encounters his greatest fear – rats – in Room 101.

Suddenly Last Summer

By 1959 Hammer had firmly established its reputation for Gothic horror. That year the company released *The Hound of the Baskervilles, The Mummy,* and *The Man Who Could Cheat Death*, all of them directed by Fisher. One can only speculate on the intriguing possibility of what Hammer films would have been sounded like if Arnold had followed in Fisher's footsteps, but one film he scored for Hollywood that year suggests a strong possibility. Joseph L Mankiewicz's adaptation of Tennessee Williams' play *Suddenly Last Summer* somewhat resembles the milieu of Hammer's psychological, as opposed to Gothic, thrillers, but it also has many Gothic elements: brain surgery, a Venus flytrap in a strange exotic garden, and a domineering mother called Mrs Venable (Katherine Hepburn), who is not so far removed from Martita Hunt's equally possessive Baroness Meinster in Fisher's *Brides of Dracula* (1960), not to mention Mrs Bates in Hitchcock's *Psycho* (1961). Like the Baroness, Mrs Venable has pampered and controlled her poet son Sebastian (whom we never see because he died 'suddenly last summer'), but instead of being a vampire, Sebastian was a homosexual, and that was considered to be much more worrying by the powers that be in Hollywood at the time. Consequently, his homosexuality could only be alluded to in a long revelation delivered by Elizabeth Taylor, who plays Sebastian's apparently mad cousin, Catherine; and it is this revelation that Mrs Venables has spent the whole film trying to prevent with her plan to have the apparently 'mad' Catherine lobotomised.

Arnold, who had more than his fair share of mental health issues, found this subject so troubling his score had to be completed by Buxton Orr; and this leads us to another fascinating set of correspondences, because Orr (a composer of several horror film scores himself) had studied composition with Benjamin Frankel, the composer of the seminal serial film score for Hammer's *The Curse of the Werewolf* in 1960. A theme associated with Sebastian in Arnold's score for *Suddenly Last Summer* and which, indeed, opens the film, consists of three notes and it bears a remarkable, though entirely coincidental, similarity to the 'werewolf' theme in Frankel's later werewolf score. Though there is obviously nothing supernatural about Sebastian, he is nonetheless described as 'predatory', and, like the Venus Fly Trap in his exotic garden, he 'consumes' people. (Stuart Walker's 1935 *Werewolf of London*, features a similar plant, which eats rabbits.) Arnold and Orr also underscore Mrs Venables' description of baby turtles being eaten by predatory birds on a beach, which epitomises not only Sebastian himself, but also the nature of reality – and Sebastian's idea of 'God' as well, with passages of chromatic terror reminiscent of the passage in Wagner's *Siegfried* I mentioned earlier.

There are different kinds of horror. Arnold became famous for his score depicting the real wartime horrors of *The Bridge on the River Kwai* – not to mention the little horrors of St Trinian's; but he was a man who knew all about horror, and his music could fully express it when the need arose.

David Huckvale

1 David Caute, *Joseph Losey: A Revenge on Life*, London: Faber and Faber, 1994, p.122

Sir Malcolm Arnold interviewed by James Cox

Sir Malcolm discusses his film career with James Cox in an interview for AMC, the American movie theatre company, in 2000.

James Cox: You have composed music for five ballets, nine symphonies, at least 25 concertos and a number of other orchestral works, but outside of the concert hall you are best known for your film scores, which number more than 80. You won an Academy Award for *The Bridge on the River Kwai* and have received numerous honours including a knighthood in 1993 for your services to British music.

Malcolm Arnold: "More than 80 films" – that's a lot of pictures! (laughter). And, yes, I did win the Oscar as well. Only one other British composer got one before me and that was Brian Easdale in the 1940s for *The Red Shoes*. And then my old friend Jock (John) Addison won for *Tom Jones* (1963) and John Barry for *The Lion in Winter* (1968). More recently two more British composers have won: Rachel Portman for *Emma* (1996) and Anne Dudley for *The Full Monty* (1997).

JC: Could you tell me how you began writing music for films?

MA: My first introduction to music was by Louis Armstrong. My sister got me hooked on him and Duke Ellington. Later, when I went to the cinema, I noticed the music in films. Writing music for films was one of the only ways for a serious composer to survive.

Composing for films also gave me good experience in conducting. My earliest pictures were conducted by Muir Matheson. [Matheson, 1911-1975, was musical director and conductor of hundreds of British films. He appeared on screen in *The Magic Box* (1951) playing Sir Arthur Sullivan.] He conducted more film scores than anyone. But as time went on, I liked to conduct myself.

My first films were all documentaries. The first dramatic feature film I scored was called *Britannia Mews* (1949; American title: *The Forbidden Street*). It was a 20th Century Fox film; and I had to write that one very quickly, as the original score which had been written by Sir Arnold Bax [1883-1953] got lost in the post and the producer needed a new one very quickly. I was on hand and enjoyed the experience. Bax was a prolific composer, but had trouble writing for films. He later became Master of the Queen's Musick.

Malcolm Arnold

JC: Can you tell me about your experiences on the *Belles of St Trinian's* comedy films of the 1950s and 1960s?

MA: They were marvellous pictures. Sidney Gilliat and Frank Launder were good to work with. [Sidney Gilliat, 1908-1994 and Frank Launder, 1906-1997, were a writing, producing and directing team responsible for more than 40 British films. Both worked on the screenplay of Hitchcock's *The Lady Vanishes* (1938) and are best remembered for the St Trinian's comedies.] A couple of the Trinian's films -- the second, *Blue Murder at St Trinian's* (1957), and *The Great St Trinian's Train Robbery* (1966) -- had songs. I just wrote the music; Sidney Gilliat wrote the words. I used only a very small chamber orchestra on most of these scores.

JC: Have you ever turned down a film score assignment or was there a film you felt didn't need a music score?

MA: Well, there is a film I did based on a Nevil Shute novel called *No Highway* (1951; US title: *No Highway in the Sky*) with Jimmy Stewart and Marlene Dietrich. I thought it only needed a bit of music: the main and end titles; I didn't think it needed anything else. The film held its own without a lot of music in it. I think Marcus Dods conducted the score, what little there was of it. Usually, for my American films, I did write for bigger orchestras, but this was a case where the film would have been hurt by having too much music in it. Some composers write too much music for a film.

JC: You worked often with director David Lean. Was the first film *The Sound Barrier* (1952)?

MA: A wonderful film. It was called *Breaking the Sound Barrier* in America. I felt the music should be like an aerial ballet. David called it my 'Spitfire Ballet' or something like that. I later used this music for my concert work the *Sound Barrier Rhapsody*. I didn't alter the music at all; I simply took the existing sections of score from the film and arranged it as a whole, complete piece.

David enjoyed my work on *The Sound Barrier* and asked me back for *Hobson's Choice* (1954). It was lovely to work on this film. I used a small chamber orchestra for this. Charles Laughton was perfect in the role of the father who owns the shoe shop. It was one of my best films.

JC: You worked with American director Mark Robson on *The Inn of Sixth Happiness* (1958) and *Nine Hours to Rama* (1963). You appear to have had a good working relationship with him as well.

MA: Yes, Mark Robson, a lovely man. One of the greatest Hollywood directors. He had already done *Peyton Place* (1957), just before *The Inn of Sixth Happiness*. Did you realise that *Inn* was supposed to take place in China, but it was shot mostly in Wales? (laughs) I won my first Novello award for that picture. Robson was very easy to work with and a very nice man. When I visited Hollywood, I would often see him at his home. He enjoyed fine art. I remember that he had some lovely sculptures in his garden.

JC: *Nine Hours to Rama* was about Mahatma Gandhi's assassination. Had you studied Indian music for this film?

MA: Yes, I did. Just as I had Chinese musicians flown in from Hong Kong to play ethnic instruments in parts of *The Inn of Sixth Happiness*, we had Indian musicians brought on board for *Rama*. I think a bit of the Indian music even made it on to the soundtrack album. It was very difficult to write down Indian music, but I think it worked well in the film. The whole film was shot in India, but the music was done in England. All of my scores were recorded in England. We have great orchestras here.

JC: You were fortunate to have worked with some other great American directors including John Huston. In 1958 you wrote the score to his film, *The Roots of Heaven*.

MA: That was a 20th Century Fox picture. It was one of their biggest productions at that time. It was about elephants and poachers and starred Errol Flynn and Trevor Howard. Sadly, I didn't see Huston very much. He basically let me get on by myself. Huston was a superb director. I admire his *Treasure of the Sierra Madre* (1948) very much. Max Steiner scored that picture. However, for *Roots of Heaven* I remember that Huston wanted a big overture for the New York premiere. Not many films had overtures anymore at that time.

JC: About the same time, you co-wrote the music for Joseph L Mankiewicz's *Suddenly Last Summer* (1959).

MA: I started writing *Suddenly Last Summer*, but found I couldn't write much music to it and Buxton Orr was brought in to complete it. It all worked together well enough. Incidentally, Buxton Orr was not only a fine composer but a licensed medical doctor as well. Katherine Hepburn and a young Elizabeth Taylor were in *Last Summer*. You could say this was an American film, but it was filmed in England and I think they might have needed a British composer for union reasons (laughs).

JC: King Vidor's *Solomon and Sheba* (1959) was scored by Mario Nascimbene, yet I believe you wrote a bit of music, uncredited, for it. Is this correct?

MA: Well, Nascimbene did in fact score that picture but the director felt he needed a bit of extra music for a scene; I think it was for a funeral, and so, as favour, I did write a short bit of music. In fact, I wasn't paid for this; I was, however, given a case of fine whiskey for it! (laughs)

JC: Another great producer-director you worked with was Sir Carol Reed.

MA: Well, of course there was *Trapeze* (1956). That had the beautiful Gina Lollobrigida as a trapeze artist. Burt Lancaster was in it as well. In fact, he was actually a circus performer himself before coming to Hollywood. Carol was another director who knew exactly what he wanted in a picture. Again, I was left to my own devices and the film's music had a lot of tunes other than my own in it. I arranged *The Blue Danube* by Strauss especially for this film. The Lola theme was very successfully recorded a number of times in America.

JC: One of your memorable scores came from *Whistle Down the Wind* (1961) directed by Richard Attenborough.

MA: Ah, Dickie Attenborough. Dickie was such a good whistler, that he whistled the tune over the main title music. This is one of my own personal favourite film pieces. I enjoy it as much as the St *Trinian's* music and *The River Kwai*. It was a rather dark film with a very bleak topic. Given that it was about an escaped murderer, I thought I had better score it in a 'lighter' fashion. The director Robert Wise once told me, "You're the man who wrote one the best film scores I have ever heard: *Whistle Down the Wind*." That was a wonderful compliment.

JC: Recently, the war film, *The Thin Red Line* (1962) was remade. You scored the original.

MA: Another of my war pictures. Andrew Marton directed it. Amazingly it was filmed in Spain and it was supposed to be in the South Pacific! But, if you watch it, I don't think you can tell. It has been recently remade? I haven't seen it.

JC: What was your experience on *Invitation to a Dance* (1956), the Gene Kelly dance film?

MA: Gene Kelly did this in London. I thought my music was very English sounding and I don't think much of it survives in the film. A young André Previn scored another segment of the picture and Johnny Green arranged yet another. Gene was a nice man. He used to go to the Cloisters [a London club] when he was in London.

JC: You were originally asked to work on the World War I aviation film, *The Blue Max* (1966)?

MA: I had been asked to score *The Blue Max*, but as I had written many war films already, I turned this one down. They got Jerry Goldsmith for this and, ironically enough, we met when I was in the studio completing *The Great St Trinian's Train Robbery* and Goldsmith needed the very same studio to start doing *The Blue Max*. His music was very good. I seem to remember that he was surprised on how I managed to get a larger sound out of such a small orchestra.

JC: You were friends with so many other film composers; you knew Bernard Herrmann when he lived in London?

MA: Well, I sponsored him to become a member of the Savile Club [an exclusive London men's club], where he was a very valued member. Trouble was, there were so many members that were composers, everybody wanted to discuss music! (Laughs) He lived in London during his later years. He had a great love of British music, particularly the music of Elgar. He wrote some of his best music for Alfred Hitchcock. He showed me the score to his opera based on *Wuthering Heights*; it was a very large score, but it was marvellous.

I used to make fun of his New York accent, but he didn't mind that. He invited me over to lunch one day to meet an old friend of his. Benny said, "I have an old friend of mine from Hollywood visiting me. You must listen to him carefully as his English has a very thick accent; he's from Hungary." And I said, "Nonsense, it's perfectly good Hungarian-English." (laughs).

Herrmann hadn't realised that I had known Miklos Rozsa from the 1950s. Rozsa was another important Hollywood composer. [Rozsa, 1907-1995, is best remembered for his scores to the epics *Quo Vadis* (1951), *Ben Hur* (1959), *El Cid* (1961) and a number of film noirs, *Double Indemnity* (1944), *Spellbound* (1945) and *The Lost Weekend* (1945).] He also wrote a violin concerto that was performed by Heifetz. A very fine work.

JC: You also had a good friendship with famed Hollywood composer Alfred Newman, the music director of 20th Century Fox.

MA: I knew Alfred Newman quite well. Al was a terrific composer. The best Hollywood had. He worked very fast, but he wrote very well. He knew how to score a film. [Newman (1901-1970) won Oscars for *Alexander's Ragtime Band* (1938), *Tin Pan Alley* (1940), *The Song of Bernadette* (1943), *Mother Wore Tights* (1947), *With a Song in My Heart* (1952), *Call Me Madam* (1953), *Love Is a Many Splendored Thing* (1955), *The King and I* (1956) and *Camelot* 1967).] Al had a beautiful house and his brother Lionel, I believe, lived right next door. In fact, Kim Novak lived very close by as well. She was a very solitary girl, but she was a beauty. She was incomparable.

JC: Of all the relationships you had with famous and talented directors, your friendship with David Lean appeared to have allowed you to write your finest film scores. We've spoken of your first two Lean films; can you tell me about your last and most successful Lean film, *The Bridge on the River Kwai?*

MA: Yes, David and I were great friends. He was a genius. No one made motion pictures like him. He knew exactly what kind of music a film needed.

JC: Yet, I understand, it was a very difficult assignment?

MA: No question that it was a difficult picture to work on. It was very rushed. I scored it all in 10 days. The producer, Sam Spiegel, wanted the film to be put out in a quick release. I worked night and day on it. A very satisfying experience though. I still feel that *The Bridge on the River Kwai* was one of the greatest anti-war films ever made.

JC: You won the Academy Award for *River Kwai*. Did you attend the Oscar ceremony?

MA: No, I was busy working on something at that time and didn't go. I really didn't think I would win either. The Oscar was delivered to London Airport and my secretary and I drove out there to retrieve it. It was pouring with rain that day and we had trouble trying to find the customs office where the Oscar was being held. I said, "I'm not going all around in this bloody rain, just for that!" But we eventually found it and I had to pay customs duties on the bloody thing! There were special custom forms that needed to be filled out, but, quite naturally, they didn't have one for an Oscar, so it took all afternoon to retrieve it. However, we later celebrated. I had no place to put it, so I later gave it to my daughter as a doorstop. (laughs). Do you remember Dimitri Tiomkin's Oscar speech? The one where he thanked Mozart, Haydn, Beethoven? Bloody marvellous sense of humour!

JC: We all know that *The Bridge on the River Kwai* was your last film for David Lean, but I understand that you were asked to score *Lawrence of Arabia* (1962) as well?

MA: I didn't work on *Lawrence of Arabia* because William Walton, Aram Khachaturian and I were all supposed to score it together, and William and I thought that the film was too long. I don't think it had been edited at this stage and it was perhaps four or five hours long. Walton, Khachaturian and I were each to score a particular part of the picture. Sam Spiegel wanted Khachaturian for the Middle Eastern sound and William for the grand British theme and I was to do everything else, including the arrangements and conducting duties.

JC: Your very last film, *David Copperfield* (1970), was for director Delbert Mann.

MA: *David Copperfield* was very dear to me, as I enjoy Dickens. The main theme in Copperfield is very melancholic, but I felt it needed to be. Delbert Mann was a very sincere man and a joy to work with. Thea King, the great clarinettist, played on that one and performed very well indeed.

JC: Why did your leave the field of film scoring?

MA: Well, for a number of reasons. The producers were always expecting a bloody theme song and I didn't always want to put in a theme song. As the 1960s wore on, every film a had a song. I didn't want that. I had also reached the point where I had written everything I cared to say in films. This allowed me to spend much more time with my serious music.

JC: You mention 'serious' music as opposed to 'film' music?

MA: Music is music, whether serious or for film. When I say 'serious' music, that is, concert music. Composers shouldn't change their style when they write different kinds of music. Some composers may 'write down' to the listeners -- making it simpler -- when scoring films. I didn't believe in this. Film music can be difficult to compose, but often it does take more thought to write serious, concert music. However, I prefer to be remembered simply as a composer, not only as film composer.

James 'Jay' Cox

John Huntley remembers

I first met Malcolm Arnold when I was working as music assistant to Muir Mathieson in the Music Department at Denham Studios shortly after World War II. Originally his work for films was done through Muir, when he was commissioned to write the scores for some editions of a Rank news magazine series called *This Modern Age*. It was 1949 and the edition I best remember was for an item called 'Women of Our Time'. One sequence that Malcolm scored depicted a scene of increasing mechanisation, showing women at work on what at the time was politely called 'light, repetitive assembly'. For this, he wrote a machine theme, somewhat in the style of Arthur Bliss, with lots of brass. He showed a skill that was soon to mark him out as something special in a piece called 'Montage: Peace and War', which involved five changes of mood in one minute four seconds. The sequence starts with scenes of modern (1940s) ballroom dancing, followed by a flash-back to rag-time; then comes a march tune depicting the part played by women in World War II, a brief shot of the British Navy at sea, and scenes of wartime destruction; as if that was not enough, the sequence ended with a musical portrait of women in peace-time Britain, enjoying afternoon tea and the pleasures of social life.

Malcolm did other scores with Muir, but his personal knowledge of the orchestra as a player and his timing skills soon made it clear that – unlike many in those days like Clifton Parker, William Alwyn, Vaughan Williams and even William Walton, who preferred to have a music director/conductor – Arnold could handle the situation on his own. As a result, he often had a very close association with film directors and could interpret their needs without an intermediary. A good case was David Lean. On *Hobson's Choice*, *The Sound Barrier* and *The Bridge on the River Kwai*, Lean's 'larger than life' approach with big-scale characters and settings was perfectly matched by Malcolm's 'larger than life' music. They both liked big tunes, too.

Apart from often seeing him in action in the recording theatre, we joined up in the dubbing theatre at the old Shepherds Bush studios sometime in the 1950s to make a BBC Schools TV programme about film music in which Malcolm gave a detailed account of how he had written the music for the opening sequence of Lean's *Hobson's Choice* and then took part in a reconstruction of the actual recording session, complete with timings to literally split seconds and the images on the screen, to which he synchronised his score to a panning shot of a line of shoes in Hobson's shop: toddlers' shoes, riding boots, ballet shoes, etc. This extraordinary piece of film remains the only record in existence that I know of which documents how things were done in that Golden Age of film music.

John Huntley

John Huntley (1921-2003) entered the film industry as a teaboy at Denham Studios around 1938. After war service in the RAF, he became an assistant to film conductor Muir Mathieson. He worked at the British Film Institute from 1952 to 1974 and set up Huntley Film Archives (www.huntleyarchives.com) in 1984.

Reconstructing Arnold's film scores

When I tell people that I have been reconstructing old film scores, a polite if somewhat blank expression usually passes over their faces. I am sure they are conjuring up images of scissors and sellotape, and, though I do indeed use such things occasionally, they are not pivotal to my endeavours. Usually in fact I require a pencil and rubber and a cassette machine, since what I am actually involved in is a series of extended aural tests.

Since the first question tends to be "Why?", I'll start there. When music was recorded for a film, no one, not even the composers, thought it would be required again, so the material was usually collected up and binned. There were obviously exceptions, and composers from the concert tradition (as opposed to those primarily involved in commercial music) sometimes saw their film music as just another composition, and saved evidence of their work in sketches, short scores or even the completed scores. But this is not to say that the 'serious' composers kept their scores while others did not; there were more factors in the equation. Remember that we are talking about a period before photocopying made it easy to keep a record of one's work. Furthermore, the film companies often saw a film score as their own physical property and kept it.

Pinewood Studios, for instance, had a treasure trove of film material. I remember the conductor Muir Mathieson telling me, shortly before his death in 1975, of the day he received a call from the studio's librarian that he should come and take anything he wanted because the building was being bulldozed the next day – with the scores still inside it! He went and retrieved William Walton's complete score for *Henry V*,amongst others. Ernest Irving, the Musical Director of Ealing Studios until his death in 1953, kept the bound scores of the films he had commissioned in his flat at the studio, but when the BBC bought the studio a few years later the scores all went on a skip – this accounts for the particular scarcity of Ealing material. I found a few scraps at the home of Irving's successor and returned them to their respective composers or estates, including those of Walton, Alwyn –and Malcolm Arnold.

Arnold has been part of my musical life for as long as I can remember; in fact, he's something of a hero of mine. When I discovered his *English Dances* around the age of 10, it was one of a handful of works (Stravinsky's *Rite of Spring* among them) which made me want to write music, and for the orchestra in particular. Meeting him, however, seemed dogged by bad luck. As a schoolboy of 16 on holiday in Cornwall, I turned up unannounced at his cottage in St Merryn to find his wife doing the weekly wash and Arnold not to be disturbed: he was writing the theme – the opening and closing title music – for a new BBC TV series *The First Lady*, starring Thora Hird.[1]

Philip Lane

A few years later, when he was appointed president of my university music society, I had a bout of flu on Presentation Day. So it was not until his final years that we actually met face to face – when he was convinced I was his son-in-law!

I soon got to know how Arnold worked as a film composer: from the lady sitting with him at the initial screening, stop watch in hand, to scoring the music itself. In this regard, as far as anyone can tell, he wrote directly into full score, with no preliminary piano score or sketches. "Why write the same thing twice?" was his attitude.[2] Having seen the work of some of his contemporaries in this field, I can report that, for example, William Alwyn sketched out in extended piano score (in his last professional years his scores were orchestrated by Muir Mathieson himself), while Richard Addinsell tended to write very little down – often just the odd melodic line – leaving the detail to associates like Roy Douglas and Douglas Gamley to write down in piano score from his piano playing and orchestrate it later!

Arnold's music is largely 'vertical' (rather than 'linear') and harmonically consistent, which is a help to the reconstructor, who is often battling sound effects and dialogue where any additional counterpoint is an unwelcome component to deal with! Having grown up with Arnold's concert music[3], I have always felt at home with his style and, in fact, have been around the music long enough it even 'infests one's psyche' so much that one ends up being able to improvise in his style quite freely. (The same thing happened when I undertook the reconstruction process for the Chandos Alan Rawsthorne film music CD – he and Arnold have an immediate fingerprint style detectable in seconds of hearing the music[4], something that could not be said, for example, of William Alwyn.)

Having written for many films, there are bound to be recurring devices and

---

[1] A BBC TV series devised by Alan Plater and first transmitted on 7 April 1968. For later episodes Arnold's theme was transcribed for brass band by Ronnie Hazlehurst.

[2] The only real exception to this was when Arnold was collaborating with Gene Kelly on the 1952 ballet film *Invitation to the Dance*, when a rehearsal score was needed for the dancers.

[3] Philip Lane has made several arrangements for Music Sales (Novello) of Arnold's concert music, including string orchestra versions of the early Recorder Sonatina and the Five Pieces for violin and piano, the latter premiere recording of which is being sponsored by the Society. In addition he has also made orchestral versions of the Three Shanties, The Duke of Cambridge March, The Padstow Lifeboat March and the two Little Suites for Brass Band (see also the article 'Arnold by Arrangement' in Beckus 98).

[4] Though stylistically poles apart, both Rawsthorne and Arnold had a predilection for the Chaconne. Indeed I have a BBC Transcription disc where Arnold conducts a performance of the slow movement (marked Chaconne) of Rawsthorne's First Piano Concerto with Louis Kentner as soloist.

Fig.1. Use of semitones: The Trek from The Bridge on the River Kwai
© Columbia Pictures Music Corporation

Fig.2a. Use of triplets: Main theme from The Heroes of Telemark
© Screen Gems-Columbia Music Inc.

Fig.2b. Use of triplets: A theme from The Inn of the Sixth Happiness
© B.Feldman & Co.Ltd/Miller Music Corporation

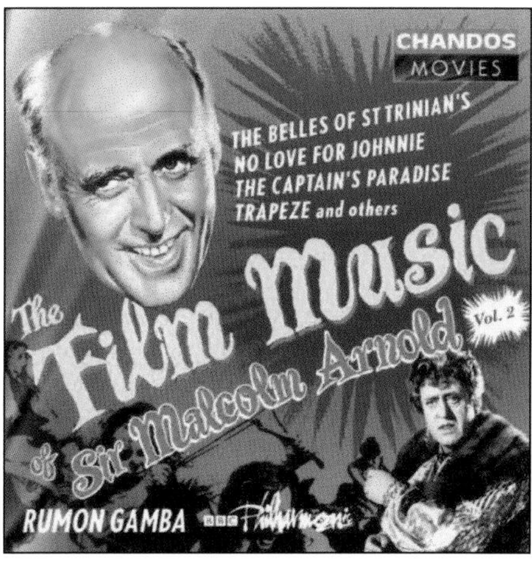

The Film Music of Malcolm Arnold, Vol.2, on Chandos

definitive fingerprints that seem to turn up in most scores (Erich Wolfgang Korngold, for instance, had a certain phrase that, it is said, he deliberately included in every one of his scores, as a kind of signature). In Arnold's case it could be accumulated semitones, usually on horns (Ex.1), or the triplet at the end of main themes (Exx.2a and 2b). Overall Arnold has been one of the most straight-forward subjects for my reconstructions, which does not in any way diminish his skill or musicianship, but simply says it as it is. There is therefore less guess-work than there might be in the works of other film composers, much of that because of questionable balance and recording.

Much of this was brought home to me when, as part of the Chandos Film Music series I was responsible for Volume 2 of Arnold's film music. It was the usual mixture of takedown and reorganisation of material, as without the full scores I had nothing to go on except the sound-tracks themselves, often issued on LP at the time of the film's release, such as the one from *Trapeze*.

However, apart from his famous 1952 Rhapsody for orchestra: The Sound Barrier Op.38, Arnold only reinvestigated one other soundtrack excerpt, which was *No Love for Johnnie.*[5] This Suite he (conveniently) conducted and recorded for the BBC, thus giving me a dialogue and sound effects-free performance from which to work, the full score having disappeared like so many others before it.

However, other titles which were to be featured on the Chandos CD did require some filtering and reorganisation of material. For *Stolen Face* for instance, given the storyline, I thought a mini-piano concerto was in order, and so I laid out the musical material to form, hopefully, a Warsaw Concerto-type movement involving the piano in parts of the score where Arnold had not used it.

In the case of *The Captain's Paradise,* I thought a musical postcard (the ones you can buy with several photographs – or in this case, themes – on the front) would suit best; then I could leave the main theme right until the end for the greatest effect.

It has always been a surprise and a tremendous help when a full score suddenly turns up and with *David Copperfield* such an occasion presented itself. Being Arnold's last cinematic score it was fitting, for a change, to have the real thing, just leaving me to do some 'topping and tailing' to make it work away from the picture.

I believe that there are still several Arnold scores which would benefit from similar treatment, not least both the TV series *War in the Air* and *Espionage,* as well as the film documentary *The Beautiful County of Ayr,* wherein lies the original version of Scottish Dance No.2. The supposedly drunken section with the solo bassoon is no such thing in the film, being an accompaniment to a particularly uncooperative cow!

Meanwhile I am happy to continue dipping my toe in the great sea of film music which I have loved and admired since I was a child. When I am asked to work on any of my absolute favourite films the job is even more rewarding; for instance, I have worked on *The Quiet Man, The Thirty Nine Steps, Kind Hearts and Coronets* and *Goodbye Mr Chips.* Whether or not the films are my favourites, the process is repeatedly satisfying, from scribbling down a piano score and orchestrating it to producing the performance in the studio.

The only bigger thrill is when the music is my own.

Philip Lane

Original 'Trapeze' soundtrack on LP

[5] Philip Lane's comments here refer to Arnold's feature films. In 1951 Arnold also re-worked the music from the 1948 documentary film *Report on Steel* into his Symphonic Study: Machines Op.30, a work not premiered until October 1984 (BBC Scottish Orchestra conducted by Sir Charles Groves).

List of feature films

Films are listed in order of release date. Here are some notes on the listings.

Feature film or documentary?

We have classified the following borderline cases as follows:

Feature films

- *The Story of Gilbert & Sullivan* (1953) – biopic of the operetta writers

Documentaries

- *The Frasers of Cabot Cove* (1949) – a picture of life in Newfoundland
- *Antony and Cleopatra* (1951) and *Julius Caesar (1951)* – abridged versions of the Shakespeare plays for educational use
- *Man of Africa* (1953) – a dramatisation of the Bakiga people's attempt to cultivate the Kigezi district of Uganda

Uncredited and rejected contributions

The following films, where Arnold had some involvement in the music, have been included for the sake of completeness:

- *The Astonished Heart* (1950) – Arnold assisted William Blezzard with the musical arrangements (uncredited)
- *Up for the Cup* (1950) – Arnold scored several sequences for Percival Mackey (uncredited)
- *The Story of Gilbert & Sullivan* (1953) – Arnold arranged the music (uncredited)
- *Invitation to the Dance* (1956) – Arnold's score was rejected and replaced by one by André Previn
- *The Barretts of Wimpole Street* (1957) – Arnold's score was rejected and replaced by one by Bronislau Kaper
- *Solomon and Sheba* (1959) – Arnold wrote some of the sequences to help Mario Nascimbene (uncredited)
- *Suddenly Last Summer* (1959) – Arnold was taken ill during the project and the score was completed by Buxton Orr
- *The Battle of Britain* (1969) – Arnold assisted William Walton with the score (uncredited) – then Walton's score was rejected (apart from the 'Battle in the Air' sequence) and replaced by one by Ron Goodwin
- *The Wildcats of St Trinian's* (1980) – Arnold's music from the previous St Trinian's films was used, with the rest of the score being written by James Kenelm Clarke

We have not included *Blind Date* [aka *Chance Meeting*] (1958), in which Arnold conducted the soundtrack which was composed by Richard Rodney Bennett.

How many film scores did Malcolm Arnold write?

You may hear various numbers quoted, and it is not possible to give an exact answer, because there are grey areas. What counts as a feature film and what counts as a documentary? Should we include films where Arnold assisted another composer or contributed a part of the score, or where his score was ultimately rejected?

This book lists 71 feature films (including 9 borderline cases, listed above) and 51 documentaries; in addition there are a couple of television series (*War in the Air*, *Espionage*) and a number of television theme tunes. So an answer to the question might be "roughly 70 feature films and 50 documentaries – 120 altogether".

Year

The year associated with a film is the year of its release. Other publications may refer to the year of production, which could be different.

Locations

Sources of information for film locations include the following websites:

- ReelStreets, www.reelstreets.com
- IMDb, www.imdb.com
- Wikipedia, www.wikipedia.org
- BFI, www.bfi.org.uk

and the following books:

- *The Worldwide Guide to Movie Locations*, Tony Reeves, London, 2006
- *London Film Location Guide*, Simon R.H. James, Batsford, London, 2007
- *Movie London*, Tony Reeves, Titan Books, London, 2008
- *Film and TV Locations: A Spotter's Guide*, Lonely Planet, 2017

There are still some films where our knowledge is sketchy, particularly for those filmed abroad, for example *The Lion* (1962), *Nine Hours to Rama* (1963), *Port Afrique* (1956) and *The Thin Red Line* (1964). We would welcome any information – contact us via **www.malcolmarnoldsociety.co.uk**

DVDs

The EAN (European Article Number) and UPC (Universal Product Code) are standard numbering systems used to identify DVD products (comparable to an ISBN for books). [The EAN is 13 digits and the UPC is 12 digits; an EAN starting with '0' is followed by the UPC.]

Region 0 and 2 DVDs are suitable for UK DVD machines. Region 1 (US) will only play on a multi-region player. All Blu-rays listed are suitable for UK.

We are grateful to Terry Cushion for providing this information.

Music notes

We are grateful to Christopher Ritchie for providing music notes for many of the films.

MAF performances

MAF refers to the Malcolm Arnold Festival, which has been held in Northampton each October since 2006. Many pieces of film music have been arranged and performed for the first time at these festivals.

www.malcolmarnoldfestival.com

References

- 'Beckus' refers to the quarterly newsletter of the Malcolm Arnold Society; see www.malcolmarnoldsociety.co.uk
- 'Maestro' refers to the annual journal of the Malcolm Arnold Society; see www.malcolmarnoldsociety.co.uk
- 'Rogue Genius' refers to Meredith, Anthony and Harris, Paul: 'Malcolm Arnold: Rogue Genius', Thames/Elkin, 2004

Badger's Green (1949)

Production Highbury Productions
Producers John Croydon and Adrian Worker
Director John Irwin
Stars Barbara Murray, Brian Nissen, Garry Marsh
Music played by London Symphony Orchestra/John Hollingsworth
Adapted screenplay
R C Sherriff from his (1930) play [*Publisher* J M Dent, 1936 and 1950]
Locations
1. The cricket match was filmed at Littlewick Green, near Maidenhead, Berkshire, with members of the local cricket team also taking part.
2. Highbury Studios, London.

Release
UK release date 28 February 1949

Location: Littlewick Green, near Maidenhead

Articles
(i) Escott, Graham: 'The Road to Badger's Green' – Beckus 72, Spring 2009

Notes
See main article 'Badger's Green: Arnold's first film score' on the next page.

Britannia Mews (1949)

***US title* The Forbidden Street**
***Alt title* The Affairs of Adelaide**
Production Twentieth Century Fox
Producer William Perlberg
Director Jean Negulesco
Stars Dana Andrews, Maureen O'Hara, Sybil Thorndike
Music played by Royal Philharmonic Orchestra/Muir Mathieson
Adapted screenplay
Ring Lardner Jnr, from the novel by Margery Sharp [*Publisher* Little Brown & Co, 1946]. Film edition: Fontana, 1954 and 1961
Locations
1. Maureen O'Hara (Adelaide Culver) meets Dana Andrews (Henry Lambert) on the bridge over St James Park, SW1, with the Foreign and Commonwealth Offices on Whitehall in the background
2. She later takes a cab to Brummel's Tea Rooms in Beauchamp Place, Knightsbridge, before walking on to the Albert Embankment having taken the steps from Westminster Bridge Road, SE1, with the Houses of Parliament in the background.
3. Adelaide Culver's large parental home – unidentified
4. London Film Studios, Shepperton, Surrey

Release
UK premiere London, 24 February 1949
UK release date 31 March 1949

Book

Poster (US)

US release date 3 May 1949
US premiere New York City, 13 May 1949
Australian release date 3 February 1950
Media
DVD EAN/UPC 0024543827375. Cinema Archives. USA. Region 0
Music notes
Arnold shows remarkable maturity in one of his first major film scores. The film itself, however, is a preposterous piece of Hollywood hokum. The highly improbable story-line tells of a well-bred girl (O'Hara) whose fascination for the sordid Britannia Mews (a forbidden street to her class) leads her into a life of poverty and squalor. If that were not bad enough, the background detail is far from convincing. The cockney characters seem straight out of a wartime Hollywood idea of old England. Thorndike is too theatrical and Andrews is uncomfortable in a dual role, of which one (a drunken painter) is the voice of another actor.

Despite his lack of film experience,

Badger's Green: Arnold's first film score

The cricketing film *Badger's Green* was particularly significant in advancing the career of the young Malcolm Arnold. It was his first feature film, and also his first (and last) with the Highbury Studios organisation. Highbury Studios were acquired by the Rank organisation, which quickly repaired the bomb damage their North London premises had suffered in 1944. Rank had originally earmarked Highbury as a special effects department and a home for its 'Company of Youth' talent school. However, it was quickly promoted to a new production company called Production Facilities (Film) under the direction of Ealing's John Croydon, where Rank's novice contract artists and technicians could develop their skills producing 45-60 minute 'programme fillers' and importantly, with a budget of around £25,000 per film [£860,000 in today's money], saving the dollars spent on American-produced second features.[1]

The first of the Highbury 'curtain-raisers' went into production in July 1947 with, ironically, a ghost story entitled *Colonel Bogey*. It was released in 1948 with Terence Fisher[2] making his directorial debut. The studio pushed the boat out with their inaugural film and felt confident enough to go to the expense of commissioning a score from the composer Norman Fulton.[3] The music was played by the London Philharmonic Orchestra conducted by the ubiquitous John Hollingsworth.[4] It is highly likely that Malcolm Arnold was still in the orchestra at the time of the recording at the end of 1947 (his final concert with the orchestra was in February 1948). By the time Arnold had returned from his Italian sabbatical in the summer of 1948 and started work on his film commission for *Badger's Green*, Rank had just announced the abandonment of their new 'B' film experiment, preferring in future to distribute films rather than make them. The closure was also part of a raft of measures designed to cure the company's insolvency crisis.

Their last two films were to be *Love in Waiting* (1948) and *Badger's Green* (1949). *Badger's Green* was a remake of the 1934 Paramount British Production directed by Adrian Brunel and starring the young Valerie Hobson. Directed by John Irwin[5] and starring Garry Marsh and Kynaston Reeves as a couple of self-important pillars of the local community, *Badger's Green* was the Highbury unit's swan-song. It was successful in relation to Highbury's mission to blood new talent, as the film's female lead, Barbara Murray, graduated to a part in Ealing's *Passport to Pimlico* (1949), but it failed as a contemporary comedy-drama. Fifteen years before,

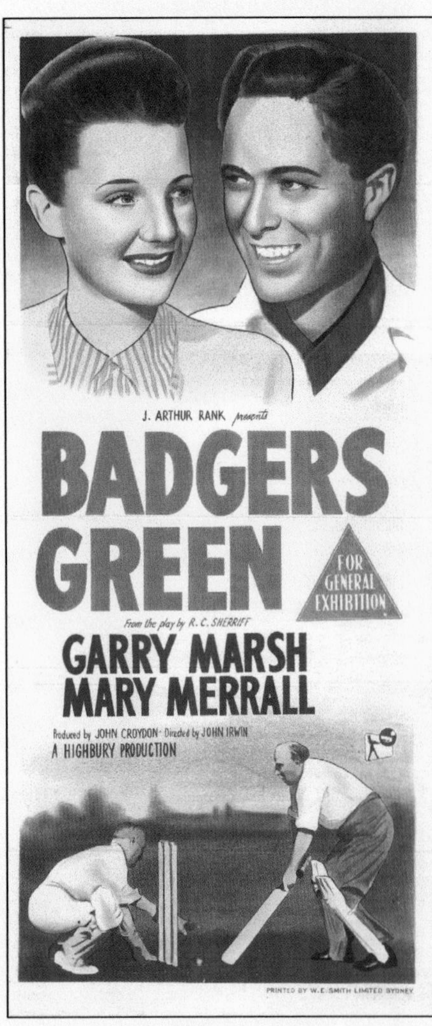

Poster for Badger's Green

its whimsical story[6] of a group of villagers putting aside their differences to unite against a threat to their way of life in the form of a modernising developer had put its finger on the concerns of a rural public. In 1949, it seemed unnecessarily reactionary.

"The theme seemed old-fashioned," commented *To-Day's Cinema*, 14 January 1949, "and a cricket match filmed at Littlewick Green, Maidenhead, Berkshire,[7] as a finale,

---

1 At the same time a duty on imported American films created a reciprocal embargo from the Hollywood studios on any UK distribution rights.

2 Terence Fisher (1904-1980) would later go on to direct three Hammer horror films with Arnold soundtracks, namely *Stolen Face*, *Wings of Danger* and *Four-Sided Triangle*.

3 Norman Fulton (1909-1980). Among Arnold's other contemporary composers vying for attention from the film production companies (and a £400 [£14,000 today] cheque for a score) would have been Doreen Carwithen, Stanley Black and Ivor Slaney. Slaney was an oboist in the war-time LPO, alongside Malcolm Arnold; he had also performed Arnold's *Suite Bourgeoise* in 1940 with the flautist Richard Adeney and the composer at the piano, to say nothing of busking on the streets of West London with the young trumpeter while they were both students at the Royal College of Music!

4 The influential conductor John Hollingsworth (1916-1963) did much to encourage Arnold to send his latest orchestral score to the Rank organisation, which probably resulted in the young composer obtaining that first all-important commission to provide the soundtrack for a Highbury Studios feature film. Hollingsworth, in fact, conducted the London Symphony Orchestra in Malcolm's very first film score, for the Jack Swain 1947 documentary *Avalanche Patrol* (qv). According to the authors of *Rogue Genius*, Paul Harris and Tony Meredith, it was "the violinist Sidney Twinn [who] constantly nagged him to 'send a score to Denham'. Malcolm [eventually] carried out Twinn's suggestion and was given a film at once. The score he had forwarded was *Beckus*."

5 The authors of *Rogue Genius* remind us that Arnold was none too pleased with Irwin's abandonment of any music during the cricket match itself, not even for the sight and sound of the ball smashing through a window as the winning runs are scored!

6 Based on an original play by R C Sherriff (1896-1975) and with a screenplay by William Fairchild. The original play was transmitted live from the BBC Television studios on 1 September 1953, produced by John Warrington and starring David Aylmer and Hugh Dempster.

7 (i) Under the headline 'Glo'ster Cricket Team were successful on *Badger's Green*', the *Gloucester Citizen* of 4 September 1950 reported:
"Playing on the village green which

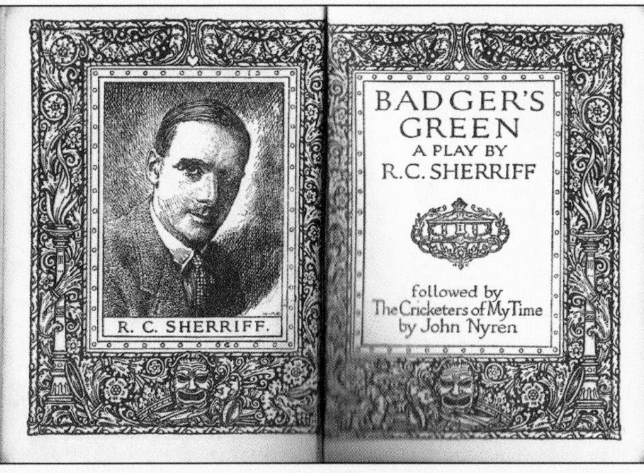

Above: The original play by R C Sherriff
Right: A still from the film. Photo: Ronald Grant Archives

provided insufficient excitement for contemporary audiences"; though *Kinematograph Weekly*, 20 January 1949, talked of the film's nostalgic appeal and its "flawless atmosphere", hailing "a modest but really English film at last".

The English obsession with cricket as a subject for 'B' movies made an early showing during the post-war period, not only in *Badger's Green* (1949) but in *It's Not Cricket* (1949), *Death of an Angel* (1952) and *Four-Sided Triangle* (1952) (another Arnold soundtrack)[8] "... and then virtually disappears. One can only speculate on the reasons, but the consideration given to the female and American audiences in conceiving the 'B' movie scenario is likely to be a significant factor."[9]

Released on 24 February 1949 and distributed by GFD (General Film Distributors), *Badger's Green* was the second feature for the main event, one of which was entitled *Eureka Stockade.*[10] It was still doing the rounds in the summer of 1951 as some local cinema advertisements would indicate.

Despite an inauspicious start with Highbury Productions, Arnold had had the opportunity not only to show his talent in providing an appropriately English score[11] – the 20-minute soundtrack, for a 60-minute film, was played by the London Symphony Orchestra (again) conducted by John Hollingsworth) – but also to network with influential contacts in the rapidly expanding world of the cinema in post-war Britain. His next foray into film would be a 60-minute soundtrack for the Twentieth-Century Fox 90-minute feature film *Britannia Mews* (1949). Here the soundtrack was played by the Royal Philharmonic Orchestra conducted by another Arnold mentor and enthusiast, Muir Mathieson (1911-1975).

Acknowledgements

Much of the material about the history of the Highbury Productions film unit was gleaned from the BFI book *The British 'B' Film* by Steve Chibnall and Brian McFarlane[12] (*Publisher* Palgrave Macmillan, 2009) and we are pleased to acknowledge their thorough scholarship and detailed researches into this hitherto unchronicled history of the movie business. Among the other 'B' movies with Arnold soundtracks discussed in their excellent publication are: *Albert RN*, *The Angry Silence*, *Drums for a Holiday*, *Four-Sided Triangle*, *Home to Danger*, *It Started in Paradise*, *Stolen Face*, *Welcome the Queen!* and *Wings of Danger*.

Alan Poulton

---

was used in the filming of the cricket scenes of *Badger's Green*, Gloucester on their Sussex tour had a fine win over Benenden."

(ii) A visitor to the 'Reel Streets' website in November 2007 enquired if there was a copy of the film available: "I happen to know that the film was made in the village of Littlewick Green. My dad was in the local cricket team [and] was asked to be in the film as apparently the actors did not have a clue how to play cricket! There is a photo of him with the cricket team and the actors, but we have never seen the film." [Sadly, the film is not available commercially, but we live in hope – Ed.]

(iii) The setting of Littlewick Green together with its pub 'The Cricketers' has often been used as a backdrop for TV dramas including *Midsomer Murders*; the nearby Redroofs Theatre School was for many years the home of Ivor Novello (1893-1951): a blue plaque on the wall describes him as 'Composer, Dramatist, Actor and Man of Theatre'.

8 Some 25 years later Arnold would write the 'Hallow Cricket Song' for his soundtrack for the 1963 feature film *Tamahine* set in an English public school.

9 *Picturegoer* of 4 June 1949 lamented: "Cricket as a basis for a film has been sadly neglected by our British producers." The situation was not helped by the release of a rather dull 1948 documentary from Ambassador entitled *It's a Great Game*. Billed as the "biggest attraction since the Royal Wedding [of Princess Elizabeth and Prince Philip on 20 November 1947] Victor Gover's [film] was one of the more static pieces of sporting cinema. Filmed at Bushey it consisted of an extended discussion about cricket by schoolboy idols Bill Edrich and Denis Compton."

10 Described in the press release as a successor to that great Australian picture *The Overlanders* (with a score by John Ireland) this tale of the gold rush in New South Wales and the battle for Eureka Hill starred Chips Rafferty and Jane Barrett.

11 Harris and Meredith's description of Arnold's score in *Rogue Genius* says: "Malcolm's music, written in the style he was shortly to make famous with his 'English Dances', lends strong support both to the comic mood and the charming rustic setting. There are some atmospheric moments early on when, to the sound of the sunniest of waltzes, the camera explores the lovely village. Various little dramas like the obstructive tactics of the local constables against the developer are neatly highlighted in the score. Everything Malcolm offers is stylish and appropriate."

12 Steve Chibnall is Professor of British Cinema at De Montfort University, UK, and Brian McFarlane is Adjunct Associate Professor at Monash University, Melbourne, Australia, and Visiting Professor, University of Hull, UK.

Arnold does his best to pull things together. The refined, cultured world of the well-bred Victorians is musically painted in warm and yet delicate colours with just the right period feel in the orchestration; a hint of what was to come in the *Hobson's Choice* score. A contrast is provided by the pianola street music of Britannia Mews and the music hall quality of the puppet theatre scenes. Many parts of the film are aided by Arnold's ability to write behind the dialogue and yet be able to reflect the changes of mood and tempo of the scenes. Several music cues are fitted so that they start on a particular piece of action, such as Dana Andrews falling down a flight of stairs; this is a favourite Arnold device. The horrible old blackmailer Mrs Mounsey (Thorndike) is represented by an ominous, unsettling motif with rhythmic beat of brass and drums. Arnold's music works particularly well in the puppet sequences where the dance-like woodwinds help bring the figures to life.

It is surprising that it took two years before Arnold worked again on another major feature film, but it is possible that Muir Mathieson's alleged interference on *Britannia Mews* led to Arnold doing more work in the field of documentaries.

Your Witness (1950)

***US title* Eye Witness**
Production Coronado Productions
Producer Joan Harrison
Director Robert Montgomery
Stars Robert Montgomery, Leslie Banks, Felix Aylmer
Music played by (London Symphony) Orchestra/John Hollingsworth

Original screenplay
Hugo Butler, Ian McLennan Hunter and Joan Harrison, with William Douglas-Home

Locations
1. It has not been possible to identify the location of the 'Coronet Cinema' which Muriel Pavlov enters
2. However, the hit-and-run moment takes place outside a shop front called 'Gladwell & Fuller', possibly EC4; also a London bus is seen on South Road
3. Warner Brothers First National Studios, Teddington, Middlesex

Release
UK premiere London, 25 January 1950
UK release date 6 March 1950
US premiere New York City, 26 August 1950
Australian release date 16 January 1953
TV premiere Finland, 19 October 1961

Media
DVD EAN/UPC 0089859061127 Kit Parker Films. USA. Region 0 [with 'Breakdown']
DVD EAN/UPC 5027626422943. Network. UK. Region 2

Poster

The Astonished Heart (1950) [arranger/uncredited]

Production Gainsborough Pictures/Sidney Box
Producer Anthony Darnborough
Director Terence Fisher
Stars Celia Johnson, Noël Coward, Margaret Leighton
Music played by London Symphony Orchestra/Muir Mathieson

Adapted screenplay
Noel Coward from his original play
Acting edition: Samuel French, 1938
Director Terence Fisher

Locations
1. Stanhope Gate and Lodges, Park Lane
2. Noel Coward and Margaret Leighton talk by the fountains overlooking the Long Water in Kensington Gardens
3. Joyce Carey meets Celia Johnson under the clock at Waterloo Station
4. Pinewood Studios, Iver Heath, Bucks

Release
US premiere Park Avenue Theatre, New York City, 15 February 1950
UK release date 2 March 1950
European release date Denmark, 12 April 1950
Australian release date 8 December 1950

Media
DVD EAN/UPC 5060105720659. ITV Studios. UK. Region 2

Sheet music
Symphonic Suite from the film arranged for piano solo, published by Chappell (1950) and now available as a reprint through Faber Music.

Articles
(i) 'Movie Review', in New York Times, 15 February 1950

Notes
(i) William Blezard was asked to provide special arrangements of Noel Coward's music and, owing to the

Poster

very tight deadlines required by the Director and Producer, Malcolm Arnold volunteered to assist Bill with the final orchestrations (their joint contribution to the film's soundtrack was uncredited).

(ii) Excerpts from the soundtrack were broadcast on 'Film Time' introduced by Leslie Mitchell – BBC Home Service, 2 March 1950

(iii) A 'Symphonic Suite' from the film was broadcast on BBC Radio 3 on 29 April 2008, the London Symphony Orchestra conducted by William Blezard.

Location: The Italian Gardens in Kensington Gardens, London

Sheet music

Up for the Cup (1950) [part/uncredited]

Production Henry Halstead Productions (Byron Films)
Producers Henry Halstead and Alan Cullimore
Director Jack Raymond
Stars Albert Modley, Mae Bacon, Helen Christie
Adapted screenplay
Jack Marks and Con West, from an original story by Robert Patrick Weston and Robert Lee[1]

Locations

1. Yorkshire and London (?)
2. Nettlefold Studios, Walton-on-Thames, Surrey

Notes

(i) Percival Mackey composed most of the music but Malcolm Arnold orchestrated several of the longer sequences to help meet the critical delivery date (uncredited)

Lobby card

1 They provided the screenplay for the original 1931 film: as song writers they were also responsible for such iconic numbers as 'Knees Up Mother Brown'(!)

No Highway (1951)

US title **No Highway in the Sky**
Production Twentieth Century Fox
Producer Louis D Lighton
Director Henry Koster
Stars James Stewart, Marlene Dietrich, Glynis Johns
Music played by Orchestra/Marcus Dods
Adapted screenplay
R C Sherriff, Oscar Millard and Alec Coppel, from the novel by Neville Shute [*Publisher* Heinemann, 1948]. Film edition: Pan Books, 1963
Locations

1. Opening shot of aircraft hangars and workers arriving/leaving by the South Gate entrance to the Royal Aircraft

Far left: Poster
Left: Book

Establishment, Farnborough Road, Farnborough, Hampshire
2. James Stewart walks down a road beside a high wall (unidentified but thought to be in Farnham, Surrey)
3. There is a shot of Gander Airport in Newfoundland seen through the blades of a propeller on a waiting aircraft
4. Further airfield scenes were filmed at Blackbushe Airport, Yateley, Hampshire
5. Denham Studios, Denham, Bucks

Release

UK premiere London, 28 June 1951

US premiere Roxy Cinema, New York City, 21 September 1951

European release date France, 5 October 1951

Australian release date 3 October 1952

UK TV premiere BBC1 Television, 16 October 1966

Media

DVD EAN/UPC 4260261432200. KSM Klassiker. Germany. Region 2

DVD EAN/UPC 0024543878162. Cinema Archives. USA. Region 1

Music notes

Despite there being no music credit on the titles, Arnold provides opening title music of about a minute and an even shorter end title. According to Arnold, he and director Henry Koster felt that the film needed only title music.

Based on the novel by Nevil Shute, the film concerns a somewhat eccentric professor (Stewart) whose research work at the Royal Aircraft Establishment leads him to believe that the tail will fall off a newly designed aircraft after a certain number of flying hours.

Arnold's title music with characteristic brass fanfares and swirling woodwinds provides the impetus for a dominant, ever-evolving theme carried by high strings and resolved by the brass section. It is so short that it can only help the audience to look forward and anticipate the nature of the story to come. Could further music have helped? Personally, I feel the domestic scenes between the professor and his young daughter (Janette Scott) would have been helped by Arnold. Also, it is particularly hard to imagine a film featuring the legendary Marlene Dietrich without music. It must have been a temptation to put something in. However, the sound department have a field day and leave little room for music. The sound of Stewart's testing of the aircraft structure and the constant hum of the engines during the transatlantic flight provide their own soundtrack. The end title music is so short that the film finishes for too abruptly. What a contrast to today's never-ending closing credits.

Notes

(i) No incidental music, only title and end-title music employed.

(ii) Excerpts from the soundtrack were broadcast on 'Film Time' – BBC Home Service, 2 August 1951

Home to Danger (1951)

Production New World Pictures/Eros Films

Producer Lance Comfort

Director Terence Fisher

Stars Guy Rolfe, Rona Anderson, Francis Lister

Music played by (Royal Philharmonic) Orchestra/Muir Mathieson

Original screenplay

Francis Edge and John Temple-Smith, with Ian Stuart Black

Locations

1. Rona Anderson (Barbara Cummings) is driven from (London?) Airport to Old Square in Lincoln's Inn Fields, WC2, for the reading of the will
2. They later journey to 'Greensleeves Manor' in Sussex (location unidentified)
3. Dennis Harkin (Jimmy) is dropped off at his home near The Cannon pub in Queen Caroline Street, Hammersmith, W6 (the pub has since been demolished)
4. Riverside Studios, Hammersmith, London

Release

UK release date August 1951

Media

DVD EAN/UPC 089859855825

Poster

Home at Seven (1952)

***US title* Murder on Monday**
Production London Films
Producer Maurice Cowan
Director Ralph Richardson
Stars Ralph Richardson, Margaret Leighton, Jack Hawkins
Music played by Royal Philharmonic Orchestra/Muir Mathieson
Adapted screenplay
Anatole de Grunwald, from the play by R C Sherriff.
Acting edition: Samuel French, 1950
Locations
1. Opening shots of London commuters going home: one shot is filmed outside Baker Street Station, NW1
2. Ralph Richardson goes for a walk in Church Road, Teddington, passing The Park Hotel in Park Road and arriving at Teddington Police Station (since rebuilt) on the corner of Luther Road and Church Road
3. British Lion Studios, Shepperton, Surrey

Release
UK release date 17 March 1952
US premiere New York City, 6 October 1953
US release date 7 October 1953
TV premiere Germany, 10 November 1962
UK TV premiere BBC2 Television, 14 October 1978
Media
DVD EAN/UPC 507626413040. Network. UK. Region 2
Blu-ray EAN/UPC 5027626824242 Network. UK Region B
Music notes
The title music's energetic character reflects the opening scenes of city workers leaving their offices for home. Busy fanfares and a hint of the bells of St Paul's develop into an attractive theme for strings and woodwinds. This short main title leads straight into a light-aired, delicate section for woodwinds accompanying Richardson's arrival home and reflecting his unconcerned manner with no warning musically or dramatically of what is about to unfold: the story of Richardson's efforts at finding again his lost 24 hours due to amnesia while extricating himself from suspicion of murder.

In the score, Arnold supplies his own distinctive touches; pompous brass accompaniment for a nosy neighbour; pensive woodwinds and solemn rhythmic drums for the discovery of the murder victim. Arnold economically uses some of his main thematic material in longer cues for Richardson's walk to his doctor's surgery and his car ride to the local police station. Eerie sustained chords provide an appropriately unsettling tone whenever Richardson tries to recall past events and find an answer to his missing day.

For what is really a filmed stage play, Arnold often only has to cement certain scenes together with short bridging cues whose origins lie in the title music. He is at his best in the tender scenes with Ralph Richardson and his wife (Margaret Leighton) providing in his music great delicacy and feeling for the characters. A nice touch in the score occurs when Arnold alerts us musically to an impending development in the story at the moment when Richardson's front door bell rings to announce a surprise visitor and the answer to those missing 24 hours.

Despite its stage origins, *Home at Seven* is still a highly enjoyable piece of British film-making that benefits from a cast that rehearsed extensively before the three-week shooting schedule on instructions from Alexander Korda. The sincere playing of Richardson, Leighton and Jack Hawkins, along with Arnold's score, make this film still worth watching today.

Articles
(i) British Film Institute, Monthly Film Bulletin, March 1952

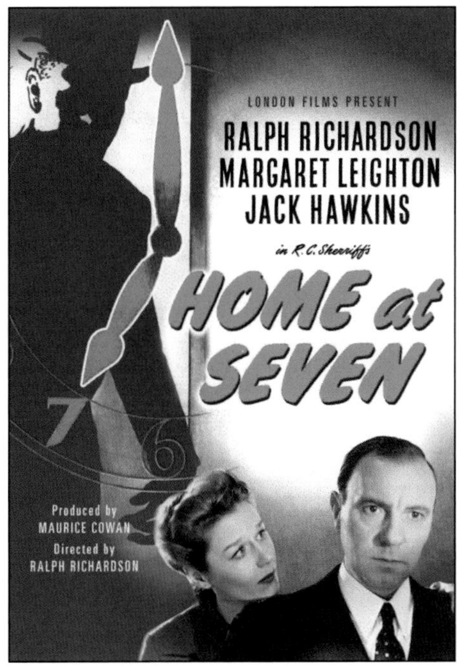

Posters: UK and US

Book

Notes
(i) Excerpts from the soundtrack were broadcast on 'Film Time' – BBC Home Service, 14 February 1952.
(ii) See main article 'Films of 1952' on page 32.

Wings of Danger (1952)

US title **Dead on Course**
Production Hammer Films
Producer Anthony Hinds
Director Terence Fisher
Stars Zachary Scott, Robert Beatty, Naomi Chance, Kay Kendall
Music played by London Philharmonic Orchestra/Malcolm Arnold

Adapted screenplay

John Gilling, based on the novel 'Dead on Course' by Trevor Dudley Smith (aka Elleston Trevor and Mansell Black) and Packham Webb [*Publisher* White Lion Publishers, 1974]

Locations

1. Rye, East Sussex
2. Riverside Studios, Hammersmith, London

Release

US premiere Los Angeles, California, 21 March 1952
US release date 1 April 1952
UK release date 26 May 1952
Australian release date 20 November 1953

Media

DVD EAN/UPC 089859056529. Kit Parker. USA. Region 0

Music notes

This is B-movie material filmed on a low budget at Riverside Studios with Hollywood import Zachary Scott in the leading role. In a professional manner, Arnold does everything that is required. The score is purely functional. The title music contains a somewhat relentless quality with dominant work from the brass. Suitably sustained chords are provided for moments of tension and there is some energetic writing for a chase. Source music is in the form of some sophisticated radio waltzes and Latin-American dance music for a restaurant scene. This is a good example of Arnold polishing his craft with a routine assignment about commercial pilots involved in a smuggling racket.

Poster

Stolen Face (1952)

Production Hammer Films
Producer Anthony Hinds
Director Terence Fisher
Stars Paul Henreid, Lizabeth Scott, André Morell
Music played by Bronwen Jones (piano)/London Philharmonic Orchestra/Malcolm Arnold

Adapted screenplay

Martin Berkley and Richard H Lanau, from an original story by Alexander Paal and Steven Vass

Locations

1. A Rolls-Royce draws up outside the 'clinic' on Belgrave Square at the corner of Chapel Street, SW1. Another shot of Belgrave Square has Wilton Crescent in the background
2. In another scene a car approaches the gates of Holloway Prison via Parkhurst Road, N7
3. Paul Henried (Philip Ritter) arrives at 'The Dog and Duck' pub (unidentified) on a rainy evening
4. Lizbeth Scott (as Lily Conover) steals a coat from Bentalls on Wood Street, Kingston-on-Thames and is apprehended
5. Later she takes the train to Plymouth; there is a shot of Surbiton Railway Station taken from Platform 2 where Lizbeth Scott (as Alice Brent) joins the train; a fight ensues, and the Bournemouth Belle locomotive is seen
6. Riverside Studios, Hammersmith, London

Release

UK release date May 1952
US release date 16 June 1952
Australian release date 26 June 1953
European release date Portugal, 29 July 1955

Media

DVD EAN/UPC 50193222. Kit Parker. USA. Region 0

Music notes

This is very much the case of a score that would appear to be too good for the picture. The attractive main title music for full orchestra and the piano soloist Bronwyn Jones is in the style of a romantic piano concerto. It is used to reflect the growing love between pianist Lizabeth Scoff and plastic surgeon Paul Henreid and in particular it illustrates a montage sequence depicting the pianist's European tour. The music provides plenty of emotional support and this film certainly needs some.

However the film does give Arnold the opportunity to write some longer musical cues. A good example is when Henreid goes on a motoring holiday; the music is light, cheerful and relaxed. He stops the night at a small inn and is subsequently kept awake by his next door neighbour who just happens to be Lizabeth Scoff and the result is the beginning of a beautiful friendship. Music underplays this whole sequence of events, never dominating but always adding just the right amount of musical support.

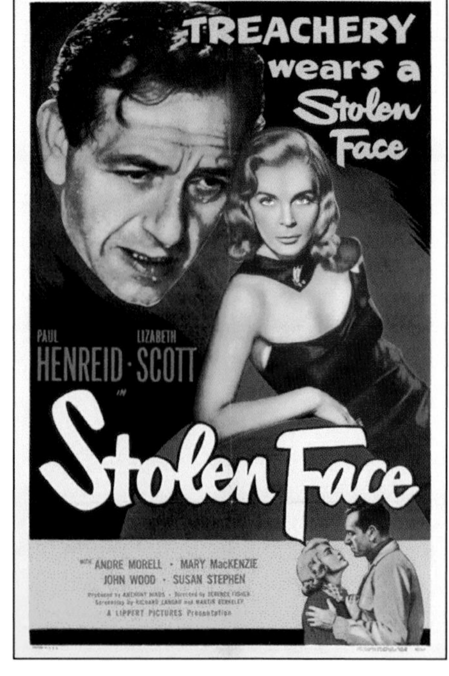

Poster

In one scene Scoff ploys the piano for Henreid. It is the concerto theme played in a slow romantic style. Now the audience only has to hear this piece to know when she is thinking of him. Arnold is also asked to supply jazz for a nightclub scene, a slow waltz number and dance-band music for a party sequence.

Amazingly the film score has survived and was found at the Royal College of Music. Did Arnold just happen to have this with him on a visit or did he feel it worth preserving? Either way the score cries out for a newly recorded suite for release on CD. It is pure Arnold in his richest melodic vein.

Autograph score

Full score (in 21 sections)

Instrumentation 3 2+bcl 2 2 – 4 3 3 0 – timp perc hp – str and solo piano

Currently at Eton College Library [MS 921 01 13]

Concert arrangement

Ballade for piano and orchestra arranged by Philip Lane (1999)

Duration 9'

Instrumentation 2 2 2 2 – 4 3 3 0 – timp perc(2) hp – str

Publisher Novello

Recording Phillip Dyson/BBC Philharmonic Orchestra/Rumon Gamba – Chandos CHAN 9831 (The Film Music of Sir Malcolm Arnold, Vol.2)

Articles

(i) Dyson, Phillip: 'Ballade of the Stolen Face' – Beckus 39, Winter 2000

(ii) Poulton, Alan: 'Bronwen Jones – pianist in *Stolen Face*' – Beckus 105, Summer 2017

Curtain Up (1952)

Production Constellation Films

Producer Robert Garrett

Director Ralph Smart

Stars Robert Morley, Margaret Rutherford, Kay Kendall

Music played by (Royal Philharmonic) Orchestra/Muir Mathieson

Adapted screenplay

Michael Pertwee and Jack Davies, from the play 'On Monday Next' by Philip King.

Acting edition: Samuel French, 1950.

Locations

1. The Industrial panoramic view of 'Drossmouth' (and its cooling tower) which opens the film has not yet been identified
2. The shots of the town centre clearly show Richmond Theatre on Little Green, Richmond, Surrey, next to the since-extended Onslow Hall as the bill poster updates the playbill
3. London Film Studios, Isleworth, Middlesex

Release

UK premiere London, 12 May 1952

US premiere New York City, 31 January 1953

UK TV premiere BBC2 Television, 17 May 1980

Media

DVD EAN/UPC 5060105724572. Strawberry. UK. Region 2

Book

Poster

DVD EAN/UPC 3984217456789. Euston. UK. Region 2

Music notes

The trials and tribulations of a small repertory company do not provide too many musical opportunities for composer Arnold. His main title does contain a swaggering comical motif for bassoon identified with producer Morley and a fluttering agitated piccolo solo for the inimitable Rutherford as the writer of the ghostly play which is in rehearsal throughout the film.

Articles

(i) British Film Institute, Monthly Film Bulletin, June 1952

(ii) 'Movie Review', in New York Times, 2 February 1953

Notes

(i) Excerpts from the soundtrack were broadcast on 'Film Time' – BBC Home Service, 15 May 1952.

The Sound Barrier (1952)

US title **Breaking (Through) the Sound Barrier**
Production London Films
Producer/Director David Lean
Stars Ralph Richardson, Ann Todd, Nigel Patrick
Music played by Royal Philharmonic Orchestra/Muir Mathieson
Original screenplay
Terence Rattigan[1]
Locations
1. We see the Regal Cinema (demolished in the 1970s) in New Zealand Avenue and the National Provincial Bank on the High Street, Walton-on-Thames (the latter now occupied by an estate agent)
2. The flying sequences were filmed at Chilbolton Aerodrome, Nether Wallop, Hampshire
3. British Lion Film Studios, Shepperton, Surrey

Release
UK release date 22 July 1952
South African premiere Johannesburg, 15 August 1952
US premiere Victoria Theatre, New York City, 6 November 1952
US release date 21 December 1952
UK TV premiere BBC1 Television, 31 December 1968

1 There is a contemporary book entitled 'The Sound Barrier' by Neville Duke [*Publisher* Cassell, 1953] which chronicles these unique events in aeronautical history

Awards
London Films – Oscar Winner for Best Sound Recording (1953)
Media
7" vinyl The Sound Barrier – Rhapsody Op.38 (1952). Royal Philharmonic Orchestra/Malcolm Arnold – Columbia SED 5542 (12/57)
DVD EAN/UPC 5055201805096. Studio Canal. UK. Region 2
DVD EAN/UPC 5055201833198. Studio Canal. UK. Region 2
DVD EAN/UPC 7321900384834. Studio Canal. UK. Region 2 (with Hobson's Choice)
Blu-ray EAN/UPC 5055201833204 Studio Canal. UK. Region B
Articles
(i) British Film Institute, Monthly Film Bulletin, September 1952
(ii) 'Movie Review' in New York Times, 7 November 1952
(iii) Ritchie, Christopher: The Arnold-Lean Trilogy, Part 1 – Beckus 27, Winter 1997 and Maestro 1, October 2014
Notes
(i) On 31 May 1952 Malcolm Arnold completed his orchestral Rhapsody 'The Sound Barrier' Op.38, based on the main themes from the film and their development follows the story line of the film.
(ii) Excerpts from the soundtrack were broadcast on 'Film Time' – BBC Home Service, 24 July 1952.
(iii) Interview with David Lean about his work on the film – BBC Television, 8 October 1952.

Poster

7" vinyl

(iv) See main article 'Films of 1952' on page 32.

It Started in Paradise (1952)

Alt title **Fanfare for Figleaves**
Production British Film-Makers
Producers Sergei Nolbandov and Leslie Parkyn
Director Compton Bennett
Stars Jane Hylton, Ian Hunter, Terence Morgan
Music played by (Royal Philharmonic) Orchestra/Muir Mathieson
Original screenplay
Marghanita Laski, with Hugh Hastings
Locations
1. Pinewood Studios, Iver Heath, Bucks

Release
UK premiere London, 28 October 1952
US release date 15 August 1953
Australian release date 25 September 1953

Left: Poster; sheet music

UK TV premiere BBC2 Television, 28 August 1969

Sheet music

Screenwriter Marghanita Laski also provided the lyrics to the romantic song 'Young Love: A Question of We'. Published by Paterson in 1952, the music was printed in an unusual negative format, with white notes on a dark green background. This is the first example of a published excerpt of Arnold's film music.

MAF performance

The song 'Young Love: A Question of We' was performed by Claire Thompson (soprano)/Scott Mitchell (piano), 19 October 2014 (MAF 9)

Media

7" vinyl On 9 December 1952, Diana Decker recorded the song "Young Love: A Question of We" with Muir Mathieson conducting a Studio Orchestra. This was issued on a Rank Film Music disc and on a BBC Sound Archive recording [BBC (SA) 18166] but, apparently, was not issued commercially in any format.

No commercial recording. View on YouTube: https://www.youtube.com/watch?v=4Xe-_Jo28ME

Notes

(i) Interviews on the film set were broadcast on 'Film Time' – BBC Home Service, 21 August 1952.

(ii) Excerpts were televised on 'Current Release', with John Fitzgerald – BBC Television, 19 November 1952.

The Ringer (1952)

***Alt title* The Gaunt Stranger**

Production London Films

Producer Hugh Perceval

Director Guy Hamilton

Stars Herbert Lom, Donald Wolfit, Mai Zetterling, William Hartnell

Music played by (Royal Philharmonic) Orchestra/Muir Mathieson

Adapted screenplay

Val Valentine, from the novel by Edgar Wallace [*Publisher* Hodder & Stoughton, 1925, as 'Gaunt Stranger']. Film edition: Pan Books, 1948-1957.

Locations

1. Shepperton Studios, Surrey

Release

European release date Sweden, 24 November 1952

UK premiere London, December 1952

UK TV premiere BBC2 Television, 27 November 1975

US premiere California, 29 August 1987 (Berkeley Art Museum & Pacific Film Archive)

TV premiere Germany, 20 August 1992

Media

DVD EAN/UPC 5027626398248. Network. UK. Region 2

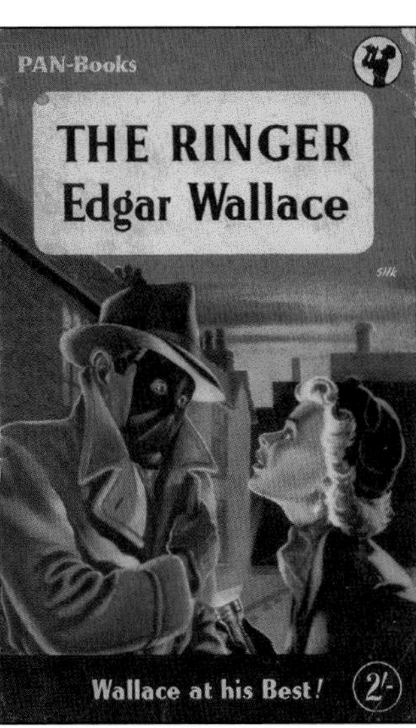

Book

Poster

Music notes

As far as the score is concerned, it is notable only for a grim, relentlessly-driven main title with a distinctly mysterious flavour in its short development. The film is a rather doted and unconvincingly acted melodrama that certainly betrays its 1930s origin.

Notes

(i) Excerpts were televised on 'Current Release' – BBC Television, 14 January 1953.

The Holly and the Ivy (1952)

Production London Films

Producer Anatole de Grunwald

Director George More O'Ferrall

Stars Ralph Richardson, Celia Johnson, Margaret Leighton

Music played by Royal Philharmonic Orchestra/Muir Mathieson

Adapted screenplay

Anatole de Grunwald, from the play by Wynyard Browne.
Acting edition: Evans Bros, 1950

Locations

1. Joyce & Matthews butcher's shop in Brompton Road, London, SW3 (now occupied by the Halifax Bank)
2. Margaret Halstan (Lydia Moncreiff) arrives at the Queen's Hotel on Kensington Gore, SW7, with the Albert Memorial in the left background
3. Hugh Williams (Lt Col Richard Wyndham) at the United Services Club looking towards St James's Palace from St James's Street, SW1
4. Postman seen making a delivery on Museum Street, Bloomsbury, WC1, with the British Museum on Great Russell Street in the background
5. Family members are seen arriving at Liverpool Street Station, EC2, for the journey to Norfolk
6. Denholm Elliott (Michael Gregory) makes his way by car to the fictional Norfolk village; shot of signpost 'Wyndenham 15 miles' (probably close to Shepperton Studios!)

Films of 1952: The Holly and the Ivy, Home at Seven and The Sound Barrier

The Holly and the Ivy

When Malcolm Arnold wrote a skilful orchestral arrangement of the traditional carol *The Holly and the Ivy* for the main title music for the film, it was for the purposes of its automatic association with its words, and hence with the title of the film, and he was probably complying with instructions from the director. This carol has become a part of the Christian celebrations of Christmas, and, through that association, the 'jolly' nature of its melody has obscured the esoteric meanings attached to the original. The deeper significance of the title and its relationship to the underlying narrative thread is further undermined by the inclusion of the tune of *The First Nowell* in his main titles arrangement. Nothing in the character of this arrangement of the two carols corresponds with the tensions and bitter undercurrents of the plot. The melody 'The Holly and the Ivy' is used throughout the film, but mainly in diegetic[1] cues involving carol singing, and the theme itself is not treated in any meaningful way that mirrors the developments of the narrative. As a dramatic interpretation, the best that can be said for the use of the main theme of this score is that, by its lack of empathy with the real dramatic situation, it serves to highlight the hypocrisy of Christmas festivities.

There is one important motif in this score which does indicate the true state of affairs that exists beneath the surface. Margaret, the sister who is perceived as cold and selfish because of her hedonistic life-style in London, is suffering deeply from the death of her child, of whose brief existence the family are in complete ignorance. Margaret tries to control her private grief through the use of alcohol and the projection of a hard persona, and this attitude, described in the film dialogue as being 'askew with the world', is the subject for a slithery motif, first heard on the bassoon (Example 1).

The first hearing of this motif occurs before Margaret has actually appeared on screen. While the phone rings in her empty flat, the camera pans to the doormat and picks out her invitation to Christmas at the family home. The motif is heard on solo bassoon over a sustained chord on strings and horns, as her name is seen on the envelope. The nature of this motif is in such marked contrast to the main theme, and to the previous music cues, that the audience is alerted to the fact that Margaret is in some way out of step with those around her. This is emphasized, in the second appearance of her motif, by the contrast between the sleazy triplet and its bustling accompaniment in duple time. The motif appears in the middle of a travel sequence showing the relatives making their way to the family home in rural Wyndenham. The bustling duple rhythm continues through the sequence, which depicts various modes of transport. Margaret is again conspicuous by her absence as the motif accompanies a shot of the empty car seat in which she should have been sitting. Played this time on solo trumpet, and with the first three notes changed to falling semitones, the motif demonstrates even more strongly Margaret's alienation from the rest of the family (Example 2).

When Margaret finally does make her first appearance on screen, nearly halfway through the film, she is seen looking out of the train window on her way to Wyndenham. Arnold chooses to illustrate this without empathy, by using a 'travel' variation of 'The Holly and the Ivy' theme. Because of the quality of Margaret Leighton's acting, the audience is left in no doubt as to her dissociation from the jolliness and eager anticipation the music suggests. One shot of her expression as she looks from the train shows that she is totally out of sympathy with the music and, therefore, with the whole spirit of Christmas celebrations.

The high standard of acting in this film makes it worth viewing, but tends to draw attention to its theatrical origins, and emphasize its uncinematic aspects. It also inhibits the composer. With actors of the quality of Ralph Richardson, Celia Johnson, Margaret Leighton and Denholm Elliott, who all tended to act on the screen with an extraordinary degree of physical restraint, the use of music becomes almost an impertinence. Only two scenes involving direct dialogue are scored with non-diegetic music cues. Scenes taking place outside the family home are used as an opportunity for scoring, in an attempt to open the film out, but these occur early on. Once all the characters are established in the main setting, the use of music becomes less plausible, and as the drama unfolds towards the end, there are no music cues at all for 18 minutes.

Arnold uses Margaret's motif four more times in the film, confirming it as a major element in the score. One of its most interesting aspects is its functioning to represent Margaret in her absence. The first and second cues using the motif are heard in conjunction with two brief shots – the invitation addressed to her, and the empty car seat. As these were both of less than 10 seconds' duration, the motif needed to be capable of creating a vivid impression of a person who is not present and who has yet to appear on screen.

The use of motifs in the absence of the character to whom they are attached was a very popular ploy of Hollywood composers. There were three main ways in which the device could be employed, each serving a slightly different function. If a motif for an absent person is heard while a visible association with him or her is present on the screen, such

Example 1. Margaret's motif from *The Holly and the Ivy*

Example 2. Margaret's motif in the travelling sequence from *The Holly and the Ivy*

1 diegetic: occurs as part of the action (rather than as background), and can be heard by the film's characters

as an empty place at the table, or some personal object, then its use may be considered gratuitous. Much depends upon the context, of course. There is all the difference in the world between the pointless repeated labelling of objects on the screen by musical codes that were prevalent in the classical Hollywood score, and the use Arnold makes of this motif in its first two appearances. When we see Margaret's name on the invitation, the motif suggests her dislocation from the rest of the family by its contrast with previous musical material, and its use serves a vital narrative function. If the envelope itself had made further appearances in the film, there would be no dramatic imperative to use the motif again, and we can be assured that Arnold would not have done so. The use of Margaret's motif in the second cue in the travelling sequence is, again, not the 'signposting' of the Hollywood composers, but the following of a narrative thread to hint at her anomalous situation.

Margaret's motif is heard for the third time in her absence during a conversation between two other characters, concerning her drinking. As she is referred to by name, and the subject of the motif, that of being 'askew with the world' is discussed, the use of her motif here is gratuitous. There is, however, a kind of motivic development by means of the change of instrumentation. On all previous occasions, her motif was played on a solo wind or brass instrument: namely bassoon, trumpet or alto flute. Here, underscoring the voices of her sister and her sister's fiancé, the motif is heard on the violins and violas – the change from the 'cold' solo instrument to the 'warmth' of a body of strings reflecting the sympathetic attitude of Jenny and David to her plight.

Of the six cues featuring Margaret's motif, three are heard in her absence, two of them before she appears on screen. The way the music is used informs the audience how powerful her influence is. This is the only narrative thread to be singled out in this way, and so it would seem to be even more surprising that the motif does not feature in the main titles. However, Arnold had a very individual approach to the writing of main titles, preferring not to put all his goods on display at once. Other composers too came increasingly to feel that a quick preview of all the main dramatic ideas of a film was neither compulsory nor entirely desirable. As audiences became more sophisticated, or at least more practised, in film viewing the notion of giving too much advance information about the nature of the forthcoming drama began to seem old-hat, particularly if the drama had tense or unexpected undercurrents to it. in 1952, the year that *The Holly and the Ivy* was released, two other films, both scored by Arnold, and both with curious parallels to it, were also released.

Home at Seven

Home at Seven was another direct translation to the screen of a successful stage play, and also starred Ralph Richardson and Margaret Leighton, this time as husband and wife. David and Janet are the ultimate representatives of respectable middle-class suburbia. David always returns home at seven in the evening from his banking job in the city, by train from Waterloo. The main titles appear over an introductory scene depicting his daily walk from the station, and are accompanied by a suitably bustling theme in the orchestra. The status quo of this diegesis is a parallel to the 'normality' of Christmas at Wyndenham, and the challenge to that status quo – a sudden attack of confusion and memory loss – is akin to the challenge posed by Margaret's 'askewness'. The motif associated with David's confusion is a peculiarly simple and eerie fragmented figure played on the cellos, under a 'mobile' of chromatic vibraphone clusters and clarinet trills (Example 3).

Just as with Margaret's motif, this representation of disruption to the status quo does not appear in the 'jolly' main titles cue. In both films, it is the dramatic element that represents the undermining of normality, the cross-current of the narrative, that is not hinted at in the main titles. By reserving the musical motif until its appropriate place in the drama, the impact of the contrast is strengthened. The first appearance of David's 'confusion' motif is particularly effective. It comes after 2 minutes of dialogue that are without music. This is the first dialogue scene in the film, so the audience are not preconditioned to make value judgments as to the characters' relative mental states. The quality of the acting distracts the attention from the stage-bound nature of this scene, with its unimaginative camera work. The restrained hysteria of Janet, who claims that David has been missing for a whole day, and David's calm reasoning with her, are acted with astonishing physical control and vocal virtuosity. It is not until the moment when the motif is heard, as David stares, totally without expression, at the date on the newspaper which supports Janet's claim, that a true moment of cinema is experienced. The juxtaposition of the image, and the unusually impressionistic music cue, inform the audience at once that all the notions they had gathered from the dialogue – Janet's instability, David's rationality – are being challenged.

Ironically, this motif is, in its economy, akin to the three-note chromatic motif of *King Kong*, the 1933 film with music by Max Steiner. Its remarkably torpid pace, however, puts it into a category of its own. The ten notes of the theme, as heard on its first appearance, occupy almost 40 seconds. Of all the film scores from the period under discussion, no other theme corresponding to a specific narrative thread is quite as attenuated as this. Because its vague, colouristic, directionless nature so perfectly illustrates David's trance-like state of confusion over his lost memory, there is no need for it to be developed extensively, and because it always represents the same situation in much the same way, it is heard virtually unchanged on each of its six further appearances. Both its nature and its function make conspicuous treatment of it unnecessary. It may have few notes, but it is neither short nor memorable, and for that reason it operates as a narrative hint on an emotional rather than an intellectual level.

The Sound Barrier

In the third film dating from 1952, Arnold demonstrates an altogether different method of 'withholding' a significant theme from the main titles music, by transforming it into something totally unrecognizable. The main titles to *The Sound Barrier* are themselves treated in an unusual way for the period, anticipating developments associated with the realism of the early 1960s. The first 2 minutes of the film are taken up with action sequences devoid of dialogue:

Example 3. David's 'confusion' motif from *Home at Seven*

The film starts with a clear sky above the cliffs of Dover, but as the camera turns we find ourselves beside the tail of a crashed aircraft on which appears a swastika. Soldiers are lounging on the cliff; we hear a mouth organ gently strumming; there is a Spitfire high in the sky. Then the music on soaring strings takes us up to the pilot who is full of the happiness of flight on a clear day, his machine racing across the sky. He goes into a dive – and suddenly the music changes into an ominous chattering sound. The plane is buffeting as it hits the sound barrier and the pilot tries frantically to pull it out of the dive. This is a fine piece of composition blended with the sound effects of the action. [Manvell and Huntley (2/1975), 135-6]

So there are two incidental music cues before the main titles, and the first cue is visibly diegetic, for the mouth organ is seen in the hands of one of the soldiers as he removes it from his lips. The use of a diegetic cue as the first piece of music in the film is both extremely unusual, and indicative of the changes that were to come in the use of music for film as the dramatic emphasis shifted towards naturalism. The main titles begin as the pilot succeeds in pulling out of the dive. The opening motif is an ominous figure played fortissimo on horns and trombones, warning of the dangers involved in the attempt to break the sound barrier (Example 4).

This motif functions in expected ways to highlight the consequences and potential threats of supersonic flight. Much of the power of this film is derived from the chilling performance of Ralph Richardson as John Ridgefield, the ruthless owner of the empire which is creating the first plane capable of breaking the sound barrier. The motif is used as a dirge at the burial of Ridgefield's son. The character of the theme is transformed by the change of instrumentation. Played legato on the cellos, it is softened into a lament. Directly after returning home from the funeral of his son, who has lost his life through fear of his father's disapproval, Ridgefield opens the package containing the model of the prototype, subsequently named Prometheus. When he holds the model up to the light, the theme is heard on muted horns, as his daughter realizes the potential threat to her husband, Tony, who will now assume the role of surrogate son to Ridgefield.

The unusual aspect of this motif is the way it is developed into something so unlike itself, that it qualifies as a separate motif altogether. Arnold effects this not by extreme measures, but by the usual methods of motivic alteration: changes to time signature, tempo and instrumentation. By transferring the motif to piccolo and celesta, and using the rhythm of a lullaby, Arnold enables it to create a completely different effect. It becomes hypnotic, as it from another world. Thematically, it is used to indicate how Tony's fascination with the challenge of breaking the sound barrier will lure him, like a siren, from his marriage to his death (Example 5).

It is first heard when Tony is discussing the mysteries of the sound barrier with the aircraft designer. and he sees the plans of Prometheus on the drawing desk. Later, when Tony debates the future of Prometheus with his father-in-law after the death of the test pilot, the audience knows what is really behind his words as he tells Ridgefield that the decision must lie with him. Because the 'siren' motif is heard at this point, it suggests that Tony is willing to sacrifice his life if the decision is made to go ahead. The night before Tony tests Prometheus, his wife sees him silhouetted against the stars as he stares towards them from the window. The 'siren' motif is heard again as she has the premonition that Tony will die. Just as in *The Holly and the Ivy* and *Home at Seven*, the motif represents the unnatural element in a character's makeup which threatens the status quo, in this case the marriage of Tony and Sue. Arnold appears to demonstrate deliberately that the motifs are two separate entities by playing them one after the other. As Sue is about to give birth on the night following Tony's death, she looks at the stars representing the mystery that has lured her husband from her.

The 'siren' motif is heard, immediately followed by the 'danger' motif. They delineate independent, but inevitably connected, threads of the drama. This is a most unusual example of a theme assuming a separate identity from its original source, both by transformation, and the manner of its application to the narrative.

Malcolm Arnold demonstrates a very sound understanding of the dramatic requirements of a film score by his manipulation of themes. Both he and William Alwyn may have suffered by being so closely associated with film, but they were gifted musico-dramatists. The ability to respond effectively in musical terms to the exigencies of the drama is not, alas, something that comes of its own accord. The technique of film scoring may be learnt empirically, much as any other musical technique, but the art of writing music that is truly in sympathy with the drama, and supports its development, is really dependent on the composer's natural affinity. An intuitive understanding of drama is a special gift, and is, unfortunately, not one of the talents granted to every composer.

Jan G Swynnoe

from 'The Best Years of British Film Music 1936-1958'
ISBN: 9780851158624
Reprinted by permission of Boydell & Brewer Ltd

Example 4. 'Danger' motif from *The Sound Barrier*

Example 5. 'Siren' motif from *The Sound Barrier*

Music examples © Paterson's/Novello

7. British Lion Studios, Shepperton, Surrey

Release

South African premiere Johannesburg, 2 December 1952

UK release date 22 December 1952

Australian release date 26 December 1952

US release date 4 February 1954

UK TV premiere BBC2 Television, 16 June 1979

Media

DVD EAN/UPC 5055201810601. Studio Canal. UK. Region 2

DVD EAN/UPC 5055201843241. Vintage Classics. UK. Region 2

Blu-ray EAN/UPC 5055201843258 Vintage Classics. UK. Region B

Music notes

Typically full of Christmas spirit – carols, chimes, percussion, bells – a time of musical rejoicing. Arnold's wonderful orchestrations make it sound as if he has written the carols himself, for they are so richly textured in his characteristic style. His music for Christmas morning in snow-covered Norfolk is full of eagerly-anticipated promise as the Gregory family find answers to their personal problems. The film is really a series of character studies and the fine cast make the most of their opportunity. Thankfully, the late Christopher Palmer put together a suite that captures much of the spirit of Arnold's original 1952 recording.

Concert arrangement

Suite arranged for orchestra by Christopher Palmer (1991). Subtitled 'Fantasy on Christmas Carols', the music is derived from the film's soundtrack as well as the carol arrangements Arnold made for the `Save the Children Fund' in 1960.

Duration 6'

Instrumentation 3 2 2 2 – 4 3 3 1 – timp perc(3) pno (cel) hp(2) – str

First performance London Symphony Orchestra/Richard Hickox – Barbican Hall, London, 21 December 1991

Publisher Novello (study score)

Recordings

(i) BBC Philharmonic Orchestra/Rumon Gambon – Chandos CHAN 9851 (The Film Music of Sir Malcolm Arnold Vol.2)

(ii) Royal Philharmonic Orchestra/John Scott – RPO Records CDRPO 7021, re-issued Alto Records ALC 1325

(iii) Royal Philharmonic Orchestra/ Anthony Inglis – RPO Records RPO 012

Poster

Notes

(i) The soundtrack includes the traditional Christmas carol 'The Holly and the Ivy', originally published by Cecil Sharp and in an arrangement by H Walford Davis.

(ii) See main article 'Films of 1952' on page 32.

The Story of Gilbert and Sullivan (1953) [arranger/uncredited]

Alt title **Gilbert and Sullivan**

US title **The Great Gilbert and Sullivan**

Production London Films

Director/Producer Sidney Gilliat/Leslie Gilliat/Frank Launder

Stars Robert Morley, Maurice Evans, Eileen Herlie

Music played by London Symphony Orchestra/Sir Malcolm Sargent, with the D'Oyly Carte Opera Company Chorus and soloists

Adapted screenplay Leslie Baily, Sidney Gilliat and Vincent Korda, based on 'The Gilbert and Sullivan Book' by Leslie Baily [*Publisher* Cassell, 1952; Spring Books, 1966]

Locations

1. British Lion Film Studios, Shepperton, Surrey

Release

European release date Sweden, 15 February 1953

UK premiere London 8 May 1953

Australian release date 5 June 1953

Left: Sheet music
Below: Book

South American premiere Argentina, 14 March 1954 (Mar del Plata Film Festival)
UK release date 17 March 1954
UK TV premiere BBC1 Television, 22 December 1976
Media
DVD EAN/UPC 5027626610449. Network. UK. Region 2
Blu-ray EAN/UPC 5027626833749. Network. UK. Region B
Sheet music
1. Piano selection, published by Chappell;
2. Set of sixteen songs, arranged for piano solo by Dudley Bayford, published by Francis, Day and Hunter.

Articles
(i) British Film Institute, Monthly Film Bulletin, June 1953
Notes
(i) Written to celebrate the Coronation of Queen Elizabeth II and the 21st anniversary of London Films.
(ii) Muir Mathieson appeared as the on-screen conductor and Malcolm Arnold was the uncredited music arranger.
(iii) An adaptation of the soundtrack for radio was broadcast on the BBC Light Programme on Christmas Day 1952.
(iv) Excerpts from the soundtrack were broadcast on 'Film Time' – BBC Home Service, 14 May 1953.

Four Sided Triangle (1953)

***Alt title* The Monster and the Woman**
Production Hammer Films
Producers Michael Carreras and Alexander Paal
Director Terence Fisher
Stars Barbara Payton, James Hayter, Stephen Murray
Music played by Royal Philharmonic Orchestra/Muir Mathieson
Adapted screenplay
Paul Tabori and Terence Fisher, from the novel by William F Temple [*Publisher* Galaxy Science Fiction Novel No.9, New York, 1951]
Locations
1. Opening shots of St Michael's Church in the High Street, followed by Ferry Road, The Old Vicarage, the Post Office and The Crown & Anchor pub, all filmed in Bray, Berkshire
2. 'Howdene' railway station is, in reality, Marlow in Buckinghamshire; another shot of 'Howdene' is in Village Road, Denham
3. Lulworth Cove in Dorset was used for the scene where Barbara Payton (Helen) goes for a swim in a suicide attempt
4. Bray Studios, Down Place, Oakley Green, Berkshire

Release
US premiere New York City, 16 May 1953
UK release date 25 May 1953
US release date 15 June 1953
Media
DVD EAN/UPC 5019322201632. Simply Media. UK. Region 2
Music notes
Four-sided Triangle is a mild forerunner of the Hammer productions of the later 1950s. Two young scientists invent a machine called a 'reproducer' that can duplicate humans as well as objects with the inevitable dire consequences.

Amazingly Arnold does find opportunities here for a worthwhile contribution.

Poster

Whether this particular film deserves it is another matter. The main theme is solidly attractive with a rich textured pastoral feeling. In fact it would not be out of place in Arnold's English Dances particularly with regard to tempo and orchestration. Another example of Arnold's worth is a short montage sequence showing the gradual development of the 'reproducer' where Arnold wisely takes the opportunity to increase the tempo of the film.

In what is really a rather slow, dreary tale, Arnold's music is like a breath of fresh air, especially when Murray and Payton take a holiday at the seaside; it is suitably romantic and idyllic. The contrived ending to a most unlikely story brings forth a very brief end title.

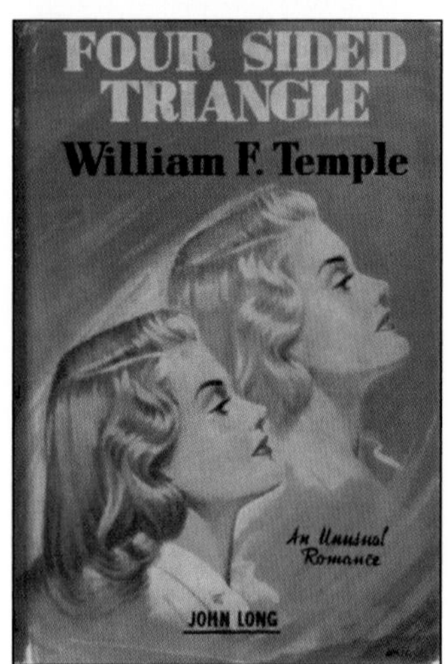

Book

Articles
(i) 'Movie Review' (WA) in *New York Times*, 16 May 1953
Notes
(i) Soundtrack includes Mendelssohn's 'Wedding March' arranged by Malcolm Arnold.

The Captain's Paradise (1953)

Original title **Paradise**
Alt title **The Captain's Progress**
Production London Films
Director/Producer Anthony Kimmins
Stars Alec Guinness, Celia Johnson, Yvonne de Carlo
Music played by Orchestra/Muir Mathieson

Adapted screenplay
Alec Coppel and Nicholas Phipps, based on a story by Alec Coppel.

Locations
1. Alec Guinness's ship 'Golden Fleece' is filmed travelling between Gibraltar and Kalique, a port in Spanish Morocco.
2. Shepperton Studios, Surrey.

Release
UK release date 9 June 1953
US release date 28 September 1953
South American premiere Argentina, 12 March 1954 (Mar del Plata Film Festival)
Australian release date 18 March 1954
TV premiere Hungary, 15 November 1962
UK TV premiere BBC1 Television 1 January 1971

Media
CD First Recording Excerpt: 'Opening titles' in compilation CD 'Hurrah for Malcolm Arnold' – Él/Cherry Red Records ACMEM95CD
DVD EAN/UPC 5060034571759. Optimum. UK. Region 2

Music notes
This is the story of a sea captain's search for true happiness with a wife at home in Gibraltar and a young woman across the sea in a North African port. Consequently Arnold's score is based on two contrasting themes.

One is firm and bold with his usual clear melodic lines to convey the spirit of home in Gibraltar with necessary brass to illustrate the military presence on the Rock. While at the fictitious port of Calique, an energetic rhythmic dance represents the exciting and exotic relationship with Yvonne de Carlo. The film is the story of how the captain's two worlds are kept apart until fate draws them together.

Arnold also supplies a Spanish flamenco dance with guitar solo as Alec Guinness as the Captain takes to the dance floor. The contrast in the Captain's lifestyle is musically illustrated with Latin American dance rhythms that suddenly cut to the formal music of a regimental brass band concert back in Gibraltar. As events take a turn for the worse, the music, still dominated by the two main themes, becomes distinctly more melancholy and slower in tempo. The main title material with its fast-moving dance rhythms is given the necessary reprise at the close. This is certainly another Arnold score that deserves some form of preservation on CD.

Concert arrangements

Opening titles
arranged by David Rose (c.1953)
Recording David Rose & his Orchestra – MGM (US) SE 4271; MGM (UK) K 1255

'Postcard from the Med'
excerpt from the film reconstructed, arranged and orchestrated by Philip Lane (c.2000)
Duration 4'
Instrumentation 2 2 2+Ten sax 2 – 4 3 4 1– timp perc(4) pno hp egtr – str
Publisher Novello
Recording BBC Philharmonic Orchestra/ Rumon Gamba – Chandos CHAN 9851 (The Film Music of Sir Malcolm Arnold, Vol.2)

Sheet music
'Flamenco' arranged by the composer for solo piano
Publisher Queens Temple Publications in in 'Piano Music Vol.2' (QT73)

MAF performance
'Flamenco' Moritz Ernst (piano), 16 October 2010 (MAF 5)

Poster

Alec Guinness and Celia Johnson

Autograph score
Full score (opening titles only); piano score ('Flamenco' only)
Instrumentation 1 1 2 1 – 3 2 2 0 – timp perc(2) gtr pno hp – str
Currently at Eton College Library [MS 921 01 13]

Notes
(i) Excerpts from the soundtrack were broadcast on 'Film Time' – BBC Home Service, 2 July 1953.

Albert R.N. (1953)

***Alt title* Spare Man**
***US title* Break to Freedom**
***US Alt title* Marlag 'O' Prison Camp**
Production Angel Productions
Producer Daniel M Angel
Director Lewis Gilbert
Stars Anthony Steel, Jack Warner, Robert Beatty
Music played by Orchestra/Philip Martell
Adapted screenplay
Guy Morgan and Vernon Harris, from the play by Guy Morgan and Edward Sammis. Both of the playwrights were British POWs in World War II.
Locations
1. The prisoner-of-war camp was built on Headley Heath in Surrey
2. Nettlefold Studios, Walton-on-Thames, Surrey

Release
UK release date 23 November 1953
US release date June 1955
UK TV premiere BBC1 Television, 27 December 1960

Media
DVD EAN/UPC 5060172961436. Cohen Film Collection. UK. Region 2
Music notes
This is the first of several Arnold scores for war films containing a resolute, onward driven main title that develops into a march for the prisoners of war which reflects their indomitable spirit even in captivity. 'Albert' is a dummy that takes the place of an escaped prisoner on the march from the wash-house back to the camp. Arnold decides against giving 'Albert' a theme of his awn. Source music in the form of a solo guitar awakens thoughts of home while some delicate work for strings provide a brief nostalgic cue. The brevity of the score may have a lot to do with the film's stage play origins.
Notes
(i) Interviews on the film set were broadcast on 'Film Time' – BBC Home Service, 20 August 1953.

You Know What Sailors Are (1954)

Production Group Film Productions
Producers Peter Rogers and Julian Wintle
Director Ken Annakin
Stars Akim Tamiroff, Donald Sinden, Sarah Lawson
Music played by Orchestra/Muir Mathieson
Adapted screenplay
Peter Rogers, from the novel 'Sylvester'[1] by Edward Solomon Hyams [*Publisher* Longmans Green, 1951]
Locations
1. Opening shots of the Lord Nelson Pub, Nothe Parade, Weymouth, Dorset, with the old Weymouth Pavilion in the centre distance.
2. The drunks pass the Holy Trinity School on Dorset Terrace, Weymouth, and go through Weymouth High Street making their way back to the Harbour, actually Portland Naval Base.
3. The air-testing scenes at the 'Navy's Mediterranean Experimental Station' were filmed on Dorset Downs.
4. Pinewood Studios, Iver Heath , Bucks (where the Presidential Palace and harem scenes with Donald Sinden (Lt Sylvester Green) and the 'President of Agraria' were shot).

Poster

Book

Release
UK premiere London, 9 February 1954
US release date 4 November 1954
UK TV premiere BBC1 Television, 17 December 1969
Media
DVD EAN/UPC 5037115257239. ITV Studios. UK. Region 2. (11 DVD Boxed Set including 'Tiger in the Smoke')

1 The dust wrapper of the novel provides us with the interesting information: "... the idea of 'Sylvester' as a film occurred to a number of critics ... the film rights have, in fact, been disposed of and at the time of reprinting [1952], a film of 'Sylvester' is in active preparation."

DVD EAN/UPC 0089859878022. Rank Collection. USA. Region 1

Music notes

The use of the popular song 'All the nice girls like a sailor' forms the main title and tells a lot about the intentions of the film makers. This dire effort relies on the audience finding the basic premise of the plot amusing: that three balls and a pram welded together could be mistaken for a vital new piece of radar technology on board a naval destroyer from the fictitious land of Agraria.

Traces of various sea shanties and 'Rule Britannia' are to be found in the first reel. Arnold gets to write a national anthem for Agraria – a pastiche of those East European anthems that possess the quality of seemingly going on forever. Amidst a harem of bright young girls and a distinctly uncomfortable Dora Bryan, Arnold provides a five-minute number (which may well have been written before filming started) for an exotically clad dancing troupe. At least he could try out a few ideas before the ballet commissions come along, There is a notable scherzo far solo clarinet which is eventually taken up by the rest of the woodwinds.

It is something of a mystery why this particular score from such a forgettable film was found residing in the archives at the Royal College of Music when other Arnold scores from worthier films are apparently lost forever.

Autograph score

Full score (in 35 sections)

Instrumentation 3 2 2 1 – 4 3 3 1 – timp perc(2) hp – str and in the Dance Band sequence: alto sax(2), tenor sax(2), tpt(4), tbn(4) gtr drums pno db

Currently at Eton College Library [MS 921 01 13]

Sheet music

'When You Love' song with words and music by Michael Carr and Leo Towers, published by Southern Music.

'Scherzetto' arranged for clarinet and piano, published by Queen's Temple Publications (QT43).

Concert arrangements

'Scherzetto'

arranged for clarinet and orchestra by Christopher Palmer (c.1991)

Duration 2'30"

Instrumentation 1 1 0 0 – 4 0 0 0 – perc(2) cel hp – str

Publisher Novello (orchestral version); Queens Temple Publications (clarinet and piano)

Recordings

(i) John Bradbury (clarinet)/BBC Philharmonic Orchestra/Rumon Gamba – Chandos CHAN 9851 (The Film Music of Sir Malcolm Arnold, Vol.2)

(ii) Thea King (clarinet)/English Chamber Orchestra/Barry Wordsworth – Hyperion CDA 66634, re-issued Helios CHD 55060

Sheet music

Notes

(i) An adaptation for radio of the soundtrack was broadcast on the BBC Home Service, 9 March 1954

Devil on Horseback (1954)

Alt title **The Boy Jockey**

Production Group 3

Producer John Grierson

Director Cyril Frankel

Stars Googie Withers, John McCallum, Jeremy Spenser

Music played by Orchestra/Malcolm Arnold

Adapted screenplay

Neil Paterson and Montagu Slater with Geoffrey Orme, based on a story by James Curtis about the jockey, Lester Piggott

Locations

1. Beaconsfield Studios, Bucks

Release

UK release date 17 March 1954

UK TV premiere BBC2 Television, 10 February 1968

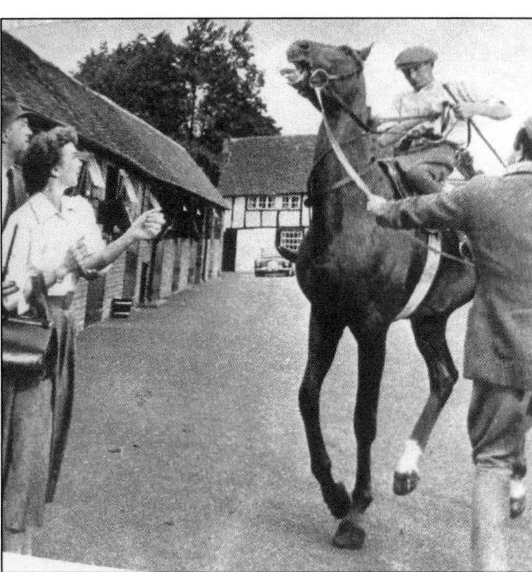

Left: Poster
Above: Still from the film

Hobson's Choice (1954)

Production London Films
Producer/Director David Lean
Stars Charles Laughton, John Mills, Brenda de Banzie
Music played by Royal Philharmonic Orchestra/Muir Mathieson

Adapted screenplay

Norman Spencer and Wynyard Browne, from the play by Harold Brighouse [*Publisher* Constable & Co Ltd, 1916].

Acting edition: Samuel French, 1960 (reprinted by Hard Press Classic Series, Florida, USA).

Locations

1. Mostly filmed in Stockport: there are several shots of Brenda de Banzie (Maggie) in Peel Park with two distinctive church spires/towers in the background. Another shot, higher up in the Park, shows part of the gardens and pathways in the shape of the Rugby League Cup (won by Salford in the 1930/40s but certainly not there in Victorian Britain).
2. Other Stockport locations show John Mills on Uxbridge Street and Waterloo Place outside The Farrier's Arms, then again on North George Street where the Band of Hope march took place; later with Maggie on the towpath by the iron railings on Canalside on their courtship walk. Clemison Street also features with the iconic chimney of the Tinsmiths works and the RC Cathedral Church of St John the Evangelist in the background.
3. Finally, an alien cooling tower makes an appearance by Hanover Chapel before the wedding scene.
4. Shepperton Studios, Surrey

Release

UK premiere London, 26 February 1954
UK release date 19 April 1954
US premiere New York City, 14 June 1954
Australian release date Sydney, July 1954
South American release date Argentina, 8 March 1956
UK TV premiere BBC1 Television, 5 May 1974

Awards

(i) Won Golden Bear at the 4th Berlin International Film Festival, June 1954
(ii) Won BAFTA for Best British Film of 1954

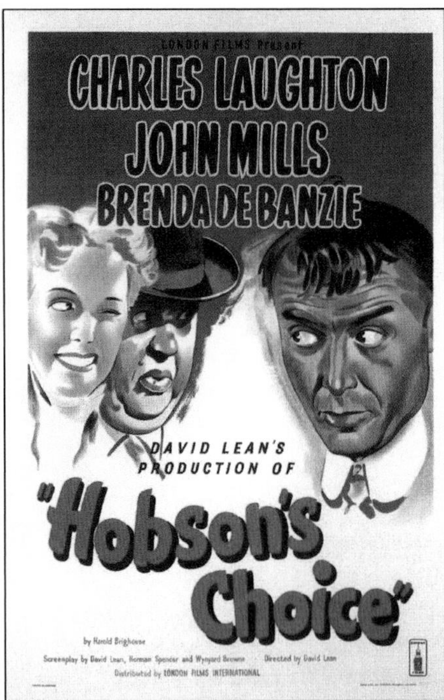

Poster

Book

Location: Maggie in Peel Park, Salford

Sheet music

Media

CD First Recording Excerpt 'Overture' in compilation CD 'Hurrah for Malcolm Arnold' – Él/Cherry Red Records ACMEM95CD

DVD EAN/UPC 5055201805089. Optimum. UK. Region 2

DVD EAN/UPC 5055201826534. Studio Canal. UK. Region 2

DVD EAN/UPC 7321900384834. Studio Canal. UK. Region 2 (with 'The Sound Barrier')

Blu-ray EAN/UPC 5055201826541. Studio Canal. UK. Region B

Sheet music

'Souvenir Selection' for piano solo with a colourful cover showing the stars of the film, John Mills, Charles Laughton and Brenda de Banzie.

***Hobson's Choice* theme** for piano solo

'Willie Mossop' theme, a song with words by Ginette Bozec in an arrangement by Tony Fones

Note All these excerpts were published by Paterson shortly after Arnold had parted company with Lengnick.

MAF performance

Suite of themes for solo piano
arranged by Tony Fones. Moritz Ernst (piano), 16 October 2010 (MAF 5)

'Willie Mossop' theme song [words: Ginette Bozec]. Claire Thompson (soprano)/Scott Mitchell (piano), 19 October 2014 (MAF 9)

Concert arrangements

Selection from the film
arranged for orchestra by Anthony 'Tony' Fones (c.1953)

Duration 17'

Instrumentation 1+picc 1 2 1 – 2 3 2 0 – timp perc hp – str

Publisher Paterson Publications (piano conductor part)

Note Performing material available from the Light Music Society Library

Concert Suite from the film
arranged for orchestra by Christopher Palmer (1992) [1. Overture and Shoe Ballet 2. Willie and Maggie 3. Wedding Night 4. Finale]

Duration 17'

Instrumentation 2 2 2 2 – 4 2 2 1 – timp perc(3) pno (cel) hp – str

Publisher Novello (study score)

First performance Royal College of Music Sinfonietta/Neil Thomson – Royal College of Music, London, 3 July 1996

Recordings

(i) London Symphony Orchestra/Richard Hickox – Chandos CHAN 9100 (CD)

(ii) Brandenburgisches Staatsorchester/Howard Griffiths – Klanglogo KL 1518 (CD)

Suite: 'Hobson's Brass'
arranged for brass band by Robin Dewhurst, Peter Graham and Derek Scott (1996)

Duration 17'

Publisher Faber

First performance Salford University Brass Band/David King – Peel Hall, Salford University, 8 November 1996

Note The suite was also performed at the Fourth Arnold Festival on 25 October 2009 by the Ipswich and Norwich Co-op Band conducted by Robin Norman

Suite arranged for piano trio
by Leslie Hogan (1995)

Duration 12'

Publisher Queens Temple Publications

Recording

(i) St Clair Trio (Detroit) – Emmanuelle Boisvert (violin), Marcy Chanteaux (cello), Pauline Martin (piano) – Koch 3-7266-2(CD)

Note This arrangement was performed by Anna Harpham (violin), Katherine Denton (cello) and Sophie Warwick (piano) at the Fourth Arnold Festival, 24 October 2009.

Articles

(i) Film review, in 'Variety', 3 March 1954

(ii) BFI, Monthly Film Bulletin, March 1954

(iii) Movie Review (B.C.), in New York Times, 15 June 1954

(iv) Ritchie, Christopher: 'The Arnold-Lean Trilogy, Part 2' – Beckus 28, Spring 1998 and Maestro1, October 2014

Notes

(i) MAS member Geoff Kindon recalls that during the filming Charles Laughton and all the crew were billeted at the Midland Hotel in Manchester.

(ii) Excerpts from the soundtrack were broadcast on 'Film Time' – BBC Home Service, 5 March 1954.

Beautiful Stranger (1954)

US title **Twist of Fate**
Production Marksman Productions
Producers Maxwell Setton and John R Sloan
Director David Miller
Stars Ginger Rogers, Herbert Lom, Stanley Baker
Music played by Orchestra/Malcolm Arnold
Adapted screenplay
Robert Westerby and Carl Nystrom, from a story by David Miller and Alford van Ronkel
Locations
1. Cannes, Alpes-Maritimes, France.
2. Shepperton Studios, Surrey.

Release
UK premiere London, 13 July 1954
US release date 5 November 1954
South African premiere Johannesburg, 4 January 1956
TV premiere West Germany, 25 September 1962
UK TV premiere BBC1 Television, 19 June 1981
Media
7" vinyl Title Song: 'Love is a Beautiful Stranger' (words: Ketti Frings; music: Jose Ferrer).
Lita Roza (the singer in the film titles) – London Records 45-1488.
Rosemary Clooney with the Wally Stott Orchestra – Columbia B.1932 (1957)
DVD EAN/UPC 5027626490348. Network. UK. Region 2

Posters: UK and US

Blu-ray EAN/UPC 5027626820848 Network. UK. Region B
Sheet music
'Love is a Beautiful Stranger' song (words: Ketti Frings; music: Jose Ferrer), published by Morris Publishing.

The Sleeping Tiger (1954)

Production Victor Hanbury Productions (Insignia Films)
Producers Victor Hanbury (aka Joseph Losey)
Director Joseph Losey
Stars Dirk Bogarde, Alexis Smith, Alexander Knox
Music played by Orchestra/Muir Mathieson
Adapted screenplay
Harold Buchman and Carl Foreman, from the novel by Maurice Moiseiwitsch [*Publisher* Heinemann, 1955][1]

Locations
1. Alexander Knox's house has been identified as being in Bridge Street near Nettlefold Studios in Walton-on-Thames
2. After the smash and grab outside William Mansell's the jewellers (located in Connaught Street, near Marble Arch) Alexis Smith is pursued by Dirk Bogarde; his car is seen parked in front of St Mary's Church Battersea, on Battersea Church Road, SW11
3. He visits Woolworths (possibly in The Strand or more likely the Walton-on-Thames branch) to get a disguise(!) and makes his way to rob the offices in Berners Street, W1, actually The Sanderson Hotel.

Book

1 He was also the biographer of Benno Moiseiwitsch in 'Biography of a Concert Pianist' [*Publisher* F Muller, 1965]

4. When Bogarde and Smith leave by car they turn off Fulham Road on to Wandon Road, SW6, passing Walsingham Mansions, then past The Jam Tree (now The Nell Gwynn, which still stands) on the King's Road
5. Nettlefold Studios, Walton-on-Thames, Surrey

Release

UK premiere London, 24 June 1954

US release date 8 October 1954

South African premiere Johannesburg, 30 December 1954

TV premiere West Germany, 2 June 1972

UK TV premiere BBC1 Television, 10 June 1983

Media

DVD EAN/UPC 089218537195. Alpha. UK. Region 2

Articles

(i) British Film Institute, Monthly Film Bulletin, August 1954

Notes

(i) Nominated for Best Film at the San Sebastian International Film Festival in 1954.

Posters

The Sea Shall Not Have Them (1954)

Production Angel Productions

Producer Daniel M Angel

Director Lewis Gilbert

Stars Michael Redgrave, Dirk Bogarde, Anthony Steel

Music played by London Philharmonic Orchestra/Muir Mathieson

Adapted screenplay

Lewis Gilbert and Vernon Harris, from the book by John Harris [*Publisher* Hurst & Blackett, Club Edition, 1956, with 20 pages of film stills]

Locations

1. Felixstowe, Suffolk
2. Alliance Film Studios, St Margaret's, Twickenham, Middlesex

Release

UK premiere London, 30 November 1954

South African premiere Johannesburg, 24 January 1955

US release date June 1955

UK TV premiere BBC Television, 15 October 1960

Media

DVD EAN/UPC 5060425350949. Screenbound. UK. Region 2

Blu-ray EAN/UPC 5060425350987. Screenbound. UK. Region B

Book

Poster

Notes

(i) The title of the film is the motto of Air-Sea Rescue High-Speed Launch Flotillas.

(ii) Film reviewed in 'The Younger Generation' – BBC Light Programme, 12 January 1956.

The Belles of St Trinian's (1954)

Production London Films
Producers Sidney Gilliat and Frank Launder
Director Frank Launder
Stars Alastair Sim, Joyce Grenfell, George Cole
Music played by Orchestra/Malcolm Arnold

Original screenplay

Frank Launder, Sidney Gilliat and Val Valentine, based on a comic strip by Ronald Searle.

Locations

1. One of the railway locations was filmed at Seer Green and Jordans station in Buckinghamshire
2. The boarded-up High Street has been identified as Stortford Road/Market Square at Great Dunmow in Essex
3. The infamous school itself was actually the All Nations College at Easneye, Stanstead Abbotts in Hertfordshire
4. Other locations include Littleton Park House (part of the Shepperton Studios complex) and the Express Dairy depot at Copse Farm in Brookshill Drive in Harrow, Middlesex
5. Shepperton Studios, Surrey.

Release

UK premiere London, 30 September 1954
US premiere The Plaza, New York City, 22 December 1954
Australian release date 5 May 1955
TV premiere West Germany, 1 December 1969
UK TV premiere BBC1 Television, 27 October 1970

Media

CD First Recording Excerpt 'Prelude' in compilation CD 'Hurrah for Malcolm Arnold' – Él/Cherry Red Records ACMEM95CD
DVD EAN/UPC 5060034577560. Studio Canal. UK. Region 2. (Boxed set with Pure Hell at St Trinian's / Blue Murder at St Trinian's / Great St Trinian's Train Robbery)
DVD EAN/UPC 5060034577768. Studio Canal. UK. Region 2
Blu-ray EAN/UPC 5055201826497. Studio Canal. UK. Region B

Autograph score

Full score (in 35 sections) and 'The St Trinian's School Song' for unison (?) voices and piano.
Instrumentation 1 1 1 1 – 0 2 1 0 – perc(2) pno duet – str
[opening titles: perc(4) pno(2)]
Currently at Eton College Library [MS 921 01 13]

Sheet music

'St Trinian's School Song': though this did not appear in print as a separate item until much later, it was included in a book entitled *The St Trinian's Story*, published by Perpetua Books in 1959; the song was reproduced directly from the composer's autograph manuscript.
March arranged for piano solo. Published by Novello (1993).

Concert arrangements

Comedy Suite `Exploits for Orchestra' arranged by Christopher Palmer (1988), edited by Philip Lane (2000) [1. Prelude 2. Train to Trinian's 3. Flash and Miss Fritton 4. Races and Games 5. Finale]
Duration 8'
Instrumentation 2 1 2 1 – 0 2 1 1 – perc(4) pno duet – str
Publisher Novello
Recordings
(i) Paul Janes (piano)/BBC Philharmonic Orchestra/Rumon Gamba – Chandos CHAN 9851 (The Film Music of Sir Malcolm Arnold, Vol.2)
(ii) Munich Symphony Orchestra/ Douglas Bostock – Classico CLASSCD 294 reissued Classico 233316

Articles

(i) British Film Institute, Monthly Film Bulletin, October 1954

Notes

(i) Film reviewed in 'The Younger Generation' introduced by Norma Ellis – BBC Light Programme, 17 November 1954.

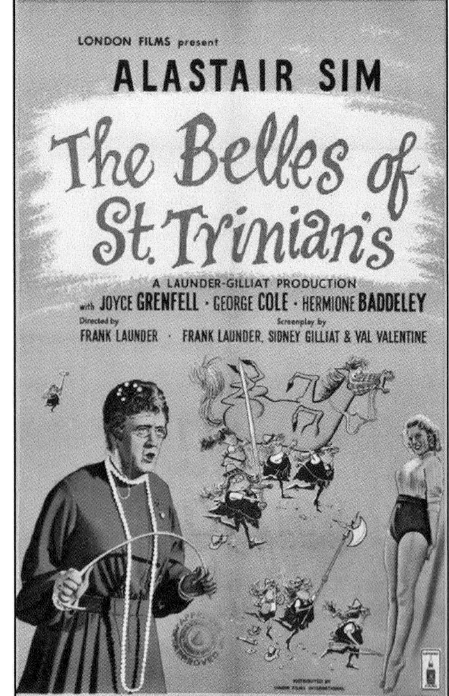

Poster

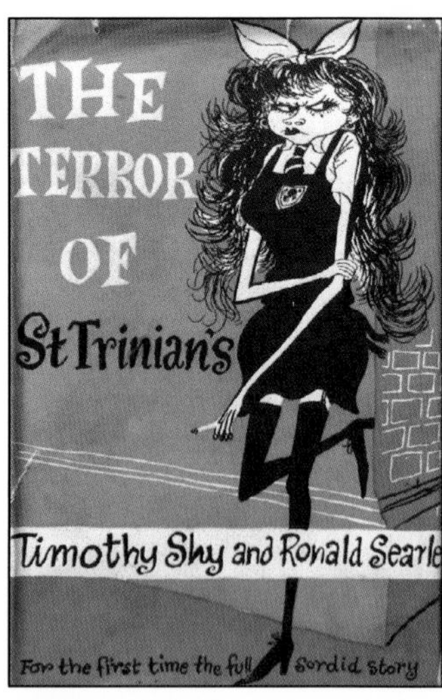

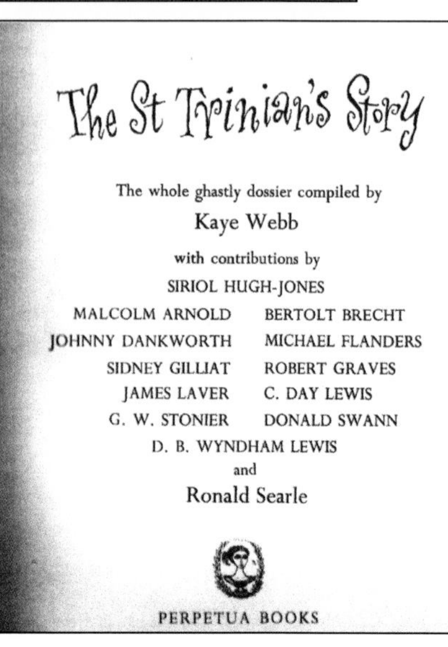

Books

Far left:
Location: All Nations College, Easneye

The Constant Husband (1955)

Alt title **Marriage à la Mode**
Production Individual Pictures
Producers Sidney Gilliat and Frank Launder
Director Sidney Gilliat
Music played by London Philharmonic Orchestra/Muir Mathieson
Original screenplay
Sidney Gilliat and Val Valentine
Locations

1. The film's opening shots were of the New Quay Hotel in New Quay (mid-Wales not Cornwall): Rex Harrison (Chris Hathaway), an amnesia victim, is seen wandering off to the Harbourside in Aberaeron, Cardigan Bay [Another source states that the opening shots are actually outside the Blue Bell Inn, South John Street in New Quay]
2. London locations include: the Charles House Offices in Studio Road, West Kensington (actually the offices of the Inland Revenue); Harrison in a car at Littleton House (actually part of the Shepperton Studios complex), then on to Kensington High Street, by Olympia, and then Milbank House, Westminster, 'The Ministry of Munitions' where Harrison worked (now the headquarters of MI5) where he is dropped off by Kay Kendall
3. Harrison is released from Wormwood Scrubs Prison on Ducane Road, East Acton, and to avoid his many wives the warden lets him out by a side entrance in Artillery Road by the Hammersmith Workhouse (now demolished)
4. The wives arrive for his trial at the Old Bailey, the old Central Criminal Court
5. The scene with Harrison and Cecil Parker is by the pond on Parkside, Wimbledon, SW19
6. Shepperton Studios, Surrey

Poster

Release
UK premiere London Pavilion, 21 April 1955
South African premiere Johannesburg, 8 June 1955
US TV premiere 6 November 1955
US film premiere 25 July 1957
UK TV premiere BBC2 Television, 26 December 1970
Awards
(i) Nominated for 'Best British Screenplay' at the BAFTA awards in 1956.
Media
DVD EAN/UPC 5055201806888. Studio Canal. UK. Region 2
Blu-ray EAN/UPC 5027626827144. Network. UK. Region B
Articles
(i) Review in The Times, 21 April 1955
(ii) British Film Institute, Monthly Film Bulletin, May 1955

Location: Rex Harrison at the Harbourside, Aberaeron, Cardigan Bay

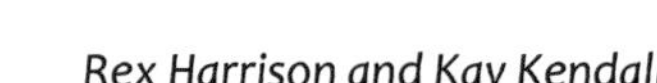

Rex Harrison and Kay Kendall

The Night My Number Came Up (1955)

Production Ealing Studios/Michael Balcon Productions
Producer Michael Balcon
Director Leslie Norman
Stars Michael Redgrave, Sheila Sim, Alexander Knox
Music played by London Symphony Orchestra/Muir Mathieson

Original screenplay

R C Sherriff, based on an actual event which occurred in the life of British Air Marshall Sir Victor Goddard. The incident was reported in the *Saturday Evening Post* on 26 May 1951, and the director, Leslie Norman, suggested it should be made into a film.

Locations

1. Kai Tak Airport in Hong Kong
2. Ealing Studios

Release

UK premiere London, 22 March 1955
South African premiere Johannesburg, 15 July 1955
US release date 19 December 1955
UK TV premiere BBC1 Television, 30 August 1981

Media

DVD EAN/UPC 5055201809841. Optimum Classic. UK. Region 2

Notes

(i) Nominated for 4 BAFTAs including 'Best British Film' in 1956.
(ii) A radio adaptation of the film soundtrack was broadcast on 'Saturday Night Theatre' – BBC Home Service, 18 February 1956.

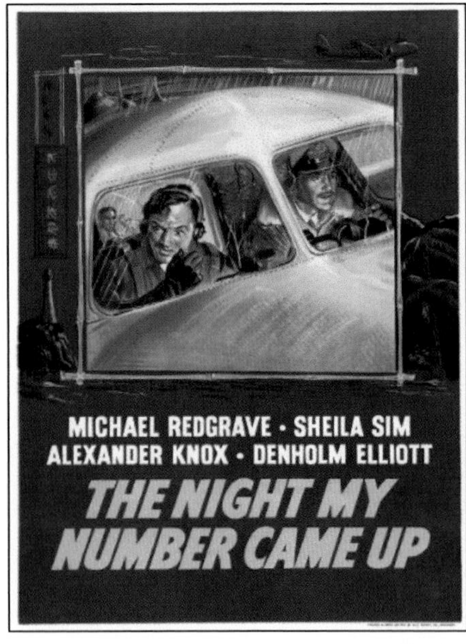

Poster

I am a Camera (1955)

Production Romulus
Producer John Woolf
Director Henry Cornelius
Stars Julie Harris, Laurence Harvey, Shelley Winters
Music played by Orchestra/Muir Mathieson

Adapted screenplay

John Collier, from the play by John van Druten, based on the short story 'Sally Bowles' by Christopher Isherwood.

Acting edition: Evans Bros, 1954, 1962.

Locations

1. Opening shots of Laurence Harvey walking in Wyndham Place, W1, at the intersection of Bryanston Place and Bryanston Square
2. Remus/Romulus Film Studios?

Release

UK release date 21 July 1955
US premiere Los Angeles, California, 21 July 1955
South African premiere Johannesburg, 17 February 1956
UK TV premiere BBC Television, 7 January 1961

Awards

There was a BAFTA nomination for Julie Harris in 1956.

Media

7" vinyl 'Who Am I?' theme song, words by Carl Sigman, music by Ralph Maria Siegel: The Taylor Maids with Frank Devol's Music – Capitol (USA) F3100 (4/55)
DVD EAN/UPC 5018755503313. Wienerworld. UK. Region 0

Sheet music

'Who Do I?' theme song, words by Carl Sigman, music by Ralph Maria Siegel, published by Berry Music in 1955.

Articles

(i) Movie Review (B.C.) in New York Times, 9 August 1955
(ii) Film review in 'Variety', New York, August 1955

Poster

Sheet music

Notes

(i) Excerpts from the film were shown on 'Film Time', with Peter Haigh – BBC Television, 25 November 1955.

Value for Money (1955)

Production Group Film Productions
Producer Sergei Nolbandov
Director Ken Annakin
Stars John Gregson, Diana Dors, Susan Stephen
Music played by Orchestra/Muir Mathieson

Adapted screenplay

R F Delderfield and William Fairchild, from the novel by Derrick Boothroyd [*Publisher* Laurie, 1953]
Film edition: J M Dent, 1955[1]

Locations

1. Opening shot of the 'Barfield Town Band' (actually the Hanwell Silver Band) marching along Taylor Street, Batley, in West Yorkshire; they continue towards the premises of 'J H Broadbent & Son' in Back Station Road.
2. After the funeral at Batley Cemetery on Cemetery Road, John Greyson (Chayley Broadbent) wanders among the gravestones
3. After a men's day-out in London the charabanc returns, arriving at Market Place, Batley, with Batley Central Methodist Church in the background
4. Gregson and Susan Stephen (his fiancée, Ethel) spend time together around the boating lake in Wilton Park on Bradford Road, Batley
5. Diana Dors (Ruthine West) is invited to open the new Civic Centre in Market Place; she arrives at Batley Station on Upper Station Road and is driven to Gregson's house on Mill Lane
6. The internal shots of the Civic Centre are actually Isleworth Swimming Baths on Twickenham Road, Isleworth, Middlesex
7. After their engagement they (Gregson/Dors) buy a new house, located at 23 Fife Road in East Sheen, SW14
8. Gregson meets the Mayor outside 'Barfield Town Hall', actually the steps of Batley Library on Market Place
9. Pinewood Studios, Iver Heath, Bucks

Poster

Book

Release

UK premiere London, 9 August 1955
South African premiere Johannesburg, 7 September 1956
US premiere New York City, 31 July 1957

Media

DVD EAN/UPC 5060105721380. ITV Studios. UK. Region 2

Music notes

The title sequence opens in rather grand manner and soon develops into a lively scherzo for woodwinds and xylophone, then moves into the strains of a popular song taken up by the brass before returning briefly to the scherzo and finishing in the grand manner The music is in danger of inflating the film beyond its reach; this not very amusing comedy about a northern businessman who falls in love with a showgirl and cannot make up his mind whether to marry her or his former girlfriend, a local journalist.

The scenes at a London stage show (with music and songs not written by Arnold) are rather stretched out and laboured. From then on, the score alternates between the title material and a popular song 'The Face of a Gentle Maiden' sung at one point by the northern businessman (Gregson) on his way home from London. The local brass band provide what little hilarity there is with their appropriately amateurish performance of 'Colonel Bogey' and 'A Life on the Ocean Wave' with players continually off-key and in the wrong tempo. All in all a British comedy of the 1950s that does not stand up very well today. Arnold is left to fill in some of the cracks.

Notes

(i) The Hanwell Silver Band appear in the opening 'funeral sequence'.
(ii) A special radio adaptation of the film was broadcast on 'Sunday Cinema' – BBC Light Programme, 11 September 1955.

1 Unusually, the 1955 edition was in hardback and had a dust-wrapper featuring scenes from the film.

The Deep Blue Sea (1955)

Production London Films
Producer Alexander Korda
Director Anatole Litvak
Stars Vivien Leigh, Kenneth More, Eric Portman
Music played by Orchestra/Muir Mathieson

Adapted screenplay

Terence Rattigan from his original play.
Acting edition: Samuel French, 1952.

Locations

1. London location shots include
   (i) Cremorne Road, Chelsea
   (ii) Cheyne Walk, west of Battersea Bridge, SW10
   (iii) Piccadilly Circus, W1
   (iv) (possibly) Flood Street, SW3 (where Vivien Leigh visits Kenneth More)
2. The skiing scenes, allegedly at Klosters in Switzerland, could well be back-projection.
3. Shepperton Studios, Surrey.

Release

UK premiere London, 23 August 1955
US premiere New York City, 13 October 1955
UK release date 17 October 1955
Japanese release date 29 October 1955
US release date 1 November 1955

Awards

(Ivor) Anatole Litvak was nominated for Best Film (Golden Lion) at the Venice Film Festival in 1956 – the film also received 2 BAFTA nominations in the same year.

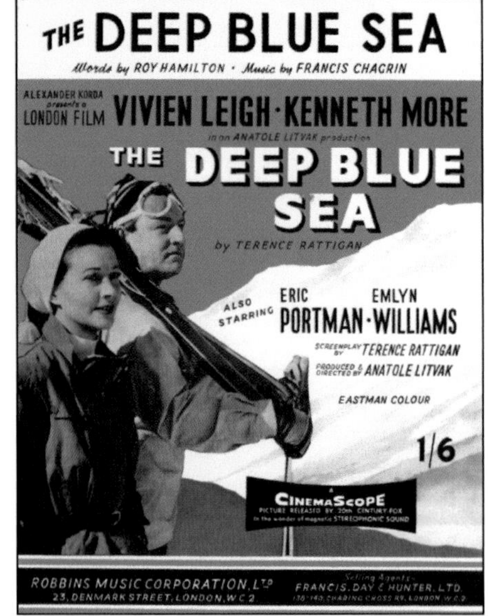

Poster *Sheet music*

Media

No commercial recording. View on YouTube: https://www.youtube.com/watch?v=aRyzAuOWATo&t=647s

Sheet music

'The Deep Blue Sea', theme song, words by Roy Hamilton, music by Francis Chagrin,[1] published by Robbins Music (1955).

Articles

(i) Film review (E.S.), in Los Angeles Times, 18 August 1957

Notes

(i) A special radio adaptation of the film was broadcast on the BBC Light Programme, 6 September 1955.
(ii) Anatole Litvak was interviewed by Gordon Gow on the programme 'Talking of Films' – BBC Home Service, 16 September 1955.
(iii) Excerpts from the film were shown on 'Film Time' – BBC Television, 30 September 1955.
(iv) A jazz version of the theme song, entitled 'Deep Sea Blues', was recorded by trumpeter Kenny Baker and trombonist George Chisholm.

1 His son, Nicholas Chagrin, appeared as a mime in the first performance of Arnold's *Song of Simeon*, given at the Theatre Royal, Drury Lane, on 5 January 1960.

The Woman for Joe (1955)

Production Group Film Productions (1955)
Producer Leslie Parkyn
Director George More O'Ferrall
Stars Diane Cilento, George Baker, Jimmy Karoubi
Music played by Orchestra/Muir Mathieson

Original screenplay

Neil Paterson

Locations

1. Nottingham Goose Fair [held in October each year at the Forest Recreation Ground, Nottingham]: establishing shots
2. The fairground scenes were possibly filmed in Ashtead, Surrey
3. Train scene (stock shot) at Hadley Wood North Tunnel in Hertfordshire

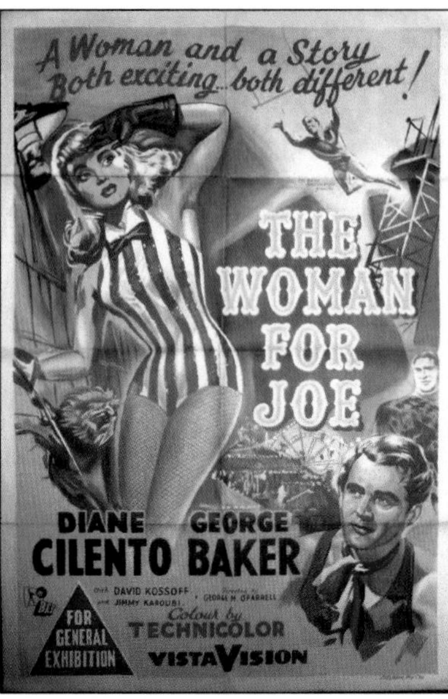

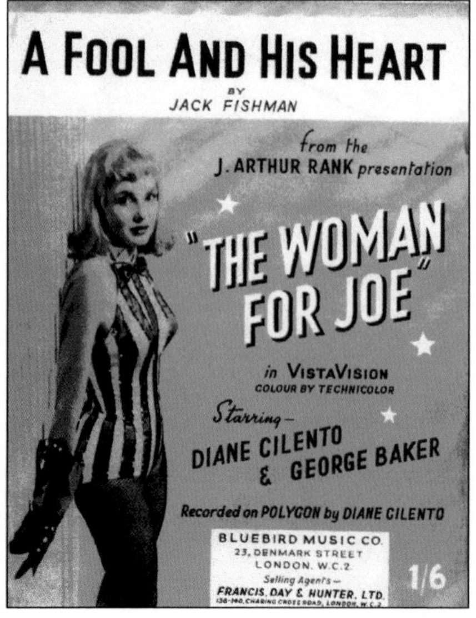

Poster; Sheet music

4. Pinewood Studios, Iver Heath, Bucks

Release

UK premiere London, 25 August 1955

UK TV premiere BBC2 Television, 21 April 1974

Sheet music

'A Fool and his Heart', theme song by Jack Fishman, performed by Diane Cilento, published by Bluebird Music.

Media

78 rpm disc 'A Fool and his Heart', theme song by Jack Fishman, was recorded by Diane Cilento on a 78 rpm disc, Polygon P1186. It is not known if this was issued on 7" vinyl.

A Prize of Gold (1955)

Production Warwick Film Productions

Producer Phil C Samuel

Director Mark Robson

Stars Richard Widmark, Mai Zetterling, Nigel Patrick

Music played by London Symphony Orchestra/Muir Mathieson

Adapted screenplay

Robert Buckner and John Paxton, from the novel by Max Catto [*Publisher* Heinemann, 1953].
Film edition: Four Square Books, 1959.

Locations

1. Richard Widmark chases Nigel Patrick from Ensign Street through Graces Alley and Wellclose Square past Wilton's Music Hall, Whitechapel; later to the swing bridge at Shadwell Pierhead (now Shadwell New Basin) where Patrick falls to his death
2. Airport Tempelhof, Berlin
3. Blackbushe Airport, Yately, Hampshire
4. Shepperton Studios, Surrey

Release

US release date 14 October 1955

UK release date 2 December 1955

Media

7" vinyl Title Song (words: Ned Washington; music: Lester Lee]:

(i) Ronnie Gaylord with an orchestra conducted by David Carroll – Mercury (USA) 70585 X45

(ii) Joan Regan with the Johnny Douglas Orchestra – Decca 45-F.10432; DFE 6278

(iii) Micki Mario – Capitol CL 14271

(iv) Chris Applewhite – Brunswick 05411

(v) Ronnie Hilton – HMV 7M 285

DVD EAN/UPC 8436569303955. Ambito. Spain. Region 2

Sheet music

Title song 'Prize of Gold', words by Ned Washington, music by Lester Lee.

'In Love in Love', words by Tommie Connor, music by Gerhard Bronner. Both published by Victoria Music. Sometimes the music was issued for the American market with a different cover (see example published by Columbia Pictures Music Corporation).

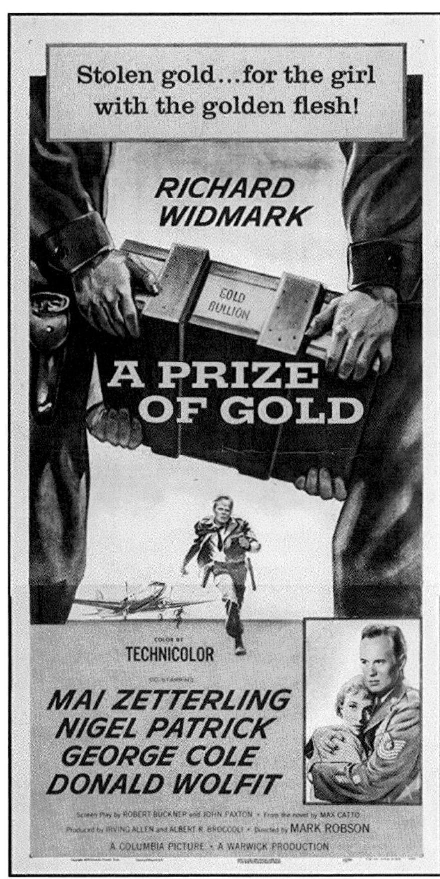

Poster

Book

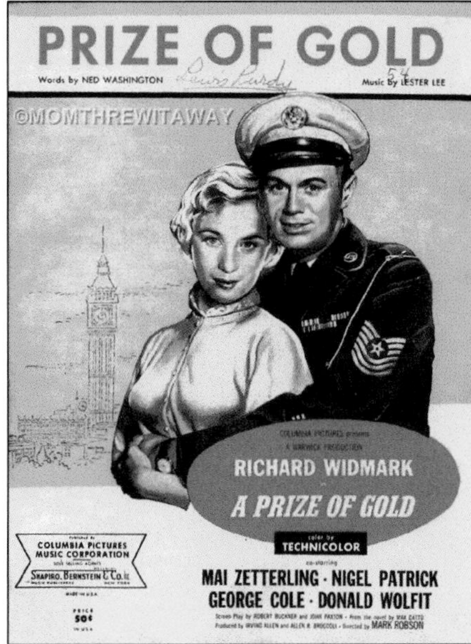

Sheet music (title song): UK and US versions

Notes

(i) Excerpts from the film were shown during the programme 'Berlin Visit' – BBC Television, 20 February 1955.

1984 (1956)

Production Holiday Film Productions
Producer N Peter Rathvon
Director Michael Anderson
Stars Edmond O'Brien, Michael Redgrave, Jan Sterling
Music played by London Symphony Orchestra/Louis Levy

Adapted screenplay

William P Templeton and Ralph Bettins, from the novel by George Orwell [*Publisher* Secker & Warburg, 1949; Penguin Books, 1954]. The book was reprinted several times between 1955 (to coincide with the film's release) and 1964.

Locations

1. London (air-raid scenes)
2. Associated British Studios, Elstree, Herts

Release

UK release date 6 March 1956
US release date September 1956

Media

DVD EAN/UPC 5013037066890. Orbit. UK Region 2

Poster

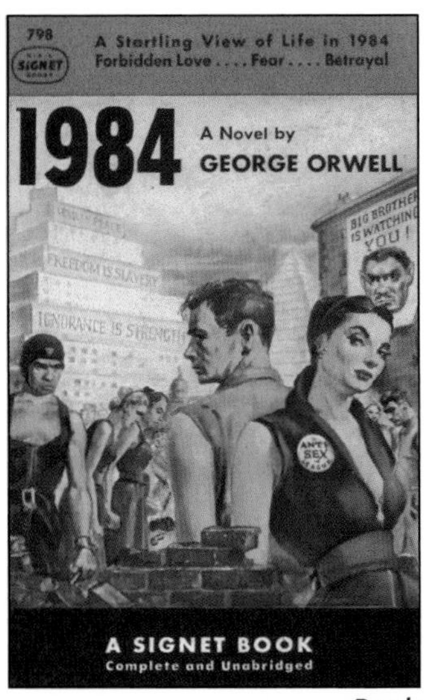

Book

Invitation to the Dance (1956) [rejected]

Production MGM
Producer Arthur Freed
Director/Choreographer Gene Kelly
Stars Gene Kelly, Igor Youskevitch, Claire Sombert
Music played by Royal Philharmonic Orchestra/John Hollingsworth

Locations

1. MGM Studios, Borehamwood, Herts

Release

US release date 15 May 1956

Media

LP First recording (Parts 1 and 2) – MGM MS 6241
DVD EAN/UPC 8436022969773. Clasicos. Spain. Region 2. (no Malcolm Arnold content)

Articles

(i) Poulton, Alan: 'Invitation to the Dance' – Maestro 4, October 2017

Notes

(i) The three parts of the ballet are:
1. 'Circus' (Jacques Ibert)
2. 'Ring Around the Rosy' (André Previn – replacing Arnold's original score)
3. 'Sinbad the Sailor' (from *Sheherazade* by Rimsky-Korsakov)

(ii) Despite Arnold providing a 20-minute ballet score entitled 'Ring Around the Rosy' for the middle movement of this three-part cinematic ballet which Kelly choreographed and later filmed, he (Kelly) and his producers were apparently dissatisfied with the music and it was summarily rejected. At that point André Previn was brought in to provide an alternative score which had to exactly match Kelly's original choreography to Arnold's now-rejected music!

(iii) See main article 'Invitation to the Dance: why was Arnold's score rejected?' on the next page.

Poster

Invitation to the Dance: why was Arnold's score rejected?

The film *Invitation to the Dance* is unusual in that there is no spoken dialogue; the characters perform their various roles entirely through dance and mime which is filmed to a series of pre-recorded music tracks. Gene Kelly appears in all three segments of this balletic film, which also features leading dancers of the era. These include Tommy Rall[1], Igor Youskevitch,[2] Tamara Toumanova[3] and Claire Sombert[4].

The first segment is entitled 'Circus' and has an exciting score by the French composer Jacques Ibert. It tells the story of a small carnival troupe set in an Italian village in the 18th century, in which Kelly plays a Clown who is hopelessly in love with another circus performer, the Equestrienne (Claire Sombert). She, however, is in love with the High Wire Walker played by Igor Youskevitch. Hoping to impress her, the Clown performs a series of highly dangerous high-wire acts during which he falls to his death. The music on the soundtrack is played by the Royal Philharmonic Orchestra conducted by John Hollingsworth.

The second segment, entitled 'Ring Around the Rosy', originally had music by Malcolm Arnold, but, as we shall see, it was replaced by an alternative score composed by André Previn, recorded on the soundtrack by the MGM Studio Orchestra conducted by André Previn, who also played the important concertante piano part. This satiric tale is a series of romantic stories of love and infidelity featuring a gold bracelet which travels from the wrist of one fickle partner to another. The bracelet is initially given by the husband to his wife and she in turn gives it to a flirtatious artist at a party; this infuriates the husband who stalks off. After giving the bracelet to a model, a series of further exchanges lead eventually to the return of the bracelet to the husband, who is reconciled to his wife (see Appendix A).[5]

1 American tap and acrobatic specialist dancer (1929-2000).

2 Ukrainian-born ballet dancer (1912–94) who joined the US Navy in 1944 and soon became an American citizen. He later joined the Ballet Russe de Monte Carlo as their Artistic Director.

3 Russian-born prima ballerina (1919–96) who became an American citizen in 1943; another member of the Ballet Russe, for whom Balanchine created several roles.

4 French-born ballerina (1935–2008) who at the time of her starring role in the 'Circus' ballet segment (aged 17) was also performing with the Paris Opera.

The final segment 'Sinbad the Sailor', with music adapted by Roger Edens from Rimsky-Korsakov's 'Sheherazade', is an Arabian Nights fantasy combining live action and animation, as Kelly, playing the part of Sinbad, dances with several Hanna-Barbera cartoon characters.[6] Carol Haney as Sheherazade and David Kasday as the Genie are other members of the cast in this segment. The conductor on the soundtrack recording was Johnny Green with orchestrations by Conrad Salinger.

Despite winning the Golden Bear for the best film at the Sixth Berlin International Film Festival in 1956, 'Invitation to the Dance' (which was commercially released in March 1957, though some sources quote May 1956) was a failure at the box office. Much of the reason for this can be put down to the long delays in its distribution to the market place. On its 'completion' in 1952–53, the film was intermittently cut and re-cut, dubbed and re-dubbed over the next three-and-a-half years in order to satisfy the MGM executives, among them producer Arthur Freed, that it would prove a viable proposition with a substantial return for the investors. (It was, after all, an art film and there were real concerns that it would only attract a minority audience.) Their misgivings were fully justified when on its release it grossed only $615,000 at the box office against accumulated costs of over $1.4 million. Clearly some of these costs can be attributed to the complete shelving of Malcolm Arnold's music for the second segment and its replacement by André Previn's score. Not only that, but *Invitation to the Dance* was, on its final release in 1957, nothing like Gene Kelly's original concept, and to understand how it changed so radically we need to look in more detail at the early planning stages of the film's creative process in the summer of 1952.

5 Kelly's only appearance in this segment was as the Marine and it was a surprisingly minor role for him. The MGM studio later bemoaned the fact that "there wasn't enough Kelly".

6 Thus pre-dating many of the ideas which re-appeared in the 1964 film *Mary Poppins*.

Original concept

Kelly's original concept, formulated in the early part of 1952, was to make a film without dialogue, shot to playbacks in four segments as follows:

i) the 'Circus' ballet to be rehearsed and filmed during August;
ii) 'Ring Around the Rosy' in September (see Appendix A);

iii) the 'Popular Song' ballet, October to mid-November (see Appendix B); and
iv) a 'Children's Ballet' to be completed by mid-December.

We know from reports to the American-based MGM producer in late July that Malcolm Arnold had already started working on the themes for his ballet 'Ring Around the Rosy' and that he had played some of them to Gene Kelly; because of the tight scheduling it was proposed that Arnold would write the music on the rehearsal stage of the MGM studios, not in Culver City, California, but in Boreham Wood, Elstree, in Hertfordshire.[7]

Jacques Ibert had already been engaged to write the 'Circus' ballet sequence and work had started on recording his score with the RPO under John Hollingsworth during mid-August. Once this was finished, rehearsals of the scenes in 'Ring around the Rosy' with Igor Youskevitch began in earnest; Youskevitch, too, was on a tight schedule, with other ballet commitments in New York.

It appears that Kelly and Arnold worked through the night on many occasions to achieve this, inevitably putting a strain on both men. Delays in getting the music contracts signed, plus set and costume design problems, meant that work on the opening number of 'Ring Around the Rosy' with Malcolm's music did not start until 9 November: by all accounts everyone was relieved to get started and thought that Arnold's sketches were "brilliant". However, by mid-October they had managed to record another sequence, namely the 'Crooner' section with its part for solo horn (imitating the Crooner's voice) played by Dennis Brain, the principal horn of the RPO. One observer on the set remarked, "[It was] brilliantly written and out-did everything anyone ever did on the horn before – you probably know that he is the most famous horn player in the world. We all heard him play with Toscanini the other night and Adolph Green[8] just couldn't believe that he would record for us."

At the end of October approval was received from the MGM producer to proceed with the 'Popular Song' segment (see Appendix B) and this prompted the search for suitable candidates to put down tracks for the ballet. These included Pearl Carr and Diana Coupland, as well as Jimmy Young and the George Mitchell Singers. From correspondence we learn that Malcolm Arnold was also assigned to do the arrangements for the 'Popular Song' ballet – there was, apparently a feeling that he was "infinitely more American" in his style of writing than the other possible choices, who were Robert Farnon and Stanley Black. It was also noted that "he writes incredibly fast" and that "his rapport with Gene is just great". The long hours put in by both composer and director/choreographer at this time led to both men being taken ill – Arnold with a nervous breakdown, which resulted in Robert Farnon being taken on to score the American song sequence. Further disaster ensued on set when Ibert, who was working on the full score for the 'Circus' ballet, had to return to Paris following the death of his daughter in a tragic accident.

Despite these set-backs, work continued on 'Ring Around the Rosy' and tracks were laid down for the 'Stage Door' sequence with Tommy Rall, and 'The Marine and The Prostitute' with Gene Kelly and Tamara Toumanova, during the third week in November. By the beginning of December the dubbed track was completed in readiness for the final recording which took place in the middle of January 1953.

It was clear, however, that the Arnold score was not to everyone's taste: it was described as "heavy-handed" and having "thick" scoring – adjectives that one seldom hears when discussing an Arnold score.[9] Admittedly the music for the 'Stage Door' number was the one exception to their criticism; it was even suggested to the composer that a quick "lightening" of the texture for the 'Bedroom' scene and the 'Hot-Dog Stand' number would make the score more acceptable (however, there is nothing to indicate that Arnold undertook any rescoring – why would he?).

The message came back from MGM in Culver City that the music was "not distinguished" enough and that the sets and costumes were merely "adequate", and, of course, there wasn't enough Gene in the 'Ring around the Rosy' segment. There was also concern about the 'Popular Song' sequence, which was labelled "uninteresting". Their best advice was for both the Ibert and Arnold scores to be dubbed to the colour footage and that Kelly should complete the remainder of the picture in their American studios.[10]

In a letter to Arthur Freed, Kelly clearly had his own misgivings about the music for 'Ring Around the Rosy' saying, "I am generally disappointed; it is orchestrated too heavily." After another delay of four or five months and despite the fact that Gene Kelly's unalterable choreography was to Arnold's music, a decision was made in the summer of 1953 to ask André Previn to provide an alternative score for the 'Ring Around the Rosy' segment. By 1954 arrangements were made to record Previn's score in England with the Royal Philharmonic Orchestra and members of

7 In an interview with *Cue* Magazine in May 1953, Kelly was asked why was it felt necessary to do the picture in Europe. He replied, "We couldn't have made it in America. For one thing, if it had been done in Hollywood, it would have been done in an entirely different way. Instead of my being the only movie star, there would have been others, because the studio would have felt it needed more box office assurance, in view of the money it cost . . . Also we are working with frozen funds, which makes it possible to be experimental." [As they couldn't take the money out of the UK they could still use the funds, provided they employed British artists and used British studios.] Kelly continues: "We are able to use a lot of talented people not known to motion picture audiences: from the Paris Opera we have Claire Sombert; Igor Youskevitch got a leave of absence from the Ballet Theatre in New York; and Tommy Rall, a young dancer I remembered from the cast of Irving Berlin's *Miss Liberty* on Broadway, has the lead in the modern dance sequence . . . This is the type of film which I feel will definitely increase the prestige of American films in Europe . . . I hope to make the Europeans believe we are aspiring artistically, so they will have a greater respect for the fine things we are attempting in our studios at home."

8 Adolph Green (1914–2002), an American lyricist and playwright who, along with his life-time collaborator Betty Comden, wrote songs and screenplays for the Arthur Freed production unit at MGM. This included Leonard Bernstein's *On the Town* for Frank Sinatra and Gene Kelly in 1944. Freed, however, scrapped much of Bernstein's score as he didn't like the music!

9 Arnold once remarked to me that he saw no reason to use the cor anglais, bass clarinet or contrabassoon in his orchestral scoring, as they tend to "thicken-up the texture". Edmund Rubbra symphonies seemed to come up later in the conversation . . .

10 Gene Kelly was also about to start work on filming the Lerner and Loewe musical *Brigadoon* with Cyd Charisse and van Johnson, and time was running out.

the Ted Heath Band[11] during October and November that year with Previn himself providing the improvisatory piano part. Previn wrote about his experience in fulfilling this unusual commission in a fascinating article published in 1956 in the summer edition of *Film Music* magazine, of which the following is an extract:

'Invitation to the Dance' was a film which certainly offered a unique opportunity for the composers involved . . . consisting of three separate and distinct ballet sequences lasting approximately 30 minutes each . . . My assignment was to compose original ballet music for the middle sequence of the picture . . . it sounded like an opportunity all too rare in the film-scoring business. However, there turned out to be several technical difficulties which made the mechanical preparation of the film almost as difficult as the writing of the music. First of all there was the following hurdle to be cleared: through a series of circumstances too involved to detail here, the picture had been shot in its entirety before I was assigned to it. There were some temporary tracks, some verbal counting and a lot of deep, dark silence. Therefore when the film was turned over to me I was faced with the problem of writing a balletic score entirely dictated by the already existing and unchangeable film. Every nuance of tempo, every meter change, had to be fitted exactly to the picture: normal procedure for the scoring of a normal film, but certainly the hard way to compose a ballet. When the final timing sheets and click track charts were put in a bundle it looked like the Manhattan City Directory. No end of credit must be given to Lela Simone, the music co-ordinator of the picture, for putting these together. She practically lived in the projection and cutting rooms and it is due to her musicianship and technical skill that not one frame was wrong on the scoring stage.

Conclusions and postscript

So what conclusions can we draw from this whole sorry episode? There was obviously some initial rapport between composer and choreographer – the music co-ordinator of the film, Lela Simone, had even reported that (his) initial sketches were "brilliant" and that Arnold was the right person to score the 'Popular Song' ballet sequence. In an interview with Peter Paul Nash in October 1991, Arnold told him that Gene Kelly had remarked to

11 The number and type of 'jazz' instrumentalists required was quite specific: 4 trumpets, 4 trombones, 5 saxophones, guitar, bass, piano and drums.

him (on the set at Elstree Studios) that "whatever you write, whether it's jazz, or anything, it always sounds as though it's by you, an Englishman . . ." Apparently, Arnold then said, "Well, you've engaged me to write it, so what the hell?"

Both were very driven creative artists and their collaboration at Elstree involved working through the night on various re-takes. Arnold confirmed this when, in an interview with Christopher Ritchie in *Soundtrack* magazine in 1987, he recalled that during the production he was given an office at the MGM studios to facilitate the creative process. However, it is what he says next in the same interview which may give us a clue as to why their relationship began to deteriorate over the next few months. Chris asked him about his collaboration with Jacques Ibert, to which Arnold replied, "(Yes), with Jacques Ibert and Robert Farnon" (who we know now was scoring the 'Popular Song' ballet sequence). He continues, "I wrote the whole of 'Ring around the Rosies' (sic) which was too advanced in its jazz idiom . . . it was Stan Kenton-type jazz with the Ted Heath Band and the Royal Philharmonic Orchestra. It was considered too advanced, so they got a young arranger at MGM to re-do it called André Previn." Arnold's advanced score may well have sounded "thick" and "heavy-handed" to those expecting a more typically Arnold divertissement. Unfortunately, the composer was not given the opportunity to re-score or lighten the orchestration, as the die was cast and Previn was swiftly hired. Arnold may well have expressed his disappointment at MGM's decision, but he may also have been relieved too. It is somewhat ironic, given the success of Arnold's score to the 1956 film *Trapeze* (qv), which told the story of another love-triangle played out on the high wire of another circus, one might speculate that things may have been so different had MGM commissioned Arnold (rather than Ibert) to compose the 'Circus' ballet sequence!

Another factor in all this was the mounting effect of Arnold's compositional workload during this time. When he was engaged (probably in the Spring of 1952) to undertake the composition of a 30-minute ballet score for *Invitation to the Dance*, he had only just put the finishing touches to a 65-minute opera *The Dancing Master* (the full orchestral score for which was only completed on 8 May 1952). In the same month he also composed an Oboe Concerto for Léon Goossens (17 May), as well as the *Sound Barrier* Rhapsody (31 May). He had also begun work on his Second Symphony, which was finally completed on 9 February 1953 – at around the time when news would have reached him concerning the rejection of his score to 'Ring Around the Rosy'. Not that this set-back halted his creative momentum, as he then completed his 40-minute ballet score *Homage to the Queen* in May 1953 in readiness for its première at the Royal Opera House, Covent Garden, on Coronation Night, 2 June, in the presence of the newly-crowned Queen Elizabeth II – talk about working under pressure!

And that's not all: during 1952 he also produced nine other film scores including *Stolen Face, The Sound Barrier, The Holly and the Ivy* and *The Four Sided Triangle*, as well as the incidental music to Sean O'Casey's play *Purple Dust*. To add to his complicated life-style, the Arnold family moved house from Twickenham to Richmond at about the same time as his nocturnal meetings with Gene Kelly at the MGM Studios in Boreham Wood during the Autumn of 1952. It's little wonder therefore that he had little appetite to tinker with the score for Kelly's ballet with so many other commissions coming his way.

So what of the whereabouts of the rejected Arnold score itself? It was hoped that Arnold's score may have been filed in the Warner Brothers archives, probably on reel to reel tape and film, but senior sources consulted[12] have advised us that it is most unlikely that there is any extant archive material. However it's clear from the article which André Previn wrote in 1956 that he certainly did have access to the 'rough cut' of the soundtrack enabling him to understand how Arnold's music was choreographed by Gene Kelly. Following several letters to André Previn via his New York agent in September 2016, we received news from Mr Previn himself that he has no information which would lead to the location of either Arnold's original soundtrack, the piano (rehearsal) score or the full score for jazz band and orchestra. Other enquiries via the Arthur Freed, Roger Edens and MGM Music Collections in the University of Southern California Cinematic Arts Library, as well as the RPO Library and the Ted Heath Music Library at the Leeds College of Music, have all drawn a blank.

Bill Lynch has continued to make regular enquiries with his US contacts as he, like me, would love to hear, if nothing else, the great horn virtuoso Dennis Brain[13] playing his solo in the two 'Crooner' sequences of Arnold's score to 'Ring Around the Rosy', now missing in action. The search goes on.

Appendix A

'Ring around the Rosy' scenes and dancers:

1. Prologue: Overture – The Husband and The Wife (David Palthengi[14] and Daphne Dale)
2. Cocktail Party (The Salon) – The Wife and The Artist (Daphne Dale and Igor Youskevitch)
3. The Studio – The Artist and The Model (Igor Youskevitch and Claude Bessy)
4. Supper Club – The Petty Gangster 'Sharpie' and The Debutante 'Hairface' (Claude Bessy, Tommy Rall and Belita)
5. Supper Club – The Debutante 'Hair Face' and The Crooner (Belita and Irving Davies[15])
6. Supper Club – The Crooner and The Hat Check Girl (Irving Davies and Diana Adams)
7. The Hat Check Girl and The Marine (Diana Adams and Gene Kelly)
8. The Marine and The Prostitute (The Girl in the Red Skirt) (Gene Kelly and Tamara Toumanova)
9. The Prostitute and The Husband (Tamara Toumanova and David Paltenghi)
10. Reunion – The Husband and The Wife (David Paltenghi and Daphne Dale)

Appendix B

The 'Popular Song' Sequence:

1. I Feel a Song Coming On (Dorothy Fields/Jimmy McHugh/George Oppenheimer)
2. Sophisticated Lady (Mitchell Parish/ Irving Mills/Duke Ellington)
3. Wedding Bells (Are Breaking Up that Old Gang of Mine) (Willie Raskin/ Irving Kahal/Sammy Fain)
4. Orange Coloured Sky (Milton de Lugg/ Willie Stein)
5. I'm Always Chasing Rainbows (Joseph McCarthy/Henry Carroll)
6. Just One of Those Things (Cole Porter)
7. The Whiffenpoof Song (Tod Galloway/George Pomeroy/Meade Minnigerode)
8. Where or When (Richard Rodgers/ Lorenz Hart)
9. On the Sunny Side of the Street (Dorothy Fields/Jimmy McHugh)
10. They Go Wild, Simply Wild, Over Me (Fred Fisher/Joseph McCarthy)
11. St Louis Blues (W.C.Handy)

Alan Poulton

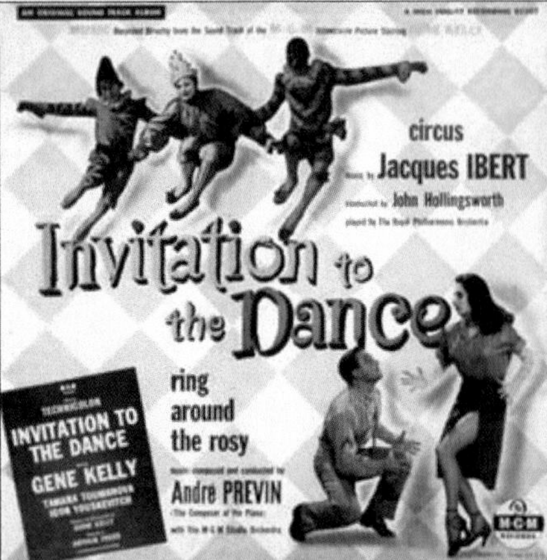

Top: Soundtrack LP includes 'Circus' and 'Ring around the Rosy' [1. 'Circus': A. Opening – Acrobats, B. Clown's Dance, C. Bacchanal – Love Duet, D. Variations – Cloak Dance, E. Consolation – Finale. 2. 'Ring Around the Rosy': A. Overture, B. Cocktail Party – Artist Studio, C. Belita – Hat Check Girl, D. Marine and the Girl in the Red Skirt – Tamara, E. Final Party] – MGM E-3027/MCA-25037 (1956).

Above: LP of Andre Previn's film music, MGM SE-4186 (1964), includes his contribution to 'Invitation to the Dance'.

---

12 Joseph Bille, Director, Music Library & Research, and George Feltenstein, Senior Vice President, Warner Brothers Pictures, Burbank, California; we are most grateful for their expertise and patience in dealing with our enquiries over several months

13 Dennis Brain can also be heard playing on the soundtrack recording of two other Arnold films released in June 1955: *The Deep Blue Sea* and *The Woman for Joe*, with the Philharmonia Orchestra conducted by Muir Mathieson.

14 David Paltenghi had choreographed some of the scenes in Arnold's 1953 score to *You Know what Sailor's Are*. His early death at the age of 41 in February 1961 much affected Arnold, who would later write that his Fifth Symphony would be "filled with memories of friends of mine who died young".

15 Irving Davies later became part of a dance group formed in 1953 called 'Three's Company', alongside Paddy Stone and Beryl Kay. The group appeared with Joyce Grenfell at the Fortune Theatre, London in her entertainment 'Joyce Grenfell Requests the Pleasure' in June 1954. One of the dance numbers was called 'Paddy's Nightmare', devised and performed by Paddy Stone to the music of Malcolm Arnold!

Port Afrique (1956)

Production Coronado Productions
Producers David E Rose and John R Sloan
Director Rudolph Maté
Stars Pier Angeli, Eugene Deckers, Pat O'Meara
Music played by Orchestra/Muir Mathieson

Adapted screenplay
Frank Patos and John Cresswell, from the novel by Bernard Vieter Dryer [*Publisher* Cassell, 1950].
Film edition: Panther Books, 1956.

Locations
1. The Casbah in Algiers
2. Tangier (Moroccan port)
3. Shepperton Studios, Surrey

Release
European release date Portugal, August 1956
US release date 7 September 1956
UK release date 18 June 1957
Australian release date 26 December 1957
South American premiere Argentina, 30 January 1958

Sheet music
'In Port Afrique' title song with words by Paddy Roberts, Geoffrey Parsons and John Turner, and music by Oscar Kinleier.
'A Melody from Heaven' song with English words by Jack Fishman and music by Luis Araque.
These formed part of the soundtrack and were sung by Pier Angeli. They were published by Chappell,

Media
7" vinyl 'In Port Afrique', title song (words: Paddy Roberts, Geoffrey Parsons and John Turner; music: Oscar Kinleiner): The Kentones (vocals) with an orchestra conducted by Ron Goodwin – Parlophone MSP 6229 (1956)
No commercial recording. View on YouTube: https://www.youtube.com/watch?v=vzKFE7sOO7Y

Poster

Book

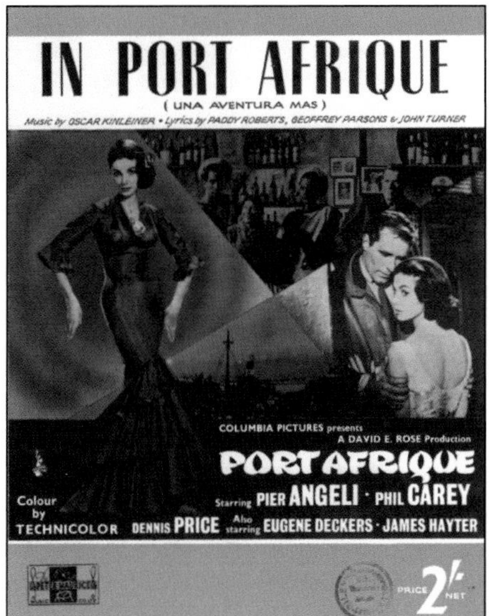

Sheet music: songs 'In Port Afrique' and 'A Melody from Heaven'

Trapeze (1956)

Production Hill-Hecht-Lancaster-Productions
Producer James Hill
Director Carol Reed
Stars Burt Lancaster, Tony Curtis, Gina Lollobrigida
Music played by Orchestra/Muir Mathieson

Adapted screenplay

James R Webb, from the novel 'The Killing Frost' by Max Catto [*Publisher* (in English) Heinemann, 1950; (in French) Robert Laffont as 'Trois Trapézistes, ou Le Disque qui tue']. Film edition: Four-Square Books, 1959.

Locations

1. Cirque d'Hiver (Bouglione), rue Amelot, Paris.
2. The circus parade was filmed along the Grand Boulevard and the Champs Elysees in front of a crowd of 9,000 Parisians.

Release

US release date 30 May 1956
European premiere Madrid, 21 December 1956
South African premiere Johannesburg, 5 June 1957
UK TV premiere BBC1 Television, 31 December 1975
European TV premiere Madrid, Spain, 24 November 1979

Awards

(i) Burt Lancaster won the Silver Bear Award for Best Actor at the Berlin International Film Festival in 1956.
(ii) Gina Lollobrigida won the Bambi Award for Best Actress in 1958.
(iii) Carol Reed was a nominee in the 'Best Director' category in the Directors' Guild of America Awards in 1957.

Poster

Book

Media

7" vinyl

Soundtrack excerpts [1. Lola's Theme 2. Mike and Lola's Love Theme]
Columbia (USA) 4-40725;
(No.1 only) Columbia (USA) EM-132 in 'Theme Songs Vol.9'

'Trapeze', title song [words: Johnny Burke; music: Paul Elie]:
Mitch Miller and his Chorus and Orchestra – Columbia (USA) 4-40715; CBS Coronet (Australia) KS-111

'Lola's theme', song with words by Al Stillman:
(i) Steve Allen and his Orchestra – Coral (USA) 9-61681; Vogue Coral 45-Q72184 (8/56); Festival (New Zealand) SP 45 1118 (5/57)
(ii) Ralph Marterie and his Orchestra – Mercury (USA) 70917 X45 (7/56)

LP

Soundtrack recording [1. Prelude 2. Lola's theme 3. Fanfare and Elephant's Waltz 4. Mike and Lola's Love theme 5. Trapeze 6. 'Washington Post March' (arr. Malcolm Arnold) 7. 'Entry of the Gladiators' (arr. Malcolm Arnold) 8. Juke Box 9. Tino's Arrival in Paris 10. 'The Blue Danube' (arr. Malcolm Arnold) 11. Above the Ring 12. 'The Stars and Stripes Forever' (arr. Malcolm Arnold)]
Columbia (US) CL 870 (m) (4/57).

Sheet music: 'Lola's Theme' in standard and accordion versions; 'Trapeze' (title song)

Later re-issued on CD – Sepia SEPIA 6001; Filmophone CD2008 (Nos. 6, 7, 10 and 12 are placed last on this disc)

CD Soundtrack excerpts [1. Prelude 2. Lola's theme 3. Juke Box 4. Mike and Lola's theme] in compilation CD 'Hurrah for Malcolm Arnold' – Él/Red Cherry Records ACMEM95CD

DVD EAN/UPC 5028836032342. Metrodome – Second Sight. UK. Region 2

DVD EAN/UPC 883904193760. MGM. UK. Region 2

Music notes

In order to illustrate the kaleidoscopic world of a European circus, Arnold's music is brimming over with musical styles: classical, jazz and popular. Despite the French locations and British composer and director, this is still a Hollywood styled picture. Filmed at the Cirque D'Hiver in Paris in the summer of 1955, director Carol Reed gets very close to an authentic atmosphere of sawdust and canvas. The training of the artists as well as the public performances are dominated by famous circus marches such as 'Washington Post', 'Stars and Stripes Forever' and 'Entry of the Gladiators' played by the Cirque D'Hiver's twelve-piece band. From the classics we hear among others Strauss and Chopin.

Wisely Arnold devotes his own score to the personal dramas of the leading players. He provides an attractive love theme for the relationship between Lancaster and Lollobrigida. In one scene Arnold uses harmonica set against hushed strings to provide some tender feeling. Tony Curtis is given a French-flavoured motif of his own for harmonica and accordion. Just as the circus needs music, so does *Trapeze* with an exciting colourful 60-minute score.

Sheet music

'Lola's Theme', song with words by Al Stillman, published by Cromwell Music.

'Lola's Theme', version for accordion solo, transcribed by Mario Mascarenhas, published in Brazil.

'Trapeze', title song with words by Johnny Burke and music by Paul Elie (not Arnold), published by Essex Music.

MAF performance

'Lola's theme': song [words: Al Stillman] Claire Thompson (soprano)/Scott Mitchell (piano), 19 October 2014 (MAF 9)

Concert arrangement

Suite from the film [1. Prelude 2. Romance 3a. Fanfare 3b. Elephant Waltz 4. Mike and Lola 5. Tino's Arrival in Paris 6. Finale] reconstructed, arranged and orchestrated by Philip Lane (1999)

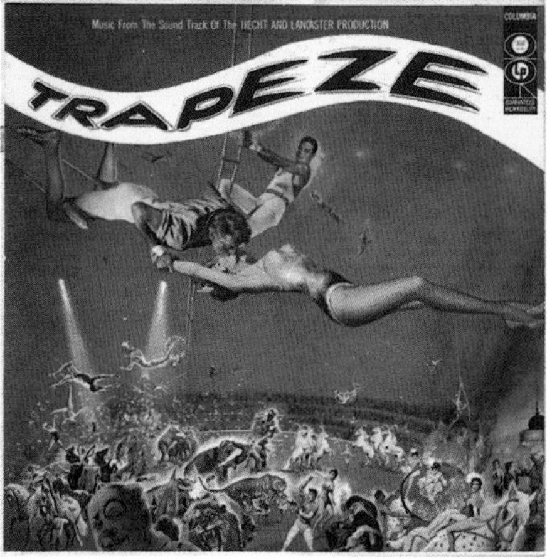

LP: Columbia CL 870

7" vinyl: 'Lola's Theme' is included on 'Theme Songs Vol.9'

Duration 13'30"

Instrumentation 2 2 2 2 – 4 3 3 1 – timp perc(3) hp acc – str

Publisher Novello

Recording

(i) BBC Philharmonic Orchestra/Rumon Gamba – Chandos CHAN 9851 (The Film Music of Sir Malcolm Arnold, Vol.2)

Articles

(i) Film review in 'Variety', New York, 31 December 1955

(ii) Movie Review (B.C.), in New York Times, 5 June 1956

Notes

(i) Basil Wright interviewed 'Three on [the] Trapeze' during the programme 'Talking of Films' – BBC Home Service, 11 November 1955.

Wicked as They Come (1956)

US title **Portrait in Smoke**

Production Frankovitch Productions (Film Locations)

Producers Maxwell Setton and M J Frankovitch

Director Ken Hughes

Stars Arlene Dahl, Philip Carey, Herbert Marshall

Music played by Sinfonia of London/Muir Mathieson

Adapted screenplay

Ken Hughes, Robert Westerby and Sigmund Miller, from the novel 'Portrait in Smoke' by Bill S Ballinger [*Publisher* Harper & Brothers/Signet Books, 1952]

Book; Poster

Locations

1. Stock shots of a busy New York ending in the backstreet slums of the city
2. Arlene Dahl (Kathleen Allenbourg) is flown to Europe from New York International Airport on Anderson Field. The plane lands at London Airport: there is a shot of the entrance to the airport on the Bath Road opposite the junction with Sipson Road
3. The Bentley passes Buckingham Palace before arriving at the May Fair Hotel in Berkeley Square.
4. Stock shots of the Arc de Triomphe in Paris
5. The murder trial venue is the Wilkins Building of University College, London, on Gower Street, WC1
6. Nettlefold Studios, Walton-on-Thames, Surrey

Release

UK premiere London, 22 May 1956
US release date February 1957
South American release date Argentina, 18 June 1957

Media

No commercial recording. View on YouTube: https://www.youtube.com/watch?v=b7E9WNUWJLU

A Hill in Korea (1956)

US title **Hell in Korea**
Production Wessex Films
Producer Anthony Squire
Director Julian Amyes
Stars Stephen Boyd, Ronald Lewis, George Baker
Music played by Royal Philharmonic Orchestra/Muir Mathieson

Adapted screenplay

Ian Dalrymple, Anthony Squire and Ronald Spencer, from the novel by Simon Kent (aka Max Catto) [*Publisher* Hutchinson, 1953]. Film edition: Arrow Books, c.1956.

Locations

1. Portugal (external shots)
2. Shepperton Studios, Surrey

Note This was Michael Caine's first credited film role (he was himself a veteran of the Korean War). He commented: "The most glaring mistake that I never brought to their notice was that Portugal did not in the least resemble Korea. If anything, Wales was more similar. I did not say anything because I wanted to stay in Portugal – I could go to Wales any old time. . ."

Release

UK premiere London, 18 September 1956
Asian premiere Hong Kong, 11 December 1958
UK TV premiere BBC1 Television, 7 December 1965

Media

DVD EAN/UPC 5055201806413. Canal Image. UK Region 2

Music notes

Brass fanfares herald in the titles and Arnold's march theme with plenty of work for brass and strings, but it is not one of his more memorable efforts. It is not really surprising since the film itself must go down as one of the worst war films made at a British studio, in this case, Shepperton and some dry-looking fields in the South of England. It is all a long way from Korea and the nearest it gets is Arnold's oriental percussion for a religious temple on the hill. Despite early film roles for Robert Shaw, Stephen Boyd and Michael Caine, this poorly scripted and directed film wastes what was an interesting cast. The score is short in length and could best be described as functional.

Poster

Book

Articles

(i) British Film Institute, Monthly Film Bulletin, January 1956

Notes

(i) Excerpts shown on 'Picture Parade' with Peter Haigh – BBC Television, 25 September 1956.

Tiger in the Smoke (1956)

Production Rank Organisation
Producer Leslie Parkyn
Director Roy Ward Baker
Stars Donald Sinden, Muriel Pavlow, Tony Wright
Music played by Orchestra/Malcolm Arnold

Adapted screenplay
Anthony Pelissier from the novel by Marjorie Allingham [*Publisher* Chatto & Windus, 1952; Hogarth Edition, 1987]

Note Chapter 1 reveals: "In the shady ways of Britain today it is customary to refer to the Metropolis of London as the Smoke." [The Smoke was also the name of an Arnold overture from 1948]

Locations
1. London and Brittany
2. PInewood Studios, Iver Heath, Bucks

Release
UK premiere London, 27 November 1956
UK TV premiere BBC1 Television, 22 May 1990

Media
DVD EAN/UPC 5037115257239. ITV Studios. UK. Region 2. (11 DVD Boxed Set including 'You Know What Sailors Are')

Music notes
1956 was not one of Arnold's most rewarding years in film scoring. On this occasion the main titles are played without music. The sounds of London and Big Ben are all that are heard on the soundtrack. In the first half the only music comes from a group of street buskers. The small ensemble comprised of two trumpets, a big drum and other percussion. Their playing has a distinctly light-jazz feel about it. There are a couple of short suspense cues with appropriate ostinato and a longer dramatic cue for the finale on the coast of Brittany. A brief flurry of orchestral chords accompany the end title.

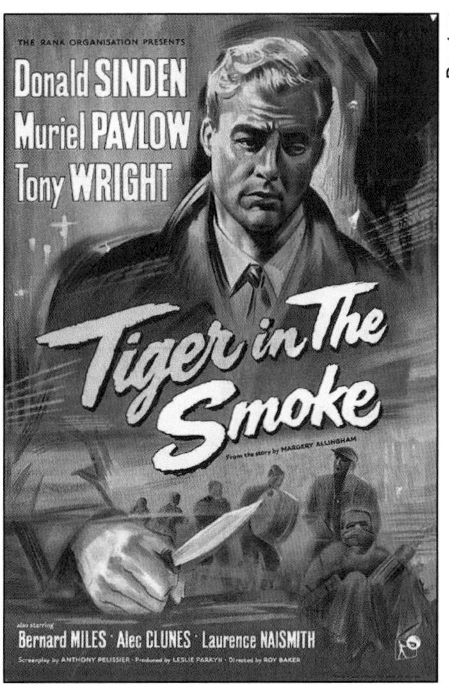

Poster

Book

Notes
(i) Excerpts and interviews were shown on 'Picture Parade' with Tony Wright – BBC Television, 20 November 1956.

The Barretts of Wimpole Street (1957) [rejected]

Production MGM British Studios
Producer Sam Zimbalist
Director Sidney Franklin
Stars Jennifer Jones, John Gielgud, Bill Travers

Adapted screenplay
John Dighton, from the play by Rudolf Besier [*Publisher* Victor Gollancz, 1930].

Locations
1. Marylebone Church, Marylebone, London
2. MGM British Studios, Borehamwood, Herts

Release
US premiere Radio City Music Hall, New York, 17 January 1957
South African premiere Johannesburg, 14 February 1957
UK release date 28 February 1957
Australian release date 18 July 1957
UK TV premiere BBC2 Television, 25 December 1971

Poster

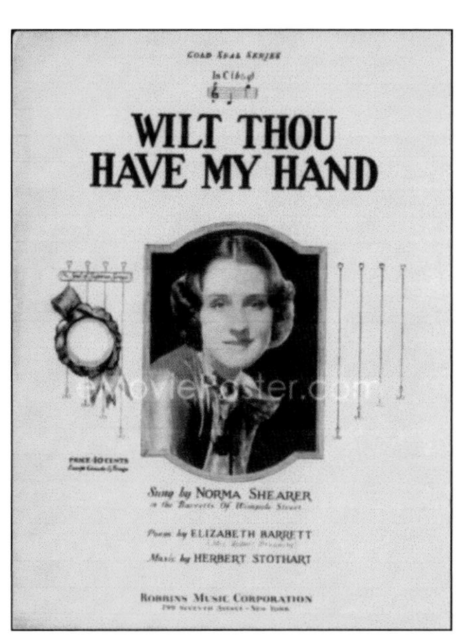

Sheet music

Articles

(i) Film review in 'Variety', New York, 16 January 1957

(ii) Movie Review (B.C.), in New York Times, 18 January 1957

(iii) British Film Institute, Monthly Film Bulletin, March 1957

Notes

(i) Arnold provided the original score and conducted his own music for this film. However, this was rejected and replaced by a score by Bronislau Kaper. There is no trace of Arnold's score despite several enquiries. In a letter to the composer dated 10 October 1956, Johnny Green, MGM's General Musical Director based In Culver City in California, says that a decision had been made for a "rather different approach to the dramatic score" and that they were now proceeding with a new one. He finishes by hoping that there will be "another opportunity for us to have the privilege of availing ourselves of your talents". Malcolm Arnold replied on 26 October 1956 from his home in Denbigh Gardens, Richmond: "I am very sorry about *The Barretts of Wimpole Street*. Fortunately this type of catastrophe has only occurred twice in my life. [The other was *Invitation to the Dance* a few years earlier.] If it had been any more I should now be busy playing the trumpet with my collection box in Regent Street!"

(ii) Excerpts shown on 'Picture Parade' with Derek Bond – BBC Television, 25 February 1957.

Sheet music

'Wilt Thou Have my Hand', song by Herbert Stothart to words by Elizabeth Barrett Browning.

Island in the Sun (1957)

Production Daryl F Zanuck Productions for Twentieth Century Fox
Producer Daryl F Zanuck
Director Robert Rossen
Stars James Mason, Joan Fontaine, Dorothy Dandridge, Harry Belafonte
Music played by Royal Philharmonic Orchestra/Malcolm Arnold

Adapted screenplay

Albert Hayes, from the novel by Alec Waugh [*Publisher* Cassell, 1956]. Film edition: Pan Books, 1959.

Locations

1. Farley Hill Mansion, Barbados (the fictional island of 'Santa Marta') [The mansion on Farley Hill National Park was gutted by fire in the mid-1960s]
2. Grenada and Trinidad
3. MGM Elstree Studios, Borehamwood, Herts

Release

US premiere New York City, 12 June 1957
UK premiere Carlton, Haymarket, London, 25 July 1957
UK TV premiere BBC1 Television, 23 October 1966

Media

7" vinyl
'Island in the Sun' title song [words: Harry Belafonte; music: Irving Burgie (Lord Burgess)]: Harry Belafonte – RCA Victor RCA 1007
DVD EAN/UPC 024543221876. Cinema Classics. USA. Region 1

Music notes

A brief Arnold fanfare is followed by a series of scenes straight out of a West Indian travelogue accompanied by a song sung by Harry Belafonte which continues into the opening titles. A curious beginning to a film that really never seems to know where it is going. The scenes

Poster

Book

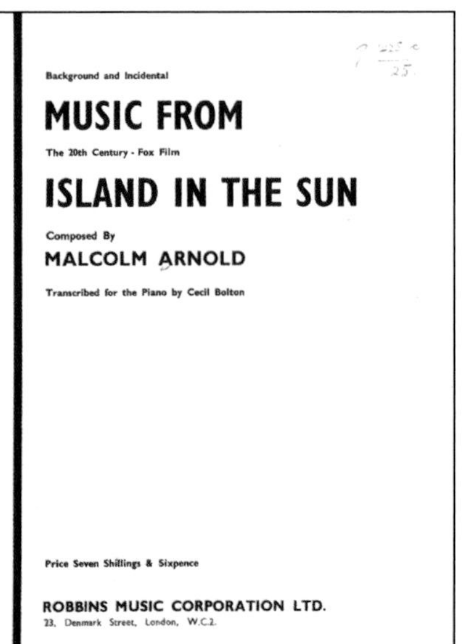
Background and Incidental

MUSIC FROM

The 20th Century - Fox Film

ISLAND IN THE SUN

Composed By

MALCOLM ARNOLD

Transcribed for the Piano by Cecil Bolton

Price Seven Shillings & Sixpence

ROBBINS MUSIC CORPORATION LTD.
35, Denmark Street, London, W.C.2.

Sheet music: Background and incidental music; 'Island in the Sun' title song.

of happy West Indians at work and at carnival time do not fit in very well with the melodramatic affairs of high society on this particular Caribbean island. There are stately and ceremonial pieces for brass band and plenty of calypso beat to supply the local colour. It is then left to composer Arnold to fill in the rest and it is not a great deal.

He dutifully supplies appropriate tremolo and ostinato sections to give some tension to the drama but it is all quite functional. The score comes to life briefly in a romantic scene between Stephen Boyd and Joan Collins but at most it gets about a minute in full orchestral splendour. The score is supposed to be 28 minutes long but certainly not on the print I watched. Was the song 'Island in the Sun' written for the film or simply a traditional calypso tune? Was much of Arnold's score cut from the final print? Even an old Lionel Newman song first heard in the 1948 *Road House* (also 20th Century Fox) is used several times as source music, put in perhaps as an afterthought by the studio. It all adds up to rather a muddle for film and score.

Sheet music

Excerpts arranged for piano solo by Cecil Bolton, published by Robbins Music [1. Fanfare; 2. Maxwell's arrival at Belfontaine; 3. Bon Marche music (Market Square); 4. Market Square; 5. Governor General's Ball; 6. Masks; 7. Euan and Jocelyn at Belfontaine; 8. Maxwell Fleury buys newspaper; 9. The Murder: Themes 1, 2 and 3; 10. Maxwell throws away wallet; 11. Maxwell drives to Police Station; 12. Euan and Jocelyn at the old fort; 13. Election Jazz- Band; 14. Maxwell's attempted suicide.][1]

'Island in the Sun', 'Cocoanut Woman', 'Don't Ever Love Me' songs with words by Harry Belafonte, music by Irving Burgie (Lord Burgess), published by Clara Music (1957).

MAF performances

'Belfontaine – the Old Fort – Return to Belfontaine', arranged for flute and piano by Alan Poulton. Ruth Morley (flute)/Scott Mitchell (piano), 19 October 2014 (MAF 9)

'Market Square (Part 1) – Governor's Ball – Market Square (Part 2)', arranged for flute and piano (with an optional part for bongos) by Alan Poulton. Alasdair Garrett (flute)/Jennifer Redmond (piano), 16 October 2016 (MAF 11)

Notes

(i) Excerpts from the film were shown on 'Picture Parade', with Peter Haigh – BBC Television, 22 July 1957.

(ii) The following week there were televised scenes recorded at the UK premiere, again on 'Picture Parade' – BBC Television, 29 July 1957.

1 The publishers prefaced these excerpts with the following remarks: "It is with great pleasure that we present the background music, transcribed for piano, from the film *Island in the Sun*. We sincerely believe this will be a useful addition to the library of the serious student of this ever-growing new medium, particularly as it is by one of England's most important composers in this field, Malcolm Arnold." These published excerpts are the most extensive for any Arnold film score: they show what can be done when a competent arranger is given access to the orchestral full score at the time of the film's release (before being burnt, shredded or just thrown away, as was often the custom).

The Bridge on the River Kwai (1957)

Production Horizon

Producer Sam Spiegel

Director David Lean

Stars William Holden, Alec Guinness, Jack Hawkins

Music played by Royal Philharmonic Orchestra/Malcolm Arnold (recorded at Shepperton Studios, 21 October 1957 – Arnold's 36th birthday)

Adapted screenplay

Carl Foreman, from the novel by Pierre Boulle, translated from the French by Xan Fielding [*Publisher* Secker & Warburg, 1954; Vanguard Press, New York, 1954].

Film edition: Bantam Books, New York, 1957 (as 'Bridge OVER the River Kwai') and Fontana Books (UK) 1956 and 1958.

Locations

1. The bridge was constructed near the village community of Kitulgala on the Masleliya Oya, a tributary of the Kelani River between Colombo and Kandy on Sri Lanka (formerly Ceylon)
2. British Headquarters was filmed at Peradeniya Botanical Gardens, Kandy District, Central Province, Sri Lanka
3. The military hospital was filmed at Mount Lavinia Hotel, Colombo, Western Province, Sri Lanka [The Mount Lavinia Hotel was originally the Governor's mansion in colonial times and served as a military hospital during WWII]

Note The cast and crew stayed at the Government Rest House in Kitulgala overlooking the site of the bridge.

Release

UK premiere London, 2 October 1957

UK release date 11 October 1957

US release date 14 December 1957

European release date Belgium and France, 20 December 1957

South American release date Brazil, 23 December 1957

Japanese release date 25 December 1957 [Merry Christmas!]

Indian release date 28 December 1957

Asian release date Hong Kong, 9 January 1958

Canadian release date March 1958

Poster

Australian premiere Sydney, 8 March 1958
Australian release date 27 March 1958
UK re-release (in 70mm) 15 May 1973
UK TV premiere BBC1 Television, Christmas Day 1974 [and subsequently televised on a regular basis by the BBC over the Christmas period]

Awards

Arnold was awarded a Hollywood Oscar for 'Best Music, Scoring' in 1958 – among the other nominations were Hugo Friedhofer for `An Affair to Remember' and Johnny Green for `Raintree Country'. Malcolm Arnold was not present at the ceremony and Morris Stoloff accepted the award on his behalf – the composer later collected his Oscar from Heathrow Airport after it had been cleared through customs.

The following year Arnold was also a Nominee for a Grammy Award for the Best Soundtrack Album (Dramatic Picture Score or Original Cast).

Media

7" vinyl

Soundtrack excerpts [1. Nicholson's Victory 2. Working on the Bridge 3. Camp Concert Dance 4. Finale] Royal Philharmonic Orchestra/ Malcolm Arnold – Philips BBE 12194 (7/58), Philips (France/Holland) 429.382 BE

Soundtrack excerpts [1. Overture 2. River Kwai March] (No.1) Royal Philharmonic Orchestra/Malcolm Arnold and (No.2) Mitch Miller and his Orchestra – CBS Sony (Japan) SOPB 236; (No.2 only) Philips 322.219 BF; CBS Coronet (Australia) KS-211

River Kwai March with Alford's 'Colonel Bogey' (selected listing)
(i) Carlson's Raiders (instrumental) led by Jack Marshall – Capitol (USA) 45-17954(12/57); Capitol (Australia) 45-CP-1276 (3/58)
(ii) Orchestra conducted by Matty Malneck (produced by William Holden) – Warner Bros. (USA) ESA 1247
(iii) Joey and his Friends (arranged and produced by Art Kaplan) – Colpix Records (USA/Australia) CP-733 (6/64)
(iv) Art Mooney and his Orchestra – MGM (USA) K12590
(v) Bavarian Wind Orchestra – Concert Hall Schlager Series (Germany) – U101 (Matrix No. C 5183)
(vi) Ron Goodwin and his Concert Orchestra – Parlophone 45-R 4391 (1958); Odeon (Germany) 45-O 29174
(vii) David Terry and his Orchestra – RCA Victor (USA) 47-7153; EPA-4250;

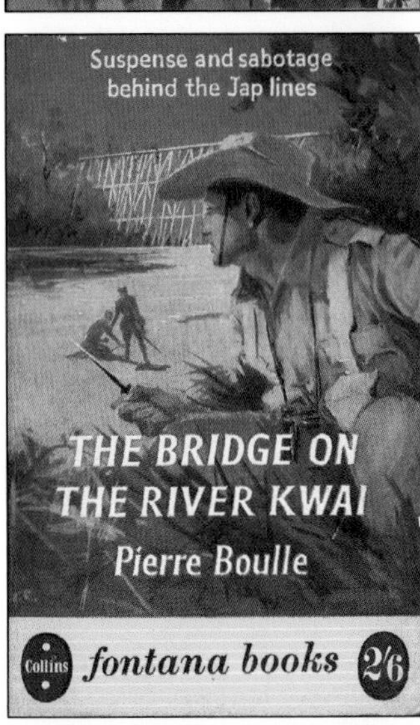

Books

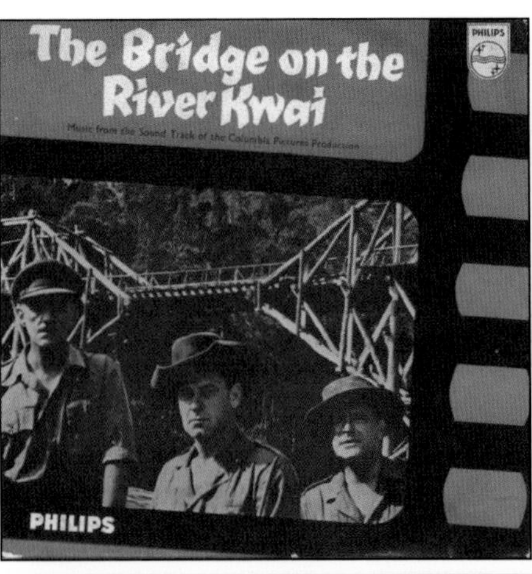

7" vinyl (top to bottom): Philips BBE 12194; Philips 429.382 BE; CBS Sony SOPB 236; RCA Victor EPA-4250

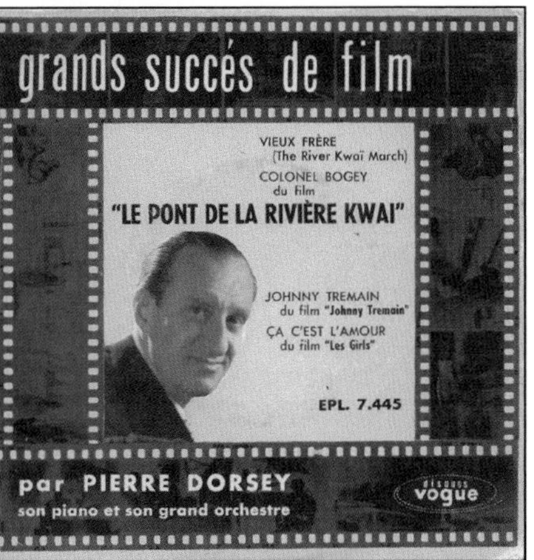

7" vinyl (top to bottom): Decca 450.070; Vogue EPL 7.445; Pathe 45 EG 375

LP: Columbia CL 1100

RCA Italiana 45M 0666 (1958) [4]
(viii) Band of the Grenadier Guards – Decca 450.070 [5]
(ix) Pierre Dorsey (piano) and his Orchestra – Vogue (France) EPL 7.445
(x) Eddie Barclay and his Orchestra – Barclay (France) 72206 (1/58); Bertelsmann (Germany) 35 411
(xii) Olavi Virta (arranged by Pauli Strom) – Philips (Finland) 427.503 PE
(xiii) Orquesta 'Huambaly' (arranged by Lucho Kuhan) – Odeon (Chile) MSOD 3015
(xiv) Leo, Leo en Leo (A Happy Holland Sound Production) – Park (Holland) BP 1095
(xv) Jack Marshall's Music – Capitol (USA) F 4197 (5/59)

'Vieux Frère' (vocal version of the 'River Kwai March') [French Words: Max Francois]: John William (vocals) with an orchestra conducted by Mario Bua – Pathe (France) 45 EG 375

LP

Soundtrack recording [1. Overture 2. Colonel Bogey March 3. Shear's Escape 4. Nicholson's Victory 5. Sunset 6. Working on the Bridge 7. Trek to the Bridge 8. Camp Concert Dance 9. Finale 10. River Kwai March 11. 'I Give my Heart to No-one but You' 12. Dance Music 13. The River Kwai March/Colonel Bogey March (Mitch Miller arrangement)] Columbia (US) CL 1100 (2/58)/CS 9426 (9/70); later re-issued on CD – Silva Screen VSD 5213; Sony SRCS 7072; Legacy/Columbia CK 66131
Filmophone CD 1001 [tracks 1,3-9,13 only]; Banda Sonora BSGZ137CD [tracks 1-9 only]

DVD EAN/UPC 5035822000131. Studio Canal. UK. Region 2

Blu-ray EAN/UPC 5050629000115. Sony. UK. Region B

4K Ultra HD EAN/UPC 5050630000111. Sony. All regions

Sheet music

River Kwai March, piano arrangement, published by Columbia Pictures Music Corporation

Colonel Bogey (Alford), piano arrangement, published by Boosey & Hawkes

Themes from the film ['Main title', 'Shear's escape', 'Nicholson's victory', 'Trek to the bridge', 'Sunset', 'Camp concert dance', 'I give my heart no one but you' (Camp concert song)], transcribed and edited by Robert C Haring, published by Columbia Pictures Music Corporation

'Vieux frère' (Old brother), song based on River Kwai March with French

Sheet music

lyrics by Max Francois, published by Francis-Day

Concert arrangements

River Kwai March

arranged for orchestra by G Green

Instrumentation 2 2 2 2 – 4 2 3 0 – timp perc hp – str

Publisher Campbell Connelly

River Kwai March

arranged for military band by Gilbert Vinter

Publisher Campbell Connelly

River Kwai Patrol

arranged for military band by R Berry An adaptation of Alford's 'Colonel Bogey' and themes from the film

Publisher Campbell Connelly

River Kwai March

arranged for concert band by Eric Osterling (1958)

Publisher Shapiro Bernstein & Co Inc

River Kwai March

arranged for junior concert band by John Higgins (1998)

Publisher Hal Leonard, 1998 (as part of 'The Big Picture – Epic Movie Themes')

River Kwai March

arranged for orchestra by John Glenesk Mortimer

Publisher Marc Reift

River Kwai March

arranged for brass band by [John Glenesk Mortimer]

Publisher Marc Reift

River Kwai March

arranged for concert band by John Glenesk Mortimer

Publisher Marc Reift

River Kwai March

arranged for concert band by Robert Longfield

Publisher Hal Leonard, 2017

Suite from the film

[1. Prelude: The Prison Camp 2. Colonel Bogey (Kenneth Alford) 3. The Jungle Trek 4. Sunset 5. Finale: The River Kwai March]

arranged for large orchestra by Christopher Palmer (1991)

Commissioned by the BBC in honour of Arnold's 70th birthday

Duration 29'

Instrumentation 3 3 3+Eflat cl 2+cbsn – 4 3 3 1 – timp perc(6) pno(2) hp(2) – str

First performance BBC Concert Orchestra/ Barry Wordsworth – Queen Elizabeth Hall, London, 26 October 1991 (70th Birthday Concert)

First European performance National Symphony Orchestra of Ireland – National Concert Hall, Dublin, 8 July 1994

Malcolm Arnold shows his Oscar for Best Musical Score for 'The Bridge on the River Kwai' to producer Sam Spiegel, 1958. Everett Collection Inc /Alamy Stock Photo

Publisher Novello

Recording

(i) London Symphony Orchestra/Richard Hickox – Chandos CHAN 9100 (The Film Music of Sir Malcolm Arnold, Vol.1)

Suite from the film

arranged by Christopher Palmer transcribed for wind band by Yoshihiro Kimura

Recording

(i) Hiroshima Wind Orchestra/Yoshihiro Kimura – Brain Music BOCD -7460

MAF performances

'Main Title' and 'Shears Escape', arranged for solo piano by Robert C.Haring: Moritz Ernst (piano), 16 October 2010 (MAF 5)

'I Give My Heart to No-one But You' – Camp Concert song [words: Dave Shand]: Claire Thompson (soprano)/ Scott Mitchell (piano), 19 October 2014 (MAF 9)

'Dawn and Trek', arranged for flute and piano by Alan Poulton (with optional segue to 'Vieux Freres', the vocal version of the 'River Kwai March' [words: Max Francois]): Alasdair Garrett (flute)/Claire Thompson (soprano)/Jennifer Redmond (piano), 16 October 2016 (MAF 11)

Articles

(i) British Film Institute, Monthly Film Bulletin, November 1957

(ii) Ritchie, Christopher: 'The Arnold-Lean Trilogy, Part 3' – Beckus 30, Autumn 1998, Maestro 1, October 2014

(iii) Poulton, Alan: 'Kwai – a cinematic review' – Maestro 2, October 2015

(iv) Dunstan, David: The Colonel Bogey saga – Beckus 118, Autumn 2020

Notes

(i) A 'pocket' edition of the film adapted for radio was broadcast on 'Movie-Go-Round' – BBC Light Programme, 21 January 1958.

(ii) 'Spiegel of the Cinema': Gordon Gow talks to Sam Speigel – BBC Home Service, 5 January 1963.

(iii) See main article 'The Bridge on the River Kwai: OST recording' on the next page.

Poster in Spanish

The Bridge on the River Kwai: OST recording

One day, out of curiosity, producer Sam Spiegel happened to purchase the novel *Le Pont de la Rivière Kwaï* by Pierre Boulle, which was, at the time, the talk of the day. He read the novel on a plane flight and by the time he arrived in London, he was determined to bring the story to the big screen. Complications arose immediately as his trusted screenwriters, Michael Wilson and Carl Foreman, were on the infamous McCarthy blacklist of people accused of Communist sympathies, and were forced to ghost-write, while Boulle, who could not speak let alone write in English, was assigned the sole writing credit. Spiegel brought in David Lean to direct the film and they assembled a stellar cast for the project, including Alec Guinness as Colonel Nicholson, Jack Hawkins as Major Warden, William Holden as Captain Shears and Sessue Hayakawa as the brutal Colonel Saito.

The story is drawn from real events in World War II where British prisoners of war were ordered to build a bridge to connect a railway line connecting Burma and Siam. Nicholson, on principle and citing the Geneva Convention, refuses Saito's order for his officers to join in manual labour. Saito tortures him, yet he refuses to succumb. Faced with a deadline, Saito acquiesces and releases Nicholson, who agrees to organise his men for the effort. Nicholson believes that this endeavour will offer enduring testimony to the strength, dignity and indomitable spirit of British soldiers under harsh circumstances. Although Nicholson is an honourable man, he becomes obsessed and we slowly begin to see the bridge shift from a testimony to the courage of British soldiers to a monument that edifies his ego. A Special Forces team is sent to destroy the bridge on the day of its inauguration during a Japanese supply train's transit. Charges are set, which Nicholson discovers and, remarkably, he alerts Saito to the danger. As they inspect the bridge a firefight ensues, killing Saito and some of the Special Forces. A shell-shocked Nicholson experiences an epiphany when viewing the dead British soldiers and utters "What have I done?", realising that he has been collaborating with the enemy. The film ends poetically as we see Nicholson collapse from his wounds on to the dynamite plunger, thus destroying the bridge as the train passes. The film was an enormous commercial and critical success, earning eight Academy Award nominations, and winning seven, among them, Best Picture, Best Director, Best Actor and Best Film Score. As fate would have it, Boulle also ended up winning the Oscar for his 'screenplay', which precipitated great controversy. In 1984 all was made right when the Academy retrospectively awarded the Oscar to Wilson and Foreman.

Spiegel had wanted to release his film by 31 December 1957, the deadline for it to be eligible for Academy Award consideration, but by early December 1957, he had still not hired a composer to score the film! He sought out British composer Sir Malcolm Arnold, who was at that point best known for his scores for *The Sound Barrier* (1952), *The Belles of St Trinian's* (1954), *Hobson's Choice* (1954), and *Trapeze* (1956), as well as his numerous ballets, symphonies and works for the British theatre. Arnold was tasked with writing the score in a mere ten days, and he rose to the occasion. Originally, Lean wanted the British troops to be introduced singing the 'Colonel Bogey March', a popular tune written in 1914 by Frederick Ricketts, a British Army bandmaster who later became the director of music for the Royal Marines, and used the pseudonym Kenneth J Alford. However, during WWII, British troops had adapted its melody to accompany bawdy new lyrics – "Hitler has only got one ball!" – and Spiegel was appalled, refusing to allow this 'vulgarity' into his film. However, Lean and Arnold were still able to make their patriotic point as they adapted the march, having the men whistle its melody.

The music (as presented on the original soundtrack recording)

The Colonel Bogey March and Arnold's River Kwai March serve as the primary thematic identities of the score. The two marches are kindred in construct in that the River Kwai March's countermelody utilises the same chord progressions as the Colonel Bogey March. The British Military Theme is rendered in two forms: the first is a classic, forthright march, carried by strings *nobilmente* and horns, in the finest traditions of the British military, but the second variant is a truly twisted rendering by dissonant and eerie

Original Soundtrack Recording

Track Listing

1. Overture
2. Colonel Bogey March
3. Shear's Escape
4. Nicholson's Victory
5. Sunset
6. Working on the Bridge
7. Trek to the Bridge
8. Camp Concert Dance
9. Finale
10. River Kwai March
11. I give my heart to no one but you
12. Dance Music (written by Dave Shand)
13. River Kwai March/Colonel Bogey March (performed by Mitch Miller & his orchestra)

Royal Philharmonic Orchestra conducted by Malcolm Arnold. Columbia (1957)

tremolo strings, which speak to us of its corruption by Colonel Nicholson's loss of perspective and egotistical obsession with the bridge. Lastly, for Colonel Saito, Arnold provides a simple motif, a dark and descending low register line, which informs us of his menace.

The opening 'Overture' is a powerful cue and a score highlight. It is a harsh, brutal and militaristic piece, which opens powerfully with horns *bellicoso*, informing us of the drama soon to unfold. It begins as the opening credits roll and we see the prisoners arriving by train. As the beleaguered men march through the sweltering jungle to the camp, Arnold juxtaposes pastoral strings and harp that speak of the jungle's beauty with martial trumpet calls alluding to the misfortunes of war. Slowly the music evolves into a *marcia brutale* as they march to their fate. A brief respite with the festive River

Kwai March lightens the moment, and ushers in spirited strings and woodwinds, which ends with a vista shot of the camp.

The Colonel Bogey March offers another score highlight. It plays as the men march into camp, and speaks to the indomitable spirit of the British military. The theme is presented in its entirety with its A-phrase emoted as a classic march, while its B-phrase is surprisingly lyrical, offering a stylish embellishment. As the men arrive and assume formation, Arnold brings in the full orchestra for a grand finish atop repeated statements of the A-phrase.

'Shear's Escape' is a complex multi-scenic cue. It reveals Shears escape from the camp, his travails and ultimate success in achieving freedom. Arnold weaves the thematic material of the overture into Shear's trek, which unfolds energetically to support his flight. We shift scenes to the Japanese guards returning to the camp with the three men that were killed, which unfolds as a grim march. Swirling strings with trumpet counters take us back to the jungle where Shears is seen struggling to crawl ashore from a raging river. As he struggles against the jungle's oppressive heat a *marcia brutale* takes form and crescendos as he reaches the sanctuary of a village. We conclude with villagers seeing him off in a boat to celebratory strings, yet the music again becomes dissonant and oppressive as he struggles in the oppressive heat. We conclude his journey to freedom with dissonant horn fare, which inform us of him reaching the ocean, and freedom.

'Nicholson's Victory' is a complex dichotomous cue. It opens on warm strings, which usher in a declaration of the first variant of the British Military Theme. This is short-lived as it mutates into the second more twisted variant on eerie tremolo strings as we witness Colonel Saito's capitulation with the release of Colonel Nicholson and his officers. This twisted and dissonant rendering of the British Military Theme plagues Saito and reflects his inner torment as he has lost face and is seen crying in solitude in his cabin. At 2:30 as the men realise Nicholson has triumphed, the music becomes celebratory and Arnold supports the moment with a festive rendering of the River Kwai March.

'Sunset' is a score highlight, a delight, and what I believe to be, its most beautiful cue. We see a contented Nicholson walking atop the completed bridge with a sense of pride and accomplishment. When Saito joins him, Nicholson lets his guard down and shares a personal moment as he recounts his life. Saito however maintains the veneer of his stoical Japanese bearing and does not respond in kind. Arnold perfectly captures the moment by stripping out the martial nature of the River Kwai March, instead providing a warm, lyrical and extended rendering with gentle strings, harp and pastoral woodwinds. Simply beautiful!

Lobby card

'Working on the Bridge' is a similarly complex cue, which features interplay between Arnold's themes. The scene reveals a now energised, determined and organised British-led labour force working on the bridge. A sparkling rendering of the River Kwai March supports the activity. An ominous interlude by Colonel Saito's motif plays as a stoic Saito looks on. The second variant of the British Military Theme then joins in interplay with the River Kwai March as Nicholson summarily rejects the doctor's suggestion that their bridge building activities could be construed as collaboration, or worse, treason. Arnold perfectly attenuates his music to the psychology of this scene.

'Trek to the Bridge' features the commando team's arduous trek through the unforgiving jungle. We open with a forthright expression of the British Military Theme, but its lustre fades and dissonance rises as they progress, thus reflecting their travails. Arnold uses nativist-sounding piccolos to reference the local Thai women bearers accompanying the team. The British Military Theme carries the men ever onward, yet it struggles in its expression, mirroring the team's struggle.

In 'Camp Concert Dance' we see a drag show as the men entertain and celebrate. Arnold offers campy source music in the spirit of Vaudeville as the men celebrate the completion of the bridge.

'Finale' features the aftermath of Nicholson's death and the bridge's destruction. It opens with ominous horns, which usher in a festive rendering of the River Kwai March, which celebrates the British victory. After an interlude of horns *nobilmente* the River Kwai March reprises as the end credits roll.

'River Kwai March' is a glorious cue, which offers a full and extended rendering of the British march in all its pomp and martial glory.

'I give my heart to no one but you' is a source song composed by Malcolm Arnold and David Shand (wrongly credited to Carl Millocker and Richard Leigh on the LP/CD). The singer is uncredited.

'Dance Music' plays as background source music for the scene where we see Shears relaxing with his girl on a beach in Ceylon.

Lastly, we have the Mitch Miller medley of 'The River Kwai March/Colonel Bogey March', which is a wonderful score highlight! It features the two marches presented with orchestral accompaniment and chorus in marvellous contrapuntal interplay! It does not get any better than this. Bravo!

While the sound quality on the Legacy/Columbia Records CD does not match current 21st century qualitative standards, the digital editing does manage to present a descent listening experience. This is a classic score well worthy of your exploration. It offers three splendid marches in the finest of military traditions, which perfectly capture the heart of this film. How Arnold attenuates his music to flesh out the underlying psychology of the film's narrative is spot on and testimony to his mastery of his craft. I believe this score to be a classic, a fine example of the Golden Age, and one essential for your collection

Craig Lysy

From the 'Movie Music UK' website
https://moviemusicuk.us
Reproduced by permission

Blue Murder at St Trinian's (1957)

Production John Harvel Productions
Producers Sidney Gilliat and Frank Launder
Director Frank Launder
Stars Terry-Thomas, George Cole, Joyce Grenfell
Music played by Orchestra/Malcolm Arnold

Original screenplay
Frank Launder, Val Valentine and Sidney Gilliat

Locations
1. The school, filmed at All Nations College at Easneye, Stanstead Abbotts in Hertfordshire
2. Several interesting locations for the filming in Rome: these included around the Forum, the Piazza Navona, the Spanish steps below the Trinity Church and several areas within the Coliseum (much of which is now no longer accessible to the general public)
3. Joyce Grenfell in shot at Melrose Road in Weybridge near the junction with Waverley Road and St Charles Primary School
4. Littleton Park House (part of the Shepperton Studios complex)
5. Shepperton Studios, Surrey

Release
UK premiere London, 19 December 1957
UK release date December 1957
US premiere New York City, 26 May 1958
UK TV premiere BBC1 Television, 3 November 1970
European TV premiere Sweden, 13 February 1973

Media
DVD EAN/UPC 5060034577560. Studio Canal. UK. Region 2. (Boxed set with Belles of St Trinian's / Pure Hell at St Trinian's / Great St Trinian's Train Robbery)
DVD EAN/UPC 5060034577775. Studio Canal. UK. Region 2

Music notes
This is the second of the St Trinian's series and probably the funniest. Alastair Sim makes only a cameo appearance and so it is left to regulars George Cole (Flash Harry) and Joyce Grenfell (Ruby Gates), ably assisted by the wonderful Terry-Thomas as a rather dubious coach operator, to keep the laughs coming.

Arnold quite rightly sticks to his successful school song which on this occasion opens proceedings with some lyrics and St Trinian's vocal support. The longest section of the score is reserved for the arrival of the new headmistress at St Trinian's. It starts with the lively school song, then receives helpings of Gilbert and Sullivan, some dramatic ostinato, all closely synchronised to the frantic action in the school, culminating in the girls welcoming their new headmistress with a rousing rendition of the school song with appropriate piano accompaniment.

When St Trinian's wins a schools competition, they head off to Europe by coach and the music illustrates the journey with snatches of the Marseillaise, a foxtrot at a French café, and Mozart in Vienna, with the school orchestra making a sudden and dramatic switch to swinging jazz. With peace having been temporarily restored a snatch of 'A Policeman's Lot is not a Happy One' is followed by a version of the school song for small instrumental ensemble over the end titles.

Sheet music
'St Trinian's School Song' is reproduced, together with several film stills, in the book 'The St Trinian's Story', compiled by Kaye Webb [*Publisher* Perpetua, 1959; Penguin Books, 1961, 1963].

Notes
(i) A 'pocket' edition of the film adapted for radio was broadcast on 'Movie- Go Round' introduced by Peter Haigh – BBC Light Programme, 12 January 1958.

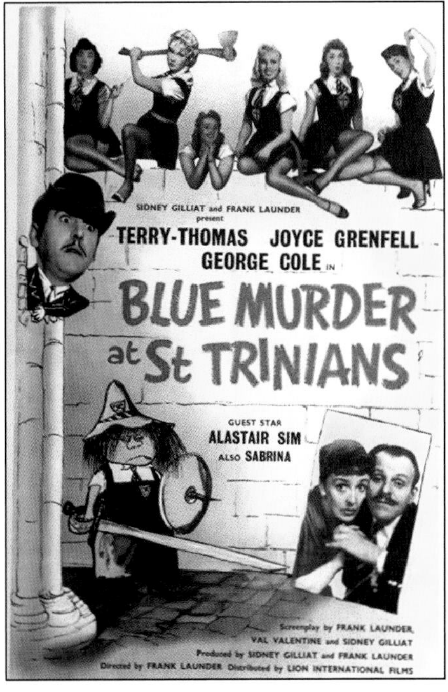

Posters

Dunkirk (1958)

Production Ealing Studios
Producer Michael Balcon
Director Leslie Norman
Stars John Mills, Richard Attenborough, Bernard Lee
Music played by Sinfonia of London/Muir Mathieson

Adapted screenplay

W P Lipscomb and David Divine, from the book 'Dunkirk' by Major J Selby Bradford and Lt Col Ewan Butler [*Publisher* Hutchinson, 1950 as 'Keep the Memory Green – The Story of Dunkirk'] and the novel 'The Big Pick-up' by Trevor Dudley Smith (writing as Elleston Trevor) [*Publisher* Heinemann, 1955; Pan Books, 1956]. Film edition: Arrow Books, 1957.

Locations

1. London locations include Downing Street and Senate House, London University and the flotilla of boats pass Blackfriars, Lambeth and Hammersmith Bridges and the Houses of Parliament
2. Bernard Lee is filmed on the Thames Embankment opposite Eel Pie Island in Twickenham: there are further meetings on the Western suspension bridge by Tough's Yard, the boat house at Teddington Lock destroyed by fire in 1999 but later rebuilt by the present owner
3. French scenes were probably filmed in Kent – there are so many oast houses in shot! These included (i) Dover Castle (the Operation Dynamo Command Centre) (ii) Sheerness Dockyards, Sheerness (iii) the blowing up of the Teston Bridge, near Maidstone, over the River Medway just as a German scout-car crosses over!
4. Camber Sands, Camber (for the Dunkirk evacuation shots) and Rye, also in East Sussex.
5. Fingringhoe, Colchester, Essex.
6. The English Channel shots were actually filmed off Plymouth Hoe.
7. MGM British Studios, Borehamwood, Herts.

Release

UK premiere Empire, Leicester Square, 20 March 1958
Australian release date 15 May 1958
South African release date 9 September 1958
US release date 10 September 1958
UK TV premiere BBC1 Television, 31 July 1983

Media

DVD EAN/UPC 7321900571616. Warner. UK. Region 2
DVD EAN/UPC 5055201802965. Studio Canal. UK. Region 2
Blu-ray EAN/UPC 9317731134180. Studio Canal. UK. Region B

Music notes

Arnold's music for *Dunkirk* is built on one of his strongest themes for a war film. After opening on brass the music quickly develops into the main theme taken up by the strings; a firm, resilient theme whose character reflects a spirit of courage and endurance. It is heard at its best when the armada of small boats, having sailed down the Thames past Big Ben and Tower Bridge, heads out into the open sea: a moment when picture and music are in perfect unison. For Arnold it is a piece of true inspiration. As with the best of his themes, it can be manipulated effectively with just a minor change in tempo or orchestration. When the soldiers at Dunkirk are filing out into the sea to await evacuation, it is the music that portrays the real tragedy of the situation. Dunkirk was both a defeat and a victory. Britain lived to fight another day and you can sense it in the music.

Articles

(i) Film review, in 'Variety', New York, 26 March 1958

Notes

(i) A review of the film by Gordon Gow broadcast on 'Home for the Day' – BBC Home Service, 23 March 1958.
(ii) Scenes at the Royal premiere in London , attended by Her Majesty the Queen, in 'Picture Parade' – BBC Television, 25 March 1958.

Poster

Books

The Key (1958)

S title **Stella**
roduction Open Road Films/Highwood Productions
roducer Carl Foreman
irector Carol Reed
tars William Holden, Sophia Loren, Trevor Howard
lusic played by Orchestra/Malcolm Arnold
dapted screenplay
Carl Foreman, from the novel 'Stella' by Jan de Hartog [*Publisher* Harper & Brothers, 1952). Film edition: Pocket Books, 1953 and 1958.
ocations
. 'Westport Dock' in the film is actually Portland Harbour, Isle of Portland, Dorset
. William Holden (Captain David Ross) is taken to the 'Seaview Apartments' on the Esplanade in Weymouth
. Sophia Loren (Stella) departs from Henley-on-Thames Station in Oxfordshire [Henley station was closed and re-sited in 1975; the old buildings seen in shot on Station Road were also demolished at that time]
. Elstree Studios, Borehamwood, Herts
elease
JK premiere London, 29 May 1958
uropean premiere Belgium, 30 May 1958 (Brussels International Film Festival)
JK release date 6 June 1958
JS premiere New York City, 1 July 1958
JK TV premiere BBC2 Television, 30 July 1988
wards
Trevor Howard won a BAFTA award for 'Best British Actor' in 1958.
ledia
" vinyl
The Key to your Heart' ('Stella') [words by Al Stillman]: Mitch Miller and his Chorus and Orchestra with Jimmy Carroll (saxophone solo) – Philips 45-PB 847 (8/58)
Chop Suey Polka':
(i) Brooke Pemberton ("The Ragtime Kid") – Warner Bros. (USA) 5010 (9/58)
(ii) Frankie Yankovic and his Yanks – Columbia (USA) 4-41232
(iii) The Texans (Square dance version) – Blue Star (USA) BS-1592
(iv) Charlie Proctor – Blue Star (USA) BS-1991
.P Soundtrack recording [1. The Key (To Your Heart) 2. U-Boat Alley 3. The Key (Theme) 4. Stella 5. Chop Suey Polka]

Book

Poster

Columbia (US) CL 1185 (8/58); later re-issued on CD – Filmophone CD1001
DVD EAN/UPC 5050582361377. Sony. UK. Region 2
Music notes
The title music is grim and unrelenting in character. A descending motif for brass develops into some fierce work for brass and strings, full of ostinato, to provide almost a documentary feel to this story of rescue tugs working off the south-west coast of England in 1941. For the many very realistic scenes at sea filmed in black and white in Cinemascope, Arnold's ability to write dramatic music in a true symphonic style is evident and he makes full use of all his orchestral resources to create perfect support for the various dramatic situations in the story. However when the occasion calls for it, he can supply an attractive and rather sad melody for Stella (Sophia Loren), given over to strings and woodwind. As William Holden, the new skipper of a rescue tug, puts his vessel through a set of testing manoeuvres, Arnold whips up a frenzied, drunken dance for the zigzag motions of the boat in the water. This particular approach is unexpected and yet surprisingly effective. As Holden gains in confidence, Arnold mirrors his mood with a brisk, march-like motif.

In a two-hour-ten-minute film it is Arnold's score that provides much needed momentum when the onshore story threatens to bog down the picture. There are several characteristic touches in his score: when Holden has a nightmare and

Sheet music

LP: Columbia CL 1185

then suddenly wakes up, tremolo strings develop into a version of the love theme (StellaS theme), and when mines are sighted at sea, brass and drums provide plenty of dramatic ostinato not unlike a similar scene at sea in the later *Heroes of Telemark*.

Later in the film, as Stella tries to rid herself of past memories, Arnold introduces us to a new, bright and attractive string theme to illustrate the change in her. The ending to *The Key* has a rather downbeat twist to it, but despite this Arnold provides some glimmer of hope for Loren and Holden with a full orchestral Hollywood-style treatment of Stella's theme. It is interesting to note that when the music was released on LP in 1958 the record tracks were formed into longer suites like the movements in a symphony.

Sheet music

'The Key to your Heart' ('Stella'), with words by Al Stillman, published by Columbia/Campbell Connelly (1958).

'Chop Suey Polka' arranged for piano published by Columbia/Campbell Connelly (1958).

MAF performances

'The Key to Your Heart', theme song [words: Al Stillman]: Claire Thompson (soprano)/Scott Mitchell (piano), 19 October 2014 (MAF 9)

Articles

(i) Film review in 'Variety', New York, 24 June 1959

Notes

(i) Extracts from the film were shown in 'Picture Parade' – BBC Television, 2 June 1958.

Malcolm Arnold plays a selection of his music for the film 'The Key' to Carl Foreman, executive producer, and Sir Carol Reed, right, director, at Elstree Studios, Hertfordshire, 16 April 1958. PA Images/Alamy Stock Photo

The Roots of Heaven (1958)

Production Darryl F Zanuck Productions for Twentieth Century Fox

Producer Darryl F Zanuck

Director John Huston

Stars Errol Flynn, Juliette Gréco, Trevor Howard

Music played by Royal Philharmonic Orchestra/Malcolm Arnold

Adapted screenplay

Romain Gary and Patrick Leigh-Fermor, from the novel 'Les Racines du Ceil' by Romain Gary (born Roman Kacew), translated by Jonathan Griffin [*Publisher* (in French) Les Editions de L'Imprimerie Nationale de Monaco, 1952; Editions Gallimard, Paris, 1956, paperback edition, 2009; (English version) Michael Joseph/Penguin Books, 1958; Simon & Schuster, New York, 1958].

Locations

1. Forest of Fontainebleau
2. French Equatorial Africa (i) Sarh, Southern Chad (ii) Belgian Congo
3. Paris, Studios de Boulogne-Billancourt

Release

US release date 15 October 1958

European release date France, 10 December 1958

UK premiere London, 15 January 1959

UK release date 22 February 1959

South American release date Uruguay, 6 April 1959

Australian release date 23 July 1959

UK TV premiere BBC1 Television, 4 June 1972

Media

7" vinyl

'The Roots of Heaven' title song [words: Ned Washington; music: Henri Patterson] (arranged by Don Costa): Johnny Nash, orchestra conducted by Don Costa – ABC Paramount (USA) 45-9989; HMV POP 597

LP

Soundtrack recording [1. Overture 2. Main Title. 3. Wild Elephant 4. Morel's Camp 5. Minna – St Denis 6. Minna's Theme 7. Jungle Clearing 8. Elephants 9. Minna's Dream 10. Ivory Poachers 11. Elephant Hunt 12. Morel's Surrender 13. The Sandstorm 14. Return to Biondi 15. Finale]
Fox (US) M.3005/S.3005 (3/59); reissued on CD: Banda Sonora

BSGZ129CD; included in compilation album 'The Cinema of Juliette Gréco' Cherry Red Records ACMEM197CD
DVD EAN/UPC 5019322889342 Simply Media. UK. Region 2
Blu-ray EAN/UPC 0851789003139 Twilight Time. UK. Region B

Autograph score

Full score (Overture only)
Instrumentation 2 2 2 1+cbsn – 4 3 3 1 – timp perc hp – str
Currently at Eton College Library [MS 921 01 13]

Sheet music

'The Roots of Heaven' title song [words: Ned Washington; music: Henri Patterson], published by Robbins Music.

Concert arrangement

'Overture' Written at the request of Darryl Zanuck for the US premiere in October 1958. The full score went missing soon after the New York performance, but was recreated in 1983-84 from the surviving parts.
Duration 5'15"
Instrumentation 2 2 2 1+cbsn – 4 3 3 1 – timp perc(2) pno (cel) hp – str
Publisher Novello
First concert performance BBC Concert Orchestra/Carl Davis – Radio 3, 21 March 1995
Recordings
(i) BBC Philharmonic Orchestra/Rumon Gamba – Chandos CHAN 9851 (The Film Music of Sir Malcolm Arnold, Vol.2)
(ii) Royal Ballet Sinfonia/Gavin Sutherland – ASV WHL 2113; Resonance CDRSB 205

Suite from the film

arranged for large orchestra by John Morgan [1. Overture 2. Main Title 3. Fort Lamy 4. The Great Elephants 5. Morel's Retribution 6. Morel's Camp 7. Minna and St Denis 8. Minna and Major Forsythe 9.The Jungle Clearing 10. The Elephant Herd 11. Minna's Dream 12. The Ivory Poachers 13. The Elephant Hunt 14. Morel's Capture 15. At the Well 16. The Sandstorm 17. Return to Biondi (Part 1) 18. Return to Biondi (Part 2)* 19. Minna's Goodbye* 20. Finale and End Titles. *Music developed by Alfred Newman]
Duration 32'30"
Recording
(i) Moscow Symphony Orchestra/William Stromberg – Marco Polo 8.225167 reissued as Naxos 8.573366

Poster

LP: Fox 3005

Book

Sheet music: title song

Notes

(i) A 'pocket' edition adapted for radio from the soundtrack was broadcast on 'Movie-Go- Round' – BBC Light Programme, 1 February 1959.

The Inn of the Sixth Happiness (1958)

Production Twentieth Century Fox
Producer Buddy Adler
Director Mark Robson
Stars Ingrid Bergman, Robert Donat, Curd Jürgens
Music played by Royal Philharmonic Orchestra/Malcolm Arnold

Adapted screenplay
Isabel Lennard, from the book 'The Small Woman: The Heroic Story of Gladys Aylward' by Alan Burgess [*Publisher* Evans Bros, 1957, 1959, rev.1969].
Film edition: Pan Books, 1959, 1966.

Locations

1. The gatehouse of Westminster City School, Palace Street, is the exterior of the 'China Missionary Office' where Ingrid Bergman (Gladys Aylward) first applies
2. Bergman looks up at the Landseer lions on Trafalgar Square
3. She later walks down Carlton House Terrace past the ICA taking the steps down to the Duke of York's column
4. Bergman arrives at Paddington Station
5. North Wales locations:
   (i) Snowdonia National Park, Gwynedd (Shanxi Province)
   (ii) Morfa, Bychan, Porthmadog, Penrhyndeudrath and Nanmor (walled city)
   (iii) Beddgelert (Sygun copper mine)
   (iv) Lake Ogwen and Capel Curig, Conway
   (v) Cwm Buchan, Llanbedr and Portmeirion
6. MGM British Studios, Borehamwood, Herts

Note Bergman stayed at the Portmeirion Hotel during the filming in North Wales.

Release
UK premiere London, 23 November 1958
US premiere New York, 11 December 1958
UK release date 11 January 1959
South American release date Argentina, 7 July 1959
UK TV premiere BBC2 Television, 24 December 1966

Awards

(i) The film score won Malcolm Arnold an **Ivor Novello** award, presented by the Songwriters Guild of Great Britain in 1959. Arnold conducted the [BBC] Concert Orchestra in his arrangement of the theme music on stage at the BBC Television Theatre – the entire ceremony was televised by the BBC on 25 May 1959.
(ii) Mark Robson was nominated for an **Oscar** in the 'Best Director' category at the Academy Awards ceremony in 1959.
(iv) The film won a **Golden Globe** in 1959 for 'Best Film promoting international understanding'(!)

Media
7" vinyl

Soundtrack excerpts [1. La Marche des Enfants (The Children's Marching Song) 2. La Theme de L'Adieu (The Parting) 3. Le Voyage Vers la Chine (Voyage to China) 4. L'Air des Muletiers (Bringing in the Mule Train)] Ingrid Bergman, Orphan's Chorus, Royal Philharmonic Orchestra/ Malcolm Arnold – 20th Century Fox Vega (France) FOXV 45 P 1972 [a]; (Nos. 1 and 2 only) 20th Century Fox (USA) 45-126 (12/58); 20th Century Fox Vega (France) FOXV 45.5028 [b]; (No.1 only) 20th Century Fox (Germany) 75 001 A

Title Song [Words: Paul Francis Webster]:
(i) The Four Aces (vocals) with an orchestra conducted by Jack Pleis – Decca 9-3082 (1/59);Brunswick OE 9458 (1/59); Brunswick 45-05773; Festival (Australia/New Zealand) FK-3073 [c]
(ii) Victor Sylvester and his Ballroom Orchestra – Columbia 45-DB 4240 (1/59)
(iii) The Wayfarers (instrumental) – Decca 45-F.11473 (6/62)

Theme (Happiness Melody) and **Children's March** (variously entitled – Nick Nack Paddy Wack/Nick Nack Song/This Old Man):
(iv) Bill Shepherd Orchestra with the Dr Barnardo's Children's Choir – Pye Nixa 45 7N-15180 (12/58); Nixa (Australia) N-15180; Vogue (France) PNV.24037 [d]
(v) Addy Andrigo and his Orchestra with Harry Gabriel (solo trumpet) – Telefunken (Germany) U 55 122
(vii) Cyril Stapleton and his Orchestra, with Bill Elliott (vocals) and 'featuring the children from the film' – London (USA) 45-1851; Decca 45-F.11094 (12/58); Decca 9.22.937

Children's Marching Song 'La Marche des Gosses' (Trad. arr. Malcolm Arnold]:
(viii) Mitch Miller and his Chorus and Orchestra – Columbia (USA) 4-41317; Columbia Hall Of Fame 4-33084;

Poster

Books

Philips (Germany) 322.385 BF; CBS Coronet (Australia) KS 299 (2/59)
(ix) Norman Leyden Child's World Orchestra (produced by Charles Green) – RCA Victor Bluebird WBY-106 (1/59);
RCA (Australia) 10640 (2/59); RCA (New Zealand) 4/60123
(x) Annie Cordy with Orchestra conducted by Roland Granier – Columbia (France) ESRF 1212 [e]
(xi) Sandpiper Chorus and Jimmy Carroll's Fife and Drums Corps – Golden Records (USA) FF 545 [f]
(xii) The Lennon Sisters with an orchestra conducted by George Cates – Brunswick (USA) 9-55113; Brunswick (Australia) BK-4016; Coral (Germany) 93 287 [g]
(xiii) The Good Fortune Cookies with the Jimmy Carroll Orchestra – Carousel (USA) (s) C-466

.P
oundtrack recordings [1. Overture 2. Journey to China 3. Bringing in the Mule Trains 4. The Meeting of Gladys and Linnan 5. Jeannie Lawson passes on 6. Prelude (Prison Riot) 7. In the Garden of the Inn 8. The Invasion 9. The Parting (Main theme) 10. Children's March from Yangcheng 11.'This Old Man' 12. Finale]
Fox (US) M.3011/S.3011 (3/59); later re-issued on CD – Filmophone CD2008
DVD EAN/UPC 5039036056656. 20th Century Fox UK. Region 2
)VD EAN/UPC 5039036020794. 20th Century Fox UK. Region 2
3lu-ray EAN/UPC 8436548868161. Feel Films. Spain. Region A,B,C (multi-region)

Ausic notes

'he Chinese will wish you five happinesses: health, wealth, long life, virtue nd a peaceful death in old age. There is lso a sixth happiness, which each of us nust find in our own hearts. The motion icture *The Inn Of The Sixth Happiness* is he story of that sixth happiness and how t came to the inn that draws its name.

This Cinemascope production from 958 is one of the best films that composer Arnold ever worked on. He wrote over o minutes of score and it is one of his nost distinctive and delightful. The story of missionary Gladys Aylward and her vork in China is given the full Hollywood reatment by American director Mark Robson, who was Oscar-nominated for his efforts.

Ingrid Bergman's ability to convey a very real sense of emotion and sincerity keeps the film from falling into

a

b

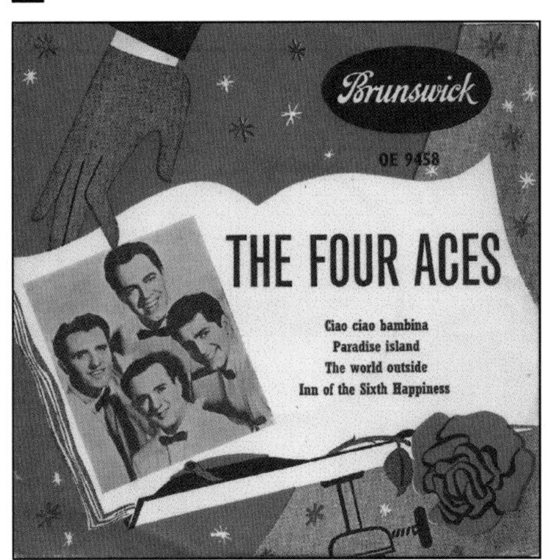

c

d

e

f

g 7" vinyl [a] to [g] – see text for details

LP: Fox 3011

sugary sentimentality. The core of the film is very much an emotional one and Arnold's score is rightly based on melody. After the Fox fanfare and a brief written prologue, the main titles, set over Bergman's arrival in London, are scored with Arnold's main theme, which is firm and assertive and is to reflect the determination and courage of Gladys Aylward's story. This theme develops into a lovely full orchestral version of the love theme primarily associated with Bergman herself. It is warm melodic writing for strings and one of the composer's most beautiful creations. An interesting example of where one might have expected to find music and in fact does not, is where Bergman says goodbye to her friends at the railway station as she heads off into the unknown. Despite no musical help, the scene still works. Your heart goes out to her.

The journey to China gave Arnold the opportunity to write music with a little flavour of the Orient with the help of appropriate percussion. A group of Chinese musicians were flown from Hong Kong to London to supplement the 70 musicians of the Royal Philharmonic Orchestra who recorded the score. A ceremonial procession introduces an oriental-flavoured motif for the local mandarin (Robert Donat). Its character has a sad, plaintive quality. As Bergman meets and is gradually drawn towards a Eurasian officer (Curt Jurgens), strings are added to the oriental flavour to provide a more romantic mood. Despite the oriental instrumentation, Arnold's melodic line remains clear. A prison riot and the ever-increasing danger of war provide opportunities for Arnold to introduce a more dramatic and harder edge to his score with brass and drums prominent.

As the film progresses, the oriental music for Jurgens and the Bergman love theme become interwoven. Ultimately the love theme takes centre stage. In particular, the scenes between Bergman and Jurgens and the scene where the mandarin (Donat) bids his farewell are among some of the most tender and emotional moments in any of the films that Arnold worked on. It is not a coincidence that he supplied some of his most beautiful music for this particular film.

At the climax of their long journey over the mountains to safety, Bergman and her orphans sing the traditional 'This Old Man' (The Children's Song) which is eventually taken over by the orchestra and transformed into the main theme. Over the closing titles, the love theme is reprised resplendent in all its orchestral glory.

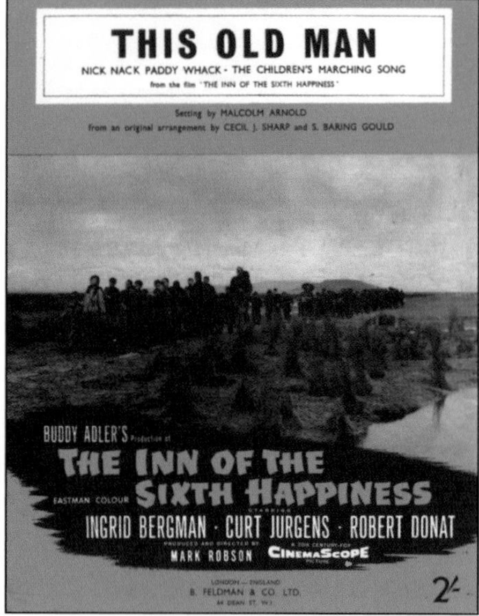

Sheet music

Arnold's score won the Ivor Novello Award that year. How it failed to be Oscar nominated is a mystery and an injustice. Arnold can be rightly proud of his contribution to the success of *The Inn Of The Sixth Happiness.*

Autograph scores

Full score

Instrumentation 2 2 2 1+cbsn – 4 3 3 1 – timp perc(2) hp(2) – str

At the Jerwood Library

Full score (title theme only) arranged by the composer for small orchestra, possibly for the Ivor Novello Awards ceremony

Instrumentation 0 1 0 0 – 1 0 0 0 – gtr perc(2) cel hp – str

Currently at Eton College Library [MS 921 01 13]

Sheet music

Title song [words by Paul Francis Webster], published in England by Feldman [27] and in America by Miller Music Corporation, both in 1958 [28]; a piano solo version was also published by Feldman in the same year [29].

'This Old Man' ('Nick, Nack, Paddy Whack') published as a unison song and piano piece with the subtitle 'The Children's Marching Song' [30]. Other published arrangements include those for orchestra, brass and military band as well as accordion solo.[1]

Title song [Swedish words by Gosta Rybrant] and 'This Old Man' ('Nick, Nack, Paddy Whack') [Swedish words by 'Ninita'], published by Reuter & Reuter Forlass AB, Sweden.

Concert arrangement

1 The brass band arrangements were made by Edrich Siebert and published in the UK by Feldman and in Australia by J Albert, both in 1958.

'This Old Man' arranged for orchestra
Instrumentation 2 2 2 2 – 2 2 3 0 – timp perc hp gtr pno – str
Publisher B Feldman, 1958
'Children's March' arranged for military band by Rodney Bashford
Recording
(i) Band of the Grenadier Guards/Lt Col Rodney Bashford – London PS 434 (LP)
Selection arranged for brass band by Edrich Siebert
Duration 6'
Publisher B. Feldman, 1958; Studio Music
Suite from the film arranged for orchestra by Christopher Palmer (1992) [1. The London Prelude 2. Romantic Interlude 3. Happy Ending (Mountain Crossing – The Children)]
Duration 14'
Instrumentation 3 2 3 2 – 4 3 3 1 – timp perc(4) pno(cel) hp(2) – str
Publisher Novello (study score)
First performance Hampshire County Youth Orchestra – Bryanston School, Blandford, Dorset, 11 April 1993
First professional performance Bournemouth Symphony Orchestra/ Richard Hickox – Wessex Hall, Poole, Dorset, 18 September 1993
First London performance Royal Academy of Music Sinfonia/Ron Goodwin – Duke's Hall, Royal Academy of Music, 18 June 1996 (British and American Film Music Festival)
Recordings
(i) London Symphony Orchestra/Richard Hickox – Chandos CHAN 9100 (The Film Music of Sir Malcolm Arnold, Vol.1)
(ii) London Philharmonic Orchestra/ Vernon Handley – LPO 0013
Suite from the film arranged by Christopher Palmer and transcribed for wind band by Munetoshi Senoo (1996)
Duration 14'
Publisher Novello
Recordings
(i) Kosei University Wind Orchestra/ Douglas Bostock – Kosei KOCD-8000
(ii) Bunko University Wind Orchestra/ Munetoshi Senoo – Brain Music OSBR 20026-7; re-issued Cafua CACG 0118 (CD)
(iii) University of Nevada-Las Vegas Wind Orchestra/ Takayoshi Suzuki – Mark Records 4867-MCD
MAF performance
'Title song' [words: Paul Francis Webster]: Claire Thompson (soprano)/Scott Mitchell (piano), 19 October 2014 (MAF 9)
Notes
(i) A 'pocket edition' adapted for radio from the soundtrack was broadcast on 'Movie-Go Round' – BBC Light Programme, 14 December 1958.
(ii) The song 'This Old Man' ('Nick, Nack, Paddy Whack') was chosen by Ingrid Bergmann from a list of six suggested by Malcolm Arnold. It was adapted from a children's song arranged by Cecil Sharp and Sabine Baring Gould.

The Boy and the Bridge (1959)

Production Xanadu Productions
Producers David Eady and Kevin McClory
Director Kevin McClory
Stars Ian Maclaine, Liam Redmond, James Hayter
Music played by Orchestra/Malcolm Arnold
Adapted screenplay
Geoffrey Orme, Kevin McClory and Desmond O'Donovan, based on a story by Leon Ware.
Locations
1. Bermondsey and Tooley Street (several scenes).
2. Most of the scenes were filmed in or around the Tower of London and Tower Bridge with the boy occupying a room at the top of the North Tower.

Release
UK premiere Curzon Cinema, London, 28 July 1959
Awards
Kevin McClory was nominated for the Golden Lion award in the 'Best Director' category at the Venice International Film Festival of 1959.
Media
No commercial recording. View/rent from the BFI: https://admin.player.bfi.org.uk/rentals/film/watch-the-boy-and-the-bridge-1959-online

Music credit in The Boy and the Bridge

Concert arrangement
Overture (Allegro and March) arranged for orchestra, probably by Tony Fones (c.1959)[1]
Duration 3'30"
Instrumentation 2+picc 1 2 1 – 2 2 3 0 – perc hp cel – str
Publisher B Feldman & Co
First concert performance Malcolm Arnold Festival Orchestra/John Gibbons – Royal & Derngate, Northampton, 17 October 2010 (Fifth Malcolm Arnold Festival)
Note Performing materials (piano conductor score and parts) are also available from the Light Music Society Library.
MAF performance
Overture (Allegro and March), arranged for flute and piano by Alan Poulton: Ruth Morley (flute)/Scott Mitchell (piano), 19 October 2014 (MAF 9)
Notes
(i) Interview with Kevin McClory on 'Movie-Go-Round' – BBC Light Programme, 9 August 1959.
(ii) See main article 'The Boy and the Bridge' on the next page.

1 I located a copy of the score together with the parts within the archives of the Light Music Society. They had acquired the material from the conductor Frank Cantell (the conductor of the BBC's West of England Light Orchestra in the fifties) and had it filed under the film's title marked "composer unidentified"! – AP

The making of The Boy and the Bridge

Prelude: Richmond, Summer 1958

The phone rang in the Arnold house. Sheila answered.

"Hello ... Yes. I'm Mrs Arnold ... He's here if you want to speak to him ... No, no trouble at all. Who shall I say is? ... Ken? ... Oh, sorry, Kevin."

By now Malcolm was in the hallway looking a little dishevelled.

"Who is it?"

Sheila put her hand over the receiver.

"It's, er, Kevin. I can hardly hear him. Sounds as if he's in a bar somewhere."

Malcolm made to grab the receiver.

"Here, give us the phone ... Hello, who is this?"

"Malcolm, it's Kevin McClory. I'm just ..."

"Kevin, just been reading about you, you old dog. What's up?"

"Gotta little proposition for you. I'm setting up my own film company, Xanadu Productions, and guess what? We want you to write the score to our first picture."

There was a moment's pause as he waited for a response but none came.

"You know you did such a great job on the Kwai bridge film. Got you an Oscar didn't it?"

"Yes, it did," said Malcolm proudly, "Couldn't go myself. Too busy on The Key. Collected it from London Airport. Took ages to get it through customs. Matter of fact, I can just see it on my desk as I speak. Well, actually, it's not on my desk at the moment; it's being used as a doorstop. The wind's getting up, I think we're going to get some rain and ..."

"Anyway, Malcolm," said McClory, interrupting him, "this film we've got in mind – wrote the screenplay myself in actual fact – it's all about another bridge which ..."

"Oh, not another bloody war film. I'm through with them!"

"No, No, Malcolm," the caller hastened to re-assure him, "it's far removed from that. It's the story of a young boy who takes refuge on a London bridge."

"Bit chilly I would have thought."

"Ah, but this is Tower Bridge. I've got three months' clearance to film there and we're shooting in a fortnight. We've found a great kid to play the lead – and then there's the seagull."

"What's his name?"

"Who, the seagull?"

"No, the boy."

"Oh, Ian Maclaine. That's not his real surname, that's McLenahan – bit of a mouthful, so I changed it when I was talking to Shirley the other day..."

"Shirley?"

"It's a long story. Anyway, I got one of your tabloid papers to find him."

"Who, the boy?"

"No, the seagull. And before you ask, he's called Sammy. He's from North Wales."

"So, what's the film called? 'Seagulls over London'?"

"Not even close. No, we're calling it The Boy and the Bridge. There's not a lot of dialogue – it'll need plenty of music for the action scenes around the Tower of London and the bridge itself. So, what do you reckon? I bet you're swamped with work."

"Matter of fact, I am, Kevin. Right in the middle of a big piece for the Hoffnung Festival."

"Hoffnung? That rings a bell. Plays the horn?"

"No, the tuba. Gerard Hoffnung, a very witty man and one of my best friends."

"What are you writing?"

"Something for four military bands and orchestra; I'm calling it 'United Nations'"

"Wow! Sounds like you've got your work cut out with that. Hey, I've just had a thought. Talking of the United Nations, I'm actually working on another film script with some other guys. It's about the theft of an atom bomb and the rest of the world held up to ransom and there's only one man who can save them. Can't say any more, it's all very hush-hush, someone may be listening in."

"Got a title yet?"

"Thunderball. Look, keep that under your hat, OK? So have a think about The Boy and the Bridge. Let me know soon, won't you? Gotta go. Oh, and one last thing, I nearly forgot..."

"You can't pay me till 1960?"

"Ha, ha, Malcolm, that's a cracker. No, my co-producer's wife – bit of a concert pianist, I hear – well, she's written this little piece, it's a waltz, I think. Anyway, she'd like you to use it as the main theme. Is that OK?"

There was a long silence.

"Look, I'll send it on to you, OK? Bye!"

"Can't wait," said Malcolm as he put the phone down. He returned to his study, the desk strewn with sheets of the Hoffnung score, some of which were now littering the floor.

"Thunderball," he mused "Great title, but that's for another day perhaps."

He reached for another blank page. He'd just remembered – Gerard was due in an hour to check on his 'United Nations'.

Producer/Director Kevin McClory

Kevin McClory was born on 8 June 1924 in Dun Laoghaire, Dublin; in 1932, the family went to live in London. During the Second World War, Kevin served in the Norwegian Marines. Then in 1946, he smooth-talked his way into a job as a £4/week boom operator and tea boy in the sound department at Shepperton Studios in Middlesex, determined to make his way to the top.

There he worked on several classic British films including *Anna Karenina* (1948) and the *Mudlark* (1950). He was soon spotted by the film producer John Huston and became his assistant, working on the *African Queen* (1951), *Moulin Rouge* (1952) and *Beat the Devil* (1953), as well as working as a location manager for Warwick Films on the *Cockleshell Heroes* (1955).

His big break came when John Huston appointed him as Assistant Director on the Herman Melville classic about the hunt for the great white whale *Moby Dick* (1956) and in the same year, on the recommendation of Huston, he was made second unit Director of Foreign Locations on the Mike Todd epic *Around the World in 80 Days* starring David Niven and Shirley MacLaine.[1]

Xanadu productions and *The Boy and the Bridge*

While on holiday in the Bahamas, Kevin happened to meet a wealthy Englishman of Inca descent, Ivar Bryce, who was married to Josephine Hartford, a fabulously rich heiress with homes in the Bahamas, United States and England. Bryce was a millionaire oil man, a real estate owner and a racehorse breeder, while his wife earned £1,000 a day from her chain-store holdings and was the world's third richest woman.[2]

---

1 At one time in the mid-fifties, Kevin McClory and Shirley MacLaine were romantically linked. Kevin remembered Shirley later: when he found Ian McLenahan to star as the boy in *The Boy and the Bridge*, he renamed him Ian Maclaine, after Shirley.

2 Ivar Bryce was the first cousin of Janet,

Kevin quickly took the opportunity to ell Bryce about a film called *The Boy and he Bridge*, which he planned to write, roduce and direct, and persuaded him o be his financial partner. They formed he company Xanadu Productions[3] with he object of establishing a multi-million-ound film industry in the Bahamas, build-ng the studios and providing all the facili-ies needed to attract major American TV nd film makers. When the press got hold f the story, they wanted to know why millionaire businessman wanted to get nto film making. McClory told them, "Ivar s a working partner, even though this is is first venture into motion pictures. He sure that motion pictures are not dying, s some people think they are. He thinks he whole trouble is that there are too nany mediocre pictures. I agree."

While in the Bahamas, McClory hanced to meet Mrs Beatrice Sigrist n a Nassau golf course. Beatrice was he mother of 'Bobo' Sigrist, the young eiress, whom Kevin had first met when he was only 16. Since then, Bobo had en-ured a stormy marriage to Gregg Jaurez, vith whom she had a young daughter alled Bianca, and was now negotiating divorce settlement. Mrs Sigrist invited evin over to the house and soon he and obo became very close friends.

By the summer of 1958 McClory and obo had both moved to London; they vere constant companions, though they vent to great lengths to conceal the fact ending the divorce proceedings, Bobo ometimes walking three paces behind im. Her mother had no such qualms, aying, "I don't see anything wrong with ou being seen together. After all, we're ll friends."

One day, Bobo arrived on the set of he *Boy and the Bridge* in a Rolls-Royce vith her own butler to serve the cast

Ian Maclaine as the boy, with Sammy the Seagull

champagne and caviar. In a later inter-view McClory remembered, "She phoned me and asked if she could call over. I said, if you can make scrambled eggs for six people, come over. She did; the eggs were delicious; it was love." However, McClory continued to exercise under-standable caution over too many appear-ances from Bobo on set and hid her away most of the time, though she did have a tiny cameo role in the film (uncredited).

Ian Maclaine and Sammy the Seagull

Filming of *The Boy and the Bridge* had been scheduled for the summer of 1958 but was somewhat delayed while the search for the leading role and accompa-nying seagull took place.

Ian Maclaine (born McLenahan), the new child star of *The Boy and the Bridge*, was described at the time by no less a person than the director, John Huston, as "the greatest find since Jackie Coogan".

Born in Brighton in July 1949, he went to school in Stoke Newington, in north-east London. According to the *Sunday Pictorial* of 19 July 1959, he was picked out from thousands of local schoolboys by Margaret Thompson, an associate of the film's producer. Brought to McClory's London office, the precocious child ap-parently stuck his head around the door and demanded, "Wot about this 'ere film part, mister!" He was signed up on the spot and his photo appeared in the *Daily Herald* on 13 November 1958 under the headline 'Ian talks his way to fame'.

So too was Sammy the seagull, whose owner was a Mrs Violet Turner from Leytonstone. However, her pet seagull was not the original choice. The *Glamorgan Advertiser* of 19 September 1958 takes up the story:

Gale force winds had caused a seagull to break both legs when landing on a busy road in Aberkenfig and it was rescued from the passing traffic by 15-year-old Barrie Evans of Bridgend, who kept him as a pet. Barrie grew very fond of the bird and some time later heard that a tame seagull was needed for a film to be directed by Kevin McClory of Xanadu Productions of London and New York. "Two months later they told me that Sammy had been chosen to star in the film from hundreds of other entries and that I was to take him to London," explained Barrie.

Barrie's journey with his pet to the capital was the start of a round of fun and excitement in the company of the filming staff. He was met at the station by the scriptwriters of the film 'Beyond the Bridge' (sic) and then taken by car to see the sights of London. Barrie stayed at Xanadu House in Mayfair where a large parrot cage had been placed on the roof especially for his pet bird. During the days that followed he appeared on television in an interview with Derek Hart on the 'Tonight' programme, visited a famous French restaurant, and attended a cocktail party to publicise the film.

Barrie is hoping to make a second visit to London to watch the filming and to see his pet for the last time; filming could not to be started until the director had found a boy to play the lead. His kind action in giving a home to a wounded bird brought him the kind of adventure that every boy dreams of experiencing.

But things were not as straightfor-ward as the local paper had reported. For a start, McClory quickly noticed that Barrie's pet gave off a highly-charged aroma. He sent it down to the palatial Moyns Park, near Steeple Bumpstead in Essex, the home of his business partner, Mr Ivar Bryce. There, to make it feel at

---

he Marchioness of Milford Haven, the nother of Ivar and George Mountbatten, vho inherited Moyns Park on the death of Ivar's wife Josephine in 1992. Ivar Bryce died in 1985; his memoirs *You Only Live Once* were published in 1975. His larger-than-life wife of 35 years, osephine, died at the age of 88 at her ownhouse in Manhattan and was buried at Black Hole Hollow Farm in Vermont. n February 2020 the farm, set within a ,000-acre forest reserve, was put up for sale; the asking price was nearly three nillion dollars.

3 'Xanadu' was the name of Ivar and Josephine Bryce's villa on New Providence Island in the Bahamas.

home, the bird was put into a moat surrounding the house, but the bird started to sink and Bryce's butler plunged in just in time to rescue it. At this point McClory decided that Barrie's bird was just not cut out to be a film star.

The search was on again, hence the hasty recruitment of Sammy the seagull from East London.

Production

Newspaper reports kept the public fully informed on the film's latest production schedule, among them the *Marylebone Mercury*, which reported on 29 August 1958 under the headline 'Mike Todd's associate makes film about London':

The film is based on a short story by an American writer, Leon Ware, who used the Golden Gate Bridge in San Francisco as the central 'character' of this tale about a boy who leaves home and takes up his abode on a bridge. McClory, who is producing and directing the film, will use London's Tower Bridge and has obtained the permission of the authorities to shoot in, on and around it, the first time this has been given to a film producer. The Boy and the Bridge will be shot almost entirely on location at Tower Bridge, Covent Garden, and in some of the City's historic streets. The musical score, which is being specially composed by Malcolm Arnold, is an important feature of the picture. The story was chosen by Kevin McClory as his first feature production because of its artistic merit, its simplicity, and because it is a type of subject – a mixture of fantasy and realism – that has seldom, if ever, been attempted before in England. Producer McClory has had to take out a heavy insurance policy against damage to Tower Bridge. He will be using the bridge for interiors and exteriors, certain scenes being actually set inside the engine room where the machinery that opens the bridge to traffic is operated.[4]

Malcolm Arnold's score made use of a waltz composed by Josephine Bryce; it is used, in various guises, as the primary theme of the soundtrack (see right).

The *Manchester Evening News*, 2 September 1958, reported: "Producer Kevin McClory is filming shots of London with hidden cameras for a new production."

Music examples © Malcolm Arnold Estate

Kinematograph Weekly, 18 September 1958, published a photo of John Huston with Kevin McClory captioned, 'Film director John Huston (left) made a flying visit to London and found time to visit his former protégé who was shooting on Tower Bridge'.

Noel Whitcomb of the *Daily Mirror* (20 September 1958) made an impromptu visit to where they were filming on Tower Bridge – an encounter which scared him witless: "The fact is that heights scare the pants off me," he wrote. Quite by chance, while crossing the bridge, he had literally bumped into the actor James Hayter, who had a small part in the film. Hayter suggested he might like to have a look round and led him into an old-style lift, concealed in the side of the bridge, which was hand-operated with a rope. After what seemed an age, the pair of them stepped out into a little room full of crew and cameras:

Kevin came up, shook me by the hand, and started telling me about this exciting picture he is making, at the same time guiding me through another door. Suddenly I looked down. We were on a suspended footway dizzily high above London with nothing between us and a 150-foot drop but a bit of wide-open ironwork. Kevin's voice went on speaking somewhere in the distance but all I could do was gulp.

Then from the other end of this catwalk I saw a girl flash out, running like Miss Guided Missile with a man in pursuit. When she got halfway across the bridge, she began climbing through the ironwork. Kevin, looking the opposite way, was saying, "They closed this high foot-bridge to pedestrians many years ago because so many people tried to commit suicide," when suddenly I let out the shout of the

4 McClory had apparently baulked at the idea of making a simple, straightforward approach to the London port authorities; rather he tried – successfully, as it turned out – to use a back-door approach through the British Ambassador in Washington. In a later newspaper interview McClory remarked, "Thank goodness I managed to borrow it (Tower Bridge). It would have cost me about a million quid to build a set."

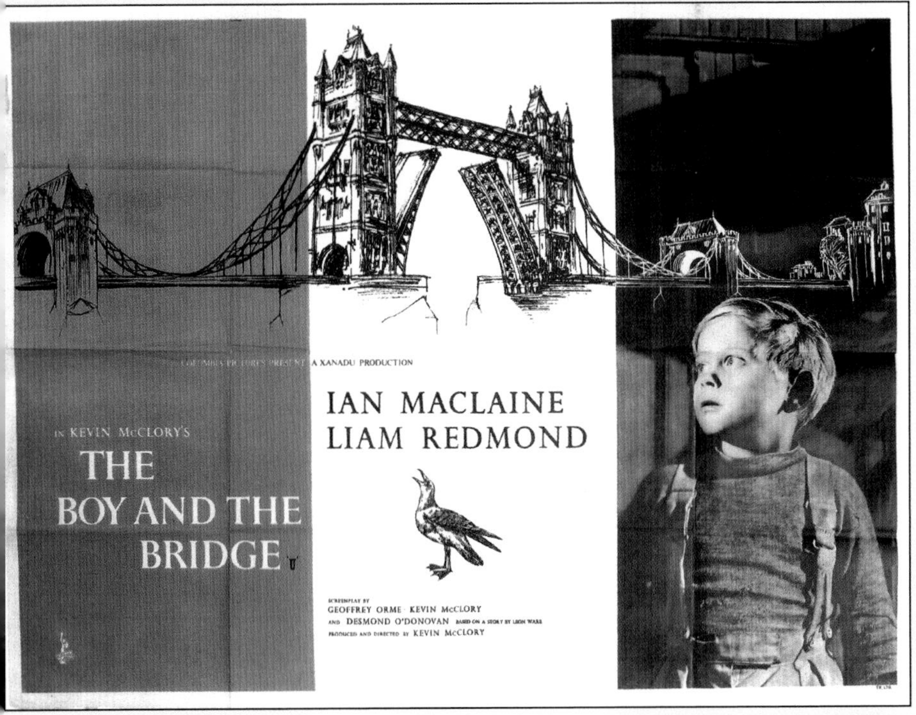

Poster

year. "Whoa!" I bellowed and made a sort of flying rugger tackle for the girl's leg to grab her away. Kevin reeled back. The girl took her leg out of the ironwork and the chappie in hot pursuit stopped dead.

And out of the far door came ace cameraman Bluey Hill with a look of puzzled fury on his face. "Whassermatter, Noel?" he shouted, "We were filming that. What the hell are you trying to do?" But I had already crawled back inside the little room, panting hard. I apologised to Bluey and Kevin and to that good actress Jocelyn Britton – the girl who was playing the part of an attempted suicide in the film, when I so rudely interrupted her. But I don't think anyone heard me apologising, because they were all rolling round the place helpless with laughter.

"Break for lunch," gasped Kevin to the unit, "and before we go I will just let Noel look down the fantastically deep cavern into which the counterweights drop when the bridge bascules are raised to let ships pass." Then they all went off to the Angel in Rotherhithe to shoot another riverside scene.

Kinematograph Weekly, 25 September 1958, brought the news:

All studio work for the Boy and the Bridge, which Kevin McClory is directing and producing for his own company, Xanadu Productions, will be at Twickenham. Most of the twelve weeks schedule, however, is being shot on location in and around London. The unit this week is shooting exteriors at Billingsgate.

Kinematograph Weekly, 20 November 1958, published an article giving some insight into McClory's business philosophy:

"A bold approach. People as they really are. Places as they really are. No glossing over." That's producer-director Kevin McClory's approach to film making. "Hope you'll see what I mean with this one," he said at a party last week, just after shooting the final sequence of the Boy and the Bridge, the first picture by his company, Xanadu Productions. "Take the French. They're masters of this natural technique and look at the progress they've made in the cinema here. We can learn a lesson from them."

But 34-year-old McClory, former protege of John Huston and an associate producer on Mike Todd's Around the World in 80 Days is still an individualist. He'll fire back a quick Irish "No!" if anyone suggest he copies Huston or Todd. "Both great men with powerful determination," he says, "I learned a lot from Huston and used those lessons with Todd. But copy them – No. I've got my own ideas and my own methods. the Boy and the Bridge is due to go out in March – round about St Patrick's Day would be ideal," says McClory.

By the end of January 1959, McClory was on his travels again, the Kinematograph Weekly (29 January) reporting:

[He] left for Nassau, Bahamas, on Saturday for a location reconnaissance in connection with an underwater adventure film he plans to make later this year as his second Xanadu Films production. He completed his first, the Boy and the Bridge, with a two-day scoring session at Shepperton studios earlier in the week, when he recorded Malcolm Arnold's original score.

The *Daily Herald* (23 February 1959) reported:

Film producer Kevin McClory's black Thunderbird sports car, in which heiress Bobo SIgrist was whisked from night-club to night-club during her recent stay in London, was wrecked yesterday. And its proud owner, 32-year-old McClory was in his Belgravia home nursing a cut head. He and his valet were on their way to the airport to bid farewell to Mike Todd Junior's attractive secretary Midori Tsuji, who was flying to Germany.

Fully recovered from the previous month's accident, Kevin and Bobo were dinner guests at the Critics' Circle in March 1959. Henry Fielding, writing in the *Daily Herald*, tells us:

Wherever the dynamic Mr McClory goes these days, the 18-year-old goes too. So I asked him if she would be accompanying him to Moscow in April when he hopes to sell the Russians his latest film the Boy and the Bridge. Mr McClory was not forthcoming (but) he went on to tell me, "I'm going to the Soviet Embassy on Thursday, and I shall be taking a copy of the film to show to officials in Moscow. There's no reason why Western films shouldn't be distributed in Russia."

Kinematograph Weekly, 30 April 1959, announced:

Producer Kevin McClory and financier Ivar Bryce, who head Xanadu Productions, are planning to build their own studio in the Bahamas. McClory recently returned from Nassau and told KINE this week that preliminary talks had been concluded and they now had the full cooperation and backing of the venture from the government of the Bahamas. They are now negotiating for a site on New Providence Island, where they plan to start with two small stages. By next year the island will be only an hour's flight from America and it is hoped to encourage both British and American producers to make their pictures there.

These are some of the attractions offered by the proposed studio: negligible tax, which will drastically cut production costs; quota ticket, levy benefits for British production companies; superb weather and climate and easy access to neighbouring territories where every type of terrain can be found – desert, mountain and jungle.

Producer McClory added that underwater photography facilities were first class and Xanadu will make use of these facilities in its first production out there. A start may be made this year.

In the same journal there was a photograph of Kevin McClory with his partner, Ivar Bryce, clinching the deal with Mike Frankovitch of Columbia Pictures, who would be handling the distribution of the *Boy and the Bridge*.

Premiere

The world premiere of the *Boy and the Bridge* took place at the Curzon Theatre, Mayfair, on 21 July 1959 in the presence of Princess Margaret. The evening was heralded with a fanfare from the Royal Military School of Music and concluded with an appeal on behalf of the Invalid Children's Aid Association by Lady Grenfell.

But it was all too much for the nine-year-old Ian Maclaine. At the afternoon preview he complained of feeling sick and was sent off to bed with a sedative. He managed to rally on the night when he was introduced to the audience by Mike Frankovitch, Chairman of Columbia Pictures. He also remembered to bow low to the princess when he was presented to her, only collapsing with nervous exhaustion shortly after the royal party left the theatre. He was sent home to rest. Too many days shooting scenes under hot arc-lamps had proved too much for the child star.

But there were other problems at home, as Jack Bentley in the *Sunday Pictorial* of 26 July 1959 pointed out:

Ian's father, Frank, is on the dole and, with a family of four young children, is almost worried out of his wits to make ends meet. I asked him what had happened to all the money paid to his son for his film star's role. "That money belongs to Ian," he replied, "It's in the Post Office in his name and I won't touch a penny of it." Ian's mother, Irene, broke in with a correction. "We did borrow £20 to fit the children out with new clothes for the film's premiere and Ian asked for another £10 to buy a train set, but the rest of the £488 8s 10d that was paid to Ian after tax deductions is still intact." Ian's father was furious about reports that he was dissatisfied with his film star son's salary. "Dissatisfied?" he exploded. "I go down on bended knees in gratitude to producer Kevin McClory. He paid my son £50 a week for teaching him to become a film actor and enjoying the experience of a lifetime."

Reviews

Early reviews were mixed, the *Daily Mirror*, 24 July 1959, reporting:

Ian Maclaine is a big-eared, tow-headed, tough little Cockney child, who may turn out to be just a one-film find. But he makes a remarkable debut. Unfortunately, the whimsical idea of this film doesn't quite come off. Ian believes that his pop is a murderer, so he runs away and secretly sets up house in Tower Bridge, London. It is 45 minutes before Ian has to say a word and meanwhile no amount of arty-crafty photography can disguise the fact that the film takes a whale of a time to get cracking. It's a near miss.

Kinematograph Weekly, 13 August 1959, described the film as a 'Children's Hour' comedy drama:

It concerns a motherless small boy who wrongly believes his improvident father is a killer, runs off and makes his home on Tower Bridge with a chirpy seagull. Ian Maclaine plays the resourceful topper naturally and the camera work is brilliant but the direction lacks discipline. The picture interleaves the antics of the lad with ceremonials and tours of the bridge's engine room, but, despite the padding and some striking Thames vistas, creaks badly as its delayed end approaches. Ian Maclaine obviously enjoys himself, but his voice grates (although) there is commendable economy of dialogue, but not, it will be observed, of footage. Kid's stuff, pure and very simple.

The *Fulham Herald* (2 October 1959) was more positive, however:

These days when most pictures are made on the principle that, so long as they are big and spectacular enough, nothing else matters. It's pleasant to find a film where the keynote is simplicity and imagination more than money has been used. Just such a picture is the Boy and the Bridge, which is a charming little movie about a boy who wrongly believes his father is a murderer. The boy runs away from home and lives in one of the turrets of Tower Bridge. His only companion is a friendly young seagull. In his secret sanctuary the little Cockney boy builds up in his imagination the kind of life he dreams of. Inevitably, of course, it all comes to an end, but happily for all concerned. The boy is played with supreme confidence by Ian Maclaine.

The *Middlesex County Times*, 3 October 1959, had some critical opinions of the film's story-line and its musical score:

The boy in the Boy and the Bridge is one of those doughy, tow-headed, little herberts who run here, there and everywhere, alone in the big city. The bridge is Tower Bridge, for he takes refuge in one of the deserted towers, when by a far-fetched coincidence he believes his father a murderer. Father, a depressingly Irish layabout (played by Liam Redmond) equally unbelievably won't be calling the police because he fears they'll regard him as an unfit parent and deprive him of his child. But all's well that ends well after predictably Carol-Reed-esque, comical, sentimental London adventures. Music by Malcolm Arnold confirming one's suspicions – developed through Dunkirk, the Key and the Inn of the Sixth Happiness – that he has of late been simply composing variations on his much-lauded score for the Bridge on the River Kwai."

Kinematograph Weekly of 20 August 1959 announced that the *Boy and the Bridge* would be screened as one of two British features[5] at the Cork International Film Festival which opened on 23 September. A week later the same journal ran an article on the Venice Festival, celebrating its twentieth anniversary:

The picture chosen for the occasion was the British entry the Boy and the Bridge and the British contingent included the producer-director Kevin McClory and the child actor of his film, Ian Maclaine. Gina Lollobrigida, however, had stolen the thunder from Ian Maclaine. An enormous crowd was at the Festival Palazzo for her arrival and broke a police cordon. In the circumstances, our own Liam Redmond and Kevin McClory could hardly compete for the fans' favour. However, during the performance Gina Lollobrigida sat next to Ian and innumerable photographs were taken of this group in the distinguished strangers' gallery, including Bobo Sigrist, David Lean, Elsa Maxwell, Robert Rossen and Ivar Bryce, the co-producer and financial backer of tonight's picture.

In the afternoon the latter invited about 50 journalists to a party on his private yacht while Kevin McClory, with his assistant director Lee Aman, entertained the British contingent to cocktails in the Excelsior Hotel. The film was well received by the public and had a round of sustained applause at the end, but, as was to be expected, critics in the Italian papers unanimously pointed out that, despite its qualities, it is not of Festival calibre."

Noel Whitcomb in the *Sunday Pictorial* of 6 September 1959 ran an article on the rapid rise to fame of 'Mr Success' Kevin McClory:

In that marvellous Venetian palace which Mrs Beatrice Sigrist has taken for the season, Kevin is being royally entertained.

5 The other film was *The Mouse that Roared* starring Peter Sellers.

Premiere programme

He is in fact being treated like a future son-in-law. His constant companion is Bobo Sigrist, the 19-year-old heiress who is assessed to be worth about 8.5 million dollars. Bobo is on a luxury yacht with him in Venice. Together, last week, they went for a wonderful cruise through the blue Adriatic, dropping anchor here and there at the romantic islands. Everywhere they stopped Bobo went off to buy dolls and toys for her daughter Bianca.

But not everything went swimmingly during their Venetian jaunt. Bob McElwaine, writing in the *Sunday Mirror* (6 September 1959):

Hot-tempered Irish producer Kevin McClory, filmdom's 'Mr Success', exploded the calm of the Venice Film Festival last week by getting involved in a bar-room rough-house with London film critic Leonard Mosley.

They published a photograph "by Pictorial cameraman, Frank Charman, showing friends struggling to restrain McClory in the crowded bar". Apparently McClory "was standing at the bar when Mosley came in. Remembering Mosley's devastating review of his film *The Boy and the Bridge*, McClory sailed into action with fists flailing. Women screamed and men shouted. For a moment there was chaos. But bystanders dragged the two men apart before any real damage was done. The following morning McClory said, "I will do it again every time I see him – as long as I can pay the fines." Mosley maintained a dignified silence."

He had recovered his composure and returned to London when *Kinematograph Weekly* of 24 September 1959 reported:

Naturally anxious to know whether The Boy and the Bridge, made with a comparatively modest budget, could compete with more expensive features, producer Kevin McClory has been keeping in daily touch with his film on its pre-release adventures. The news that he and [the distributor] Columbia have been receiving has been encouragingly good, he tells me. In nearly every situation its takings have beaten those of more expensive features and (a most encouraging point) the box office has built up each day. In Cambridge, for instance, the box office took four times as much on Saturday as it did on Monday; and the manager of the cinema has asked for a return booking. Kevin is now negotiating for a New York release at Christmas, but well before then the film, either dubbed or sub-titled, will be going the rounds on the Continent.

Kevin McClory and James Bond

Ivor Bryce was a close friend of Ian Fleming[6], and in 1958 Fleming approached Kevin McClory to produce the first Bond film. McClory rejected all of Fleming's books but developed the James Bond character into a screenplay (to be called Thunderball) and went into pre-production.

However, *The Boy and the Bridge* was not performing as well as expected, and Bryce and Fleming lost their confidence in the young Irishman's ability to handle the production of their first James Bond film, and forced him out of the film.

In 1961 Fleming turned the screenplay into a novel without crediting McClory, leading to a court case in 1963, as a result of which McClory received damages. Harry Saltzman and Albert R. Broccoli's production company Eon Productions, who made the first James Bond film Dr No in 1962, later made a deal with McClory for Thunderball to be made into a film in 1965, with McClory producing.

If Thunderball had gone ahead as planned and appeared as the first James Bond film in 1959, would McClory have asked Malcolm Arnold to write the score? Had he done so, he might have found the composer 'unavailable' and still recovering from nervous exhaustion owing to overwork. Arnold had only just started writing the soundtrack to Sam Spiegel's *Suddenly Last Summer* when he was taken ill, leaving Buxton Orr to complete the score. However, by 1960 Arnold had recovered sufficiently to score four more movies that year. If Arnold had done the first James Bond film, he would no doubt have done many more. However, by 1965 John Barry was firmly established as the Bond soundtrack composer, and would go on to score 12 of the films in the series.

Postscript

And what of the boy star of the 1959 film *The Boy and the Bridge*, the nine-year-old Ian Maclaine? It appears that he never made another film again. We do know that he got married in July 1975 in Southend-on-Sea. His bride was Cutina Drake, born in Stoke Newington, North-East London, in July 1957, with whom he would have two children, Stuart (b. August 1976) and Alastair (b. November 1978). The family later lived on Canvey Island in the Thames estuary, some 30 miles downstream from the Tower which must have changed their lives over 60 years ago.

Alan Poulton

---

6 Ivar Bryce and Ian Fleming first met on holiday in Cornwall in 1917 and they resumed their friendship at Eton College. During the Second World War, Bryce was living in Jamaica with his wife Sheila, who owned a large house on the island called Bellevue. During 1941 Fleming visited Bryce on the island and determined to live there after the war. Bryce helped him find a house and twelve acres of land on the coast. Fleming called it 'Goldeneye' after his wartime project in Spain.

Solomon and Sheba (1959) [part/uncredited]

Production Edward Small Productions for United Artists
Producer Ted Richmond
Director King Vidor
Stars Yul Brynner, Gina Lollobrigida, George Sanders
Music played by Orchestra/Franco Ferrara

Adapted screenplay
Anthony Veiller, Paul Dudley and George Bruce, from the book by Jay Williams [*Publisher* Macdonald, 1959]. Film edition: Corgi Books, 1960.

Locations
1. Madrid, Spain
   (i) Monasterio de San Lorenzo de El Escorial
   (ii) Castillo de Manzanares El Real
   (iii) San Martin de la Vega
2. Valdespartera, Zaragoza, Aragon, Spain

Release
UK premiere London, 27 October 1959
Australian premiere Sydney, 9 December 1959
US premiere New York City, 25 December 1959
UK TV premiere BBC1 Television, 29 December 1976

Media
LP Soundtrack Recording United Artists (US) UAL 4051/UAS 5051 (1960); later re-issued on CD. No Malcolm Arnold content on recording.
DVD EAN/UPC 5050070020236. MGM 10001023 MZI. UK. Region 2
Blu-ray EAN/UPC 811956020437. Twilight Time. USA. All regions

Sheet music
United Artists published the film's main theme in 1959 (with words by Johnny Lehmann).

Articles
(i) Film review in 'Variety', New York, 31 December 1959.

Notes
(i) Though Mario Nascimbene is credited with the entire score, Malcolm Arnold was brought in by the producer at the last minute in to write 3 cues, totalling around 3 mins 45 secs.
(ii) A 'pocket' edition adapted for radio from the soundtrack was broadcast on 'Movie-Go-Round' – BBC Light Programme, 1 November 1959.

Poster

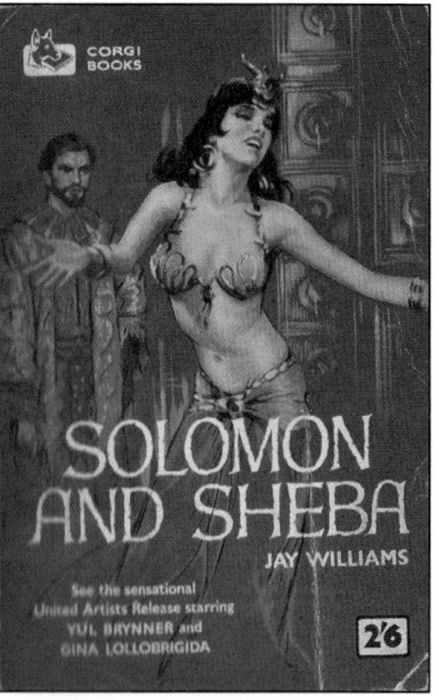

Book

LP: United Artists UAL 4051/UAS 5051

Sheet music

Suddenly Last Summer (1959) [part]

Production Columbia Pictures/Horizon
Producer Sam Speigel
Director Joseph L Mankiewicz
Stars Elizabeth Taylor, Katharine Hepburn, Montgomery Clift
Music played by Orchestra/Buxton Orr

Adapted screenplay
Gore Vidal, from the play by Tennessee Williams [*Publisher* New Directions, 1958].
Film edition: Signet Books, 1960 (with 8 pages of stills from the film).

Locations
1. Catalonia, Spain (locations for the beach/village and old castle scenes): (i) Begur, Gerona (ii) S'Agaro (iii) Costa Brava(iv) Castell-Platja d'Aro
2. Majorca, Balearic Islands
3. Shepperton Studios, Surrey

Release
US premiere New York City, 22 December 1959
Canadian release date 15 February, 1960
South American premiere 16 March 1960 (Mar del Plata Film Festival)
UK premiere; London, 12 May 1960
Australian release date 13 May 1960

Awards
(i) The music was nominated for a Golden Laurel Award in 1960 – it eventually finished in 4th place.
(ii) Both Katherine Hepburn and Elizabeth Taylor were nominated for an Oscar in the 'Best Actress' category at the Academy Awards ceremony in 1960.
(iii) Elizabeth Taylor won a Golden Globe in 1960 for her performance in the film (Hepburn was also a nominee).

Media
DVD EAN/UPC 5050582359459. Columbia Classics. UK. Region 2
Blu-ray EAN/UPC 5060697920833. Powerhouse. UK. Region B

Music notes
Arnold started work on the score for this doom-laden Tennessee Williams drama but then decided to hand over to Buxton Orr to complete the job. Arnold was going through a period of depression at the time due to the loss of several close friends in the music world. As he usually worked chronologically from the main titles to the end credits, it is likely that the early parts of the score are entirely his. The only major theme of the film is contained in the music for the opening credits; a slow moving development for strings with gradual support from the brass giving it the necessary sombre quality. Later in the film the music is often associated with the memories of 'last summer' and has a dream-like tone with drifting strings and woodwind and fragments of unsettling brass in keeping with the rather unpleasant story-line of what is very much a filmed stage play.

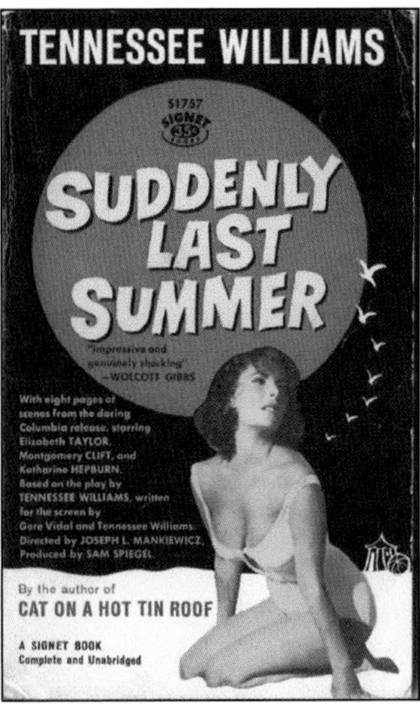

Poster

Book

Autograph score
Full score (opening titles only); short score (sketches of 'themes', some incomplete); piano score (sketch of title theme); also the 78 rpm records created in the studio of Arnold's contribution to the soundtrack (sent to Alan Poulton by Buxton Orr's widow).

Currently at Eton College Library [MS 921 01 13]

MAF performance
Title song [words: Howard Dietz] edited and arranged for high voice and piano by Alan Poulton: Claire Thompson (soprano)/Scott Mitchell (piano), 19 October 2014 (MAF 9)

Articles
(i) Review in 'Variety', New York, 16 December 1959
(ii) The Screen review (B.C.), in New York Times, 23 December 1959
(iii) British Film Institute, Monthly Film Bulletin, June 1960

Notes
(i) Arnold was taken ill during the composition of the soundtrack, having completed only about one-fifth in full score. However, he did leave a number of sketches of various 'themes' and 'characters' from which Buxton Orr was able to complete the process of assembling the finished score.
(ii) Excerpts from the film were shown on 'Picture Parade' – BBC Television, 10 May 1960.
(iii) 'Joseph L Mankiewicz: A Film Profile' – BBC Television, 18 October 1960.

The Angry Silence (1960)

Production Beaver Films
Producers Richard Attenborough and Bryan Forbes
Director Guy Green
Stars Richard Attenborough, Pier Angeli, Michael Craig
Music played by Orchestra/Malcolm Arnold

Adapted screenplay

Bryan Forbes from the novel by John Burke [*Publisher* Hodder & Stoughton, 1961].
Film edition: Hodder Books, 1962.

Locations

1. The opening titles were shot at Willesden Junction Railway Station, with the car-park sequence filmed on Station Approach, Willesden, NW10
2. Other London locations included Brackenbury Primary School, Dalling Road, Hammersmith, W6, and Lincoln's Fish Shop in Hayes, Middlesex (now a Somali restaurant)
3. Ipswich location shots (external): the main factory entrance for 'Martindale Engineering' was probably filmed at Ransome's and Rapier Waterside Works [Ransome's and Rapier were manufacturers of railway equipment and cranes – the factory closed in 1987]; other locations identified were Cowell Street (where the 'picket line' was filmed), Tyler Street, Hawes Street, and Wherstead Road (several of these served as background to Richard Attenborough and others making their way to work)
4. Ipswich location shots (internal): the factory scenes were filmed at Reavell & Co on the Ranelagh Road with several employees involved in the background (apparently Attenborough went to Ipswich to be taught how to operate the machine he worked on during the filming) [Reavell & Co were manufacturers of compressed air machinery and were a major employer in the town; when production was moved to Redditch, the factory was finally demolished in 2006 to be replaced by flats, retail outlets and a hotel]
5. Shepperton Studios, Surrey

Release

UK premiere London, 10 March 1960

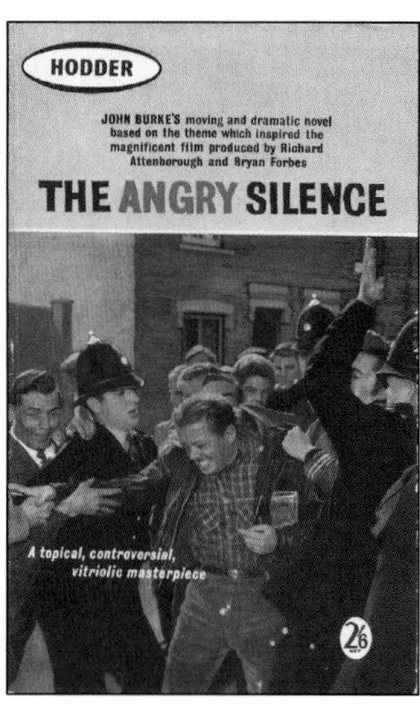

Book

Poster

UK release date 15 March 1960
South African release date 9 September 1960
Australian release date 25 November 1960
US release date 12 December 1960
South American release date Argentina, 28 March 1961
Canadian release date 14 July 1961
UK TV premiere BBC1 Television, 1 November 1965

Awards

(i) Shown at the 10th International Film Festival in Berlin in June 1960 where it won the Fipresci Prize for director Guy Green.
(ii) Nominated for an Oscar at the Academy Awards ceremony in 1961 for 'Best Screenplay'.

Media

DVD EAN/UPC 5060021171528. Momentum. UK. Region 2
Blu-ray EAN/UPC 5055201831729. Studio Canal. UK. Region B

Music notes

This film is a product of its time: a story of one ordinary worker who refuses to go on strike when a communist agitator causes unrest at a small northern engineering firm. With a strong feeling of almost documentary-like realism, *The Angry Silence* has a very short seven-minute Arnold score. The basis of the opening material is a nagging two-note motif that predominates the title music; a relentless dramatic section that is given over to the brass suggesting the northern industrial locale. This material usually returns in similar form at moments of violence and unrest with noticeable work for solo horn. This becomes the symbol of the lone worker (Attenborough), a man who sticks to his principles. The end titles are accompanied by this solitary horn, now the symbol of a quiet victory not without cost.

Articles

(i) British Film Institute, Monthly Film Bulletin, April 1960
(ii) The Screen Review (BC), in New York Times, 13 December 1960

Notes

(i) Interview with Richard Attenborough and excerpts from the film were shown on 'Picture Parade' – BBC Television 15 March 1960.
(ii) Interviews with Michael Craig and John Boulting on the film – 'Wednesday Magazine'. BBC Television 23 March 1960.
(iii) Scenes from the film were televised by the BBC direct from the 10th International Film Festival in Berlin on 4 July 1960.

Tunes of Glory (1960)

Production Knightsbridge Films
Producer Colin Lesslie
Director Ronald Neame
Stars Alec Guinness, John Mills, Susannah York
Music played by Orchestra/Malcolm Arnold

Adapted screenplay
James Kennaway, from his novel 'Jock' [*Publisher* Putnam, 1956; Corgi, 1959].
Film edition: Corgi Books, 1960.

Locations
1. Set in Stirling Castle, Stirling, and Falkirk in Scotland.
2. The major's home is, in reality, in Long Walk, Windsor, at the junction with Park Street; other scenes were shot in Windsor Old Town.
3. The major visits the theatre, actually the Theatre Royal in Thames Street, Windsor.
4. Shepperton Studios, Surrey

Release
European premiere Venice, 4 September 1960 (10th International Film Festival)
UK premiere London, 1 December 1960
US premiere New York City, 20 December 1960
Canadian release date 9 February 1961
South African release date 31 May 1961
Australian release date 23 June 1961
South American release date Argentina, 6 September 1961
UK TV premiere BBC2 Television, 13 November 1975

Awards
(i) Nominated for an Oscar for 'Best Screenplay' at the 1961 Academy Awards ceremony.
(ii) 5 BAFTA nominations in 1961 including one for Ronald Neame in the category 'Best British Film'
(iii) John Mills won the Volpi Cup for 'Best Actor' at the 1960 Venice International Film Festival. Ronald Neame was also nominated for 'Best Film'.

Media
7" vinyl
(a) Soundtrack excerpts:
[Five Marches – 1. Tunes of Glory 2. Dixie 3. Yankee Doodle 4. The Girl I Left Behind Me 5. The Bandit]
Mitch Miller and his Orchestra – Philips (France) 435.101 BE [16]
(b) Other excerpts:
Title Song [Words: Mel Mandel and Norman Sachs]:
(i) Mitch Miller and his Chorus and Orchestra – Columbia (USA) 4-41941;

Poster

Philips PB 1107/328.714 BF
(ii) Cambridge Strings and Singers conducted by Malcolm Lockyer – London (USA)45-1960; Decca 45-F.11303 (2/61)
(iii) Andy Stewart with the Michael Sammes Singers and Orchestra conducted by Frank Cordell – Top Rank JAR-565 (1961); HMV 7EG 8950 (1966)
(iv) Terry Snyder and his Orchestra, Chorus and Bagpipes, (arranged and produced by Don Costa) – United Artists (USA/New Zealand) UA 298 (1/61)
(c) 'The Black Bear':
(i) Frank Cordell and his Orchestra – HMV POP 824 (3/61)
(ii) Terry Snyder and his Orchestra, Chorus and Bagpipes – United Artists (USA/New Zealand) UA 298 (1/61)
(iii) Pipe Major Reid's Pipe Band (arranged by Pipe Major Reid) – Beltona BL 2729

LP Soundtrack Recording United Artists (US) UAL 4086/UAS 5086 (1960/61) (awaiting a CD re-issue) [1. Tunes of Glory 2. The Last Straw 3. The Highland Regiment 4. I'll Never Forget You 5. Lullaby 6. The Regimental March 7. End Title 8. Dark Mood 9.

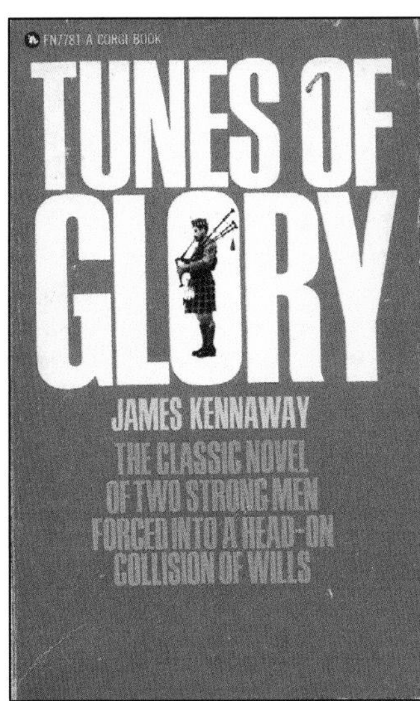

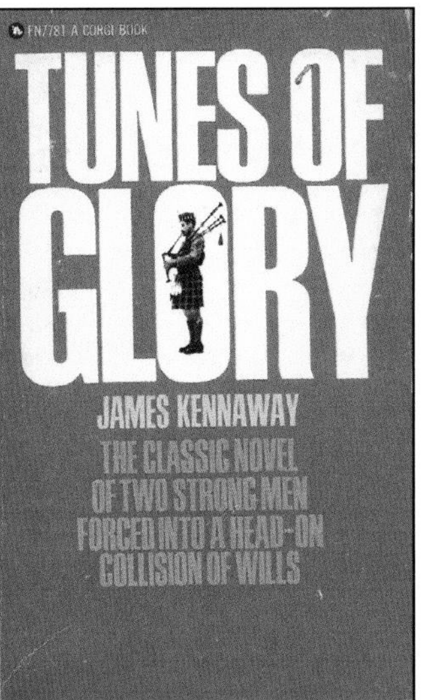

Book

7" vinyl

LP: United Artists UAL 4086/UAS 5086

Sheet music

Main Title Theme 10. Prologue 11. With the Brigade 12. Listen to the Pipers]

DVD EAN/UPC 5055002531347. In2Film. UK. Region 2

Blu-ray EAN/UPC 8436532913808. New Line. USA. All regions

Music notes

A lone Scottish piper and the sound of a winter wind blowing across a snow-covered landscape accompany the main titles of this excellently written and performed drama about the conflict over command at a Scottish regiment. Musical support is minimal. Several old Scottish pipe tunes form the necessary background for a band practice in a snowy courtyard, at a cocktail party, and most effectively during the poignant finale where the 'Black Bear', 'Scotland the Brave' and others illustrate the traditions of the regiment; the emotional pull of the *Tunes of Glory*. The film ends with a slow, moving rendition of the 'Black Bear' for pipes and drums and closing brass fanfares.

Autograph score

Full score (titles only)

Instrumentation 1+picc 1 3+bcl 0 – 4 3 3 1 – timp perc(2) hp pno – str. (vcs and dbs only) at Eton

Currently at Eton College Library [MS 921 01 13]

Sheet music

Title theme (Arnold's arrangement of 'Scotland the Brave' to words by Mel Mandel and Norman Sachs)

'The Black Bear' (Arnold's piano solo arrangement of the bag-pipe tune)

'Tunes of Glory' arrangement by Andy Stewart and Neil Grant (sung and recorded by Andy Stewart).

All published by United Artists.

Articles

(i) Movie Review (B.C.) New York Times, 21 December 1960

(ii) Film Review in 'Variety', New York, 1 January 1961

Notes

(i) Excerpts from the film were shown on 'Picture Parade' – BBC Television, 29 November 1960.

Location:
The major's home is, in reality, in Long Walk, Windsor; Stirling Castle was added into the background.

The Pure Hell of St Trinian's (1960)

Production Hallmark/Tudor/Vale Productions
Producers Frank Launder and Sidney Gilliat
Director Frank Launder
Stars Cecil Parker, George Cole, Joyce Grenfell
Music played by Orchestra/Malcolm Arnold

Original screenplay

Frank Launder, Val Valentine and Sidney Gilliat

Locations

1. After the St Trinian's Academy for Young Ladies is burnt down all the pupils and staff appear at the Old Bailey, EC4
2. In another scene Joyce Grenfell (Ruby Gates) rushes towards 'Barchester' Police Station (actually, Chobham Police Station on the Bagshot Road)
3. 'Hannington Manor', the new home of St Trinian's' was filmed at Littleton House, Shepperton (part of the Shepperton Studios)
4. Shepperton Studios, Surrey (including all the scenes in the harem)

Release

UK release date 22 December 1960
South African premiere Johannesburg, 10 April 1961
US premiere 25 September 1961
TV premiere Denmark, 3 December 1967
UK TV premiere BBC1 Television, 7 July 1973

Media

DVD EAN/UPC 5060034577799 Studio Canal. UK. Region 2
DVD EAN/UPC 5060034577560. Studio Canal. UK. Region 2. (Boxed set with Belles of St Trinian's / Blue Murder at St Trinian's / Great St Trinian's Train Robbery)

Music notes

The third entry in the series, in which the old school is burned down and a new headmaster takes over with modern ideas on how to tame the terrors of St Trinian's. All the familiar favourites from Arnold's previous scores are here including the school song (or is it march?) sung by the school chorus and taken up by woodwind with eventual support from brass, chimes, piano and timpani. When a festival of culture takes place at the new school headquarters, Arnold supplies string quartet support for a fashion show and jazz-flavoured piano for a strip-tease 'Hamlet' (female version). There are many brief musical cues for small ensemble in the form of string quartet, piano, guitar with percussion and drums for middle-eastern colour as well as fragments of the school song and Flash Harry's (George Cole) off-key piano motif. One new entry is used as a therapeutic device by the stressed-out members of the Ministry of Education, who take turns in dancing to a dainty pastoral waltz in the form of source music from a gramophone. It is with this that the end titles bring events to a close.

Poster

Articles

(i) Movie Review, in 'Variety', New York, 1 January 1961

Notes

(i) Excerpts were shown on 'Picture Parade' – BBC Television, 28 December 1960.

No Love for Johnnie (1961)

Production Five Star Films
Producer Betty E Box
Director Ralph Thomas
Stars Peter Finch, Stanley Holloway, Mary Peach
Music played by Orchestra/Malcolm Arnold

Adapted screenplay

Nicholas Phipps and Mordecai Richler, from the novel by Wilfred Fienburgh [*Publisher* Hutchinson, 1959]. Film edition: Arrow Books, 1960.

Locations

1. Bolton Abbey, North Yorkshire
2. Peter Finch (Johnnie Byrne) is seen campaigning in 'Earnley', actually New Bank, Halifax, from where he is driven to Halifax Station in Church Street/Shevie Road. He arrives on Platform 6 at Euston Station, NW1, and is driven to Towcester Mansions (actually Bryanston Mansions, York Street, Marylebone)

Poster

Book

3. Finch is later interviewed in Parliament Square, SW1, with the Houses of Parliament in the background; he talks to colleagues on the members' terrace of the House of Commons with Westminster Bridge in the right background (the latter may be studio shots)
3. Mary Peach (Pauline West) catches a taxi at Knox Street, Marylebone, after attending Fenella Fielding's party
4. Finch contrives a meeting with Mary Peach at Fagg's Studios on the corner of Sussex Place and Hyde Park Garden Mews in Paddington, W2; they take a river bus from Westminster Pier on the Victoria Embankment passing under Tower Bridge and landing at Greenwich Pier, SE10. They admire the Cutty Sark and sit under the Colonnade of the Queen's House, Park Row, Greenwich
5. When Finch sees off Peach at Euston Station there is a shot of the Doric Arch on Drummond Street, NW1
6. Finch walks up a steep hill to visit Dr West's surgery back in 'Earnley', actually shot in Priory Road, High Wycombe, with Priory Road County Primary School in the background; a former pupil remembers the rain being provided by a rain machine and they watched the filming from their classroom windows
7. Pinewood Studios, Iver Heath, Bucks

Release

UK premiere Leicester Square Theatre, London, 9 February 1961

UK release date 14 February 1961

European premiere Berlin, June 1961 (Berlin Film Festival)

South African premiere Johannesburg, 23 June 1961

US premiere New York City, 12 December 1961

TV premiere East Germany, 31 October 1970

UK TV premiere BBC2 Television, 28 February 1986

Awards

Peter Finch won a BAFTA for 'Best British Actor' in 1961 and a Golden Berlin Bear in the same category at the Berlin Film Festival in June 1961. Ralph Thomas received a nomination for 'Best Director' at the same Festival.

Media

7" vinyl

Title song [words: Leslie Bricusse]: Garry Beckles (vocals) with the Johnny Douglas Orchestra – Oriole 45-CB 1606 (2/61)

DVD EAN/UPC 5060105720871. ITC Studio. UK. Region 2

Music notes

Arnold decides on a quick march for brass band as his title music to this story of a Labour MP (Finch) and his personal and political problems. This march 'To The Hustings' suggests the battle for re-election to his constituency and the use of brass band is a nod to Yorkshire. Former trumpeter Arnold is in his element when writing for this particular ensemble. When Finch's wife walks out on him, Arnold introduces his Johnnie Byrne theme as Finch restlessly visits a pub and striptease club, and has an unsuccessful encounter with a prostitute. All these scenes are scored with this edgy, nervous motif for strings and woodwind, then turned over to percussion and drums and finally driven on with the help of injections of jagged brass. With no dialogue, the music carries the montage sequence and suitably reflects the state of mind of this lonely and insecure man. Even when Finch goes to a party, the source music is provided by a jazz version of Johnnie's theme that nags away so much it even irritates the hostess. When Finch meets a young girl (Mary Peach) at the party, the tone of the music becomes warmer as their friendship grows. When Johnnie's theme quietly moves into this new love theme we know that he Is thinking of her. It is not what he says but what the music is telling us.

The best and longest musical cue is for the boat ride down the Thames to Greenwich. The music is bright, sunny and optimistic in tone. Under the dialogue the woodwinds sound pensive. Romantic-sounding strings take up the love theme; a woodwind solo for Johnnie's theme; romantic strings again (love theme); brass enter as the boat passes Tower Bridge; as dialogue resumes, the music interchanges between Johnnie's theme and the love theme, depending on what is being said. The music is under the dialogue and working with it; a fine example of Arnold's skill as a musical dramatist. When Greenwich Pier is reached, the love theme is allowed full expression; the tone is rich and warm. Finally there is delicate scoring for strings under the dialogue and a slow rendition of the love theme as Johnnie and his girl return home.

Another boat ride, this time on the Serpentine, provides some tender writing for woodwind. A short patriotic motif is used as a tribute to the Houses of Parliament and for another party scene there are echoes of *Trapeze* in the scoring for jazz piano. For the love scenes, fairly torrid for 1960, Arnold gives them an overwhelmingly passionate treatment with full orchestral development of the love theme material.

As Johnnie Byrne takes up a new government post, it is his theme that is played over the end titles. With Peter Finch in fine form in the central role, director Ralph Thomas gives his composer Arnold the opportunity to write a fine score.

Sheet music

Sheet music

Title song with words by Leslie Bricusse, published by Film Music Publications (1961)

'To The Hustings' orchestral interlude [there appears to be no extant copy].

MAF performance

Title song [words: Leslie Bricusse]: Claire Thompson (soprano)/Scott Mitchell (piano), 19 October 2014 (MAF 9)

Concert arrangement

'To the Hustings'

arr. for orchestra by Johnny Douglas (c.1961)

Publisher Film Music Publishing, 1961

Suite from the film

reconstructed and orchestrated by Philip Lane (c.2000)

Duration 10'30»

Instrumentation 2 2 2 2 – 4 2 3 1 – timp perc(3) cel hp – str

Publisher Novello

Recording

(i) BBC Philharmonic Orchestra/Rumon Gamba – Chandos CHAN 9851 (The Film Music of Sir Malcolm Arnold, Vol.2)

Articles

(i) British Film Institute, Monthly Film Bulletin, January 1961

(ii) Movie Review, in 'Variety', New York, February 1961

Notes

(i) Excerpts were shown on 'Picture Parade' – BBC Television, 7 February 1961.

(ii) 'Peter Finch – Film Profile' – BBC Television, 6 June 1962.

Whistle down the Wind (1961)

Production Allied Film Makers/Beaver Films
Producer Richard Attenborough
Director Bryan Forbes
Stars Alan Bates, Bernard Lee, Hayley Mills
Music played by Orchestra/Malcolm Arnold

Adapted screenplay
Keith Waterhouse and Willis Hall, from the novella by Mary Hayley Bell (Hayley Mills's mother), illustrated by Owen Edwards [*Publisher* V T Boardman, 1958; Chivers Press, 1989; Sceptre Paperback, 1997]

Locations
1. The New Line Reservoir, Bacup, Lancashire
2. A railway bridge on the Bacup to Rochdale line; the signal box is at Britannia, south of Bacup, looking from Stubbylee Moss Moor
3. Downham village near Burnley: the main street and the bridge over Downham Beck
4. The main farmyard scenes, where Alan Bates is discovered, were filmed at Worsaw End Farm on Pendle Hill
5. Abel Street, Burnley, next to Barden Secondary Modern School in Barden Lane
6. Salthill Quarry between Clitheroe and Chatburn (it is now an industrial estate)
7. 'The Stable Cafe' on Todmorden Road, Townley Park in Burnley
8. Local schoolchildren from the Lancashire villages around Burnley and Clitheroe were used as extras; children from Chatburn Primary School played the 'disciples'.
9. PInewood Studios, Iver Heath, Bucks.

Release
UK premiere Odeon, Leicester Square, London, 20 July 1961
UK release date 6 August 1961
Canadian release date; 25 December 1961
Australian release date 17 February 1962
South American premiere 26 March 1962 (Mar del Plata Film Festival)
US premiere New York City, 21 April 1962
TV premiere West Germany, 4 April 1969
UK TV premiere BBC1 Television, 18 January 1978

Awards
Winner of 4 BAFTAS in 1962 including one for 'Best Film' for Bryan Forbes. He was also similarly nominated at the Mar del Plata Film Festival in Argentina in March 1962.

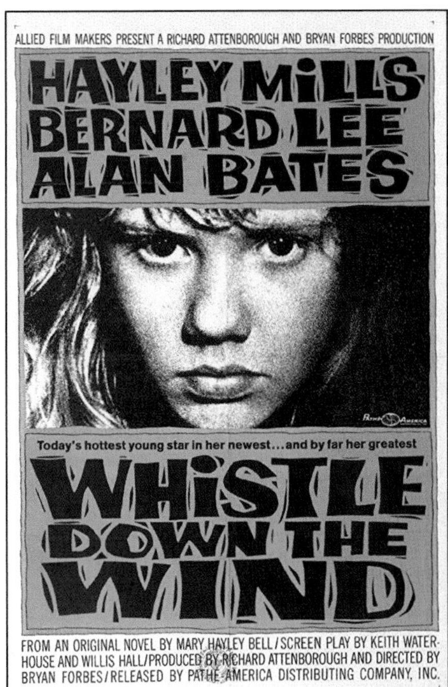

Book

Poster

Media
7" vinyl
Title Song [words: Marge Singleton]:
(i) Mantovani & his Orchestra – London (USA) 45-LON 9520
(ii) The Wayfarers (instrumental) – Decca 45-F.11370 (7/62)
(iii) The Krewkats (instrumental/vocal quartet) – HMV (France) 7 EMF 338
March – 'We Three Kings':
Jonny Keating and the 'Z' Men – Piccadilly 7N 35071 (10/62); Piccadilly NEP 34011 (12/62); Pye (New Zealand) 7N-35071
DVD EAN/UPC 5037115059833. ITV Studios. UK. Region 2

Music notes
This is a small intimate film about a group of children (brought up on a regular diet of Sunday School) mistaking a criminal on the run for Jesus. It is filmed in black and white amidst a bleak Lancashire landscape.

Composer Arnold quickly realises that what is needed is a simple melody for small ensemble over the titles. The lightness of touch is supplied by glockenspiel, chimes, guitar, harmonium and whistler (producer Richard Attenborough). Strings eventually take over from the whistler and they in turn are replaced by the woodwind who complete the opening title sequence. There is a brief woodwind-strings motif for the farmhouse and then several short fragments of the main theme given in turn to various soloists: glockenspiel, celesta, guitar and harp. Arnold turns 'We Three Kings' into a joyous dance as the children run off and are silhouetted against the skyline.

As the police search the countryside for the criminal (Bates) the scoring develops a more dramatic character, the style of which is very much Arnold. In contrast, guitar, celesta and chimes play 'The Grand Old Duke of York' at the farmhouse birthday party. However the inevitable capture of 'Jesus' provides a sad and poignant finale and is due in no small measure to the emotional strength of Arnold's delightful music, no doubt inspired by the performances of Hayley Mills and her young co-stars.

Autograph score
Full score. Held by the Sir John Trevelyan estate.

Sheet music
Main theme for piano. Published by Henrees Music (1961)
Main theme as a song with words by Margie Singleton[1]. Publshed by Harvard Music (US).
Main theme. Orchestral version by Johnny Arthey and his Orchestra. Published by Feldman.
'We Three Kings of Orient Are' arranged as 'March for piano and orchestra'. Published by Henrees Music.

MAF performance
'Title theme' for solo piano: Moritz Ernst (piano), 16 October 2010 (MAF 5)

1 Marge (Margie) Singleton (b. Louisiana, 1935) was an American country music singer and songwriter of the sixties.

Concert arrangement
Theme
arranged for orchestra by Johnny Arthie (c.1961)
Publisher B Feldman
March 'We Three Kings of Orient are'
arranged for piano and orchestra (1962)
Publisher Henrees Music, 1962
Suite from the film
arranged for small orchestra by Christopher Palmer (1991) [1. Prelude (Theme) 2. The Three Kings 3. Finale]
Duration 9'
Instrumentation 2 1 2 0 – 2 0 0 0 – perc(2) pno(cel) hp gtr – str (max 8 6 4 4 2)
Publisher Novello
First performance Perth Youth Orchestra – City Hall, Perth, Scotland, 11 April 1993
First professional performance London Symphony Orchestra/Richard Hickox – Barbican Hall, London, 16 December 1993
Recording
(i) London Symphony Orchestra/Richard Hickox – Chandos CHAN 9100 (The Film Music of Sir Malcolm Arnold, Vol.1)

Sheet music

Articles
(i) British Film Institute, Monthly Film Bulletin, September 1961

Notes
(i) Excerpts were broadcast on 'Movietime' – BBC Light Programme, 8 August 1961.
(ii) Filming on location and film excerpts were shown on 'Blue Peter' – BBC Television, 21 August 1961.
(iii) Matthew Taylor's 'Fantasy on a theme by Arnold' for piano is based on the theme from 'Whistle Down the Wind'. Its first performance was by Moritz Ernst (piano), 16 October 2010 (MAF 5)

Locations. Left: The farmhouse where the children lived. Right: The phone box which Auntie Dorothy ran to

On the Fiddle (1961)

***US title* Operation Snafu** (Situation Normal – All Fouled Up)
***US Alt title* Operation War Head**
Production Coronado Productions
Producer Benjamin Fisz
Director Cyril Frankel
Stars Alfred Lynch, Sean Connery, Victor Maddern
Music played by Orchestra/Malcolm Arnold

Adapted screenplay
Harold Buchman, from the novel 'Stop at a Winner' by R F Delderfield [*Publisher* Hodder & Stoughton, 1961; Simon and Schuster, New York, 1961, 1978].
Film edition: Hodder Books, 1961.

Locations

1. The RAF enlisting station has been identified as 85-88 Minories, London, EC3 (occupied in 1954 by the Institute of Marine Engineering)
2. Alfred Lynch and Sean Connery pass The Cable Cafe in Cable Street by Mill Yard, London E1; later they walk past The Blue Cafe in Ensign Street
3. Lynch and Connery board a Brighton and Hove bus to their hotel in Bedford Square, Brighton (in reality The Bedford on King's Road, which caught fire under mysterious circumstances in 1964)
4. The Lodge at Littleton House, Squires Bridge Road, Shepperton (part of the Shepperton studios) is also used as a location shot
5. Village scenes were filmed at the butcher's shop in Shere, Newark Mill in Pyrford, and The Black Swan pub in Ockham – all in Surrey.
6. Horsell Common in Woking was used for the battle scenes [Horsell

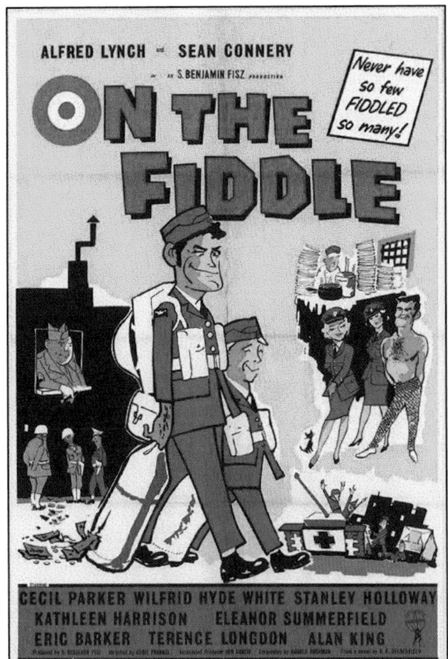

Poster

Book

Sheet music

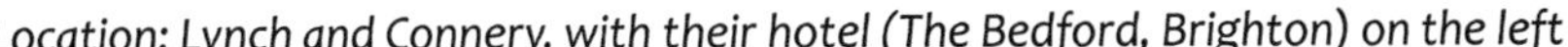
Location: Lynch and Connery, with their hotel (The Bedford, Brighton) on the left

Common was, of course, the site for the alien landings in H G Wells's 'War of the Worlds'!]
7. Shepperton Studios, Surrey

Release

UK release date 10 October 1961

US release date 21 May 1965

TV premiere Germany, 14 October 2006

Media

DVD EAN/UPC 5027626386047. Network. UK. Region 2

Music notes

For this rather feeble comedy about two con-men's wartime antics, Arnold provides a boisterous swaggering march for military band which at least gets the film off to a bright start. After that everything is downhill all the way. Apart from some fragments of this material, the rest is made up of Strauss, Sousa and some wartime songs.

Sheet music

Title theme arranged for piano. Published by Henrees Music (1961).

MAF performance

Title theme, arranged for flute and piano by Alan Poulton: Ruth Morley (flute)/ Scott Mitchell (piano), 19 October 2014 (MAF 9)

Articles

(i) 'Screen' (H.T.), in New York Times, 22 May 1965

Notes

(i) Excerpts from the film were broadcast on 'Move-Go- Round' – BBC Light Programme, 5 November 1961

The Inspector (1962)

***US title* Lisa**

***US Alt title* Lisa and the Police Inspector**

Production Red Lion Films

Producer Mark Robson

Director Philip Dunne

Stars Stephen Boyd, Dolores Hart, Leo McKern

Music played by Orchestra/Malcolm Arnold

Adapted screenplay

Nelson Gidding, from the novel by Jan de Hartog [*Publisher* Hamish Hamilton, 1960]

Film edition: Four Square Books, 1963

Locations

1. Amsterdam, Tangier, Israel and London.
2. The final scene was shot at Three Cliffs Bay, Gower Peninsula, South Wales.

Release

UK release date May 1962

US release date 24 May 1962

Awards

Nominated for a Golden Globe in the 'Best Motion Picture' category in 1963.

Media

7" vinyl

'Lisa's Theme' (produced and arranged by Don Costa):

(i) Ferrante & Teicher (two pianos) with an orchestra conducted by Nick Perito – United Artists (USA/Canada/ New Zealand) UA 470 (5/62); United Artists (Spain) HU 067-67; HMV POP 1028 (6/62) [17]

(ii) The Wayfarers (instrumental) – Decca 45-F.11473 (6/62)

DVD EAN/UPC 024543873907. Cinema Archives. USA. Region 1

Sheet music

'Lisa's Theme' for piano solo, published by Henrees Music [also published in the Netherlands (Francis-Day Muzikuitgevers) and Spain (Canciones)]

Poster

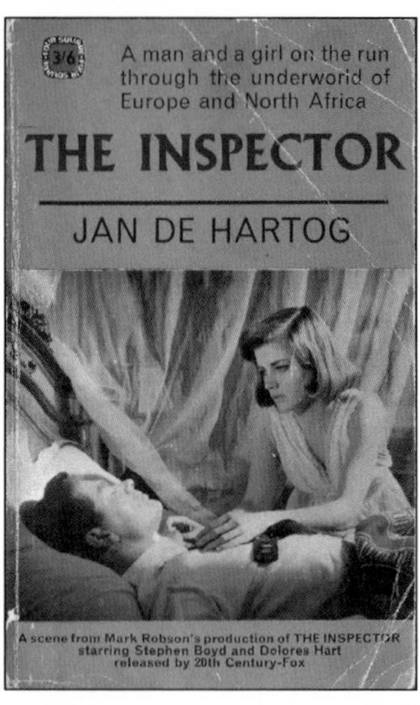

Book

7" vinyl

Sheet music

MAF performance

'Lisa's theme', arranged for flute and piano by Alan Poulton: Ruth Morley (flute)/Scott Mitchell (piano), 19 October 2014 (MAF 9)

Concert arrangement

'Lisa's theme' arranged for orchestra by K Papworth (c.1962)

Instrumentation 2 2 2 2 – 4 3 3 0 – timp perc hp pno – str

Publisher Henrees Music, 1962

rticles

) Review in 'The Philadelphia Inquirer', 31 May 1962

Notes

(i) Excerpts from the film were broadcast on 'Movie-Go Round' – BBC Light Programme, 8 July 1962.

he Lion (1962)

roduction Samuel G Engel Productions for Twentieth Century Fox

roducer Samuel G Engel

irector Jack Cardiff

tars William Holden, Trevor Howard, Capucine

lusic played by Orchestra/Malcolm Arnold

dapted screenplay

Irene and Louis Kamp, from the novel by Joseph Kessel [*Publisher* Dell Pubs, New York, 1959; (in French) Gallimard-Jeunesse, 2005, with illustrations by Philippe Mignon].

Film edition: Dell, 1962.

ocations

. Nanyuki and the Mount Kenya Safari Club in Kenya (the club was co-owned by William Holden)

. Tanzania and Uganda

. TCF Studios, Los Angeles

elease

K premiere London, 26 July 1962

K release date 19 August 1962

S premiere New York City, 21 December 1962

ledia

he Lion (1962)

" vinyl

oundtrack excerpts [1. Opening Music 2.Love Theme 3.Dance of Happiness 4. Death of King 5. End Title] Orchestra/Malcolm Arnold – Decca DFE 8507 (12/62)

P

oundtrack Recording London (US) M.76001 (2/63); later re-issued on CD (with Nine Hours to Rama) – Artemis ART-F009; Vocalion CDLK 4371 [1. Opening title music 2. Tina's theme (Love theme) 3. Drum Dance – Tina at Night 4. King: Dance of Happiness 5. Tina's theme – End title]

DVD EAN/UPC8420266948243. Cinema Classics. Spain. Region 2

Music notes

Forget the story-line; this is all about Africa, wildlife, the wide open spaces and Arnold's marvellous score that supplies so much of what is missing in the script. The score is basically made up of three themes. The main 'Lion' theme with full blooded work for brass and drums highlights the wildness and savagery of

Poster

Sheet music (UK and US)

Book

7" vinyl

LP: London M.76001

Africa, then develops into a more expansive section for strings, which illustrates the breadth and splendour of the landscape and in particular the Kenyan game reserve where the story is set. Arnold produces a playful, high spirited theme for Tina (the young daughter of Holden and Capucine) who has been brought up with the lion; and there is the love theme, restrained and yet with very effective writing for strings.

In spite of being filmed in Africa, *The Lion* is really one of the occasional Hollywood-type pictures that Arnold worked on. Big stars and production values bring out the best in Arnold. Despite obvious weaknesses in the script, the score carries the picture, and the way he develops his thematic material is really quite wonderful. One of his very best scores and most deserving of the LP that was issued back in 1962, even if the record company did get the track titles mixed up.

Sheet music

Main theme for piano solo, published by Miller Music (US) and Henrees Music (UK)

Articles

(i) Review in *The Times*, 26 July 1972

Nine Hours to Rama (1963)

***US Alt title* Nine Hours to Live**

Production Red Lion for Twentieth Century Fox

Producer/Director Mark Robson

Stars Horst Buchholz, José Ferrer, Valerie Gearon

Music played by Orchestra/Malcolm Arnold

Adapted screenplay

Nelson Gidding, from the novel by Stanley Wolpert [*Publisher* Random House, New York and Hamish Hamilton, London, 1962]

Film edition: Four Square Books, 1962 (with 8 pages of film stills).

Locations

1. India
2. MGM Studios, Borehamwood, Herts

Release

UK release date 21 February 1963

US release date 3 April 1963

TV premiere Hungary, 10 February 1978

UK TV premiere BBC1 Television, 7 August 1977

Awards

Nominated for a BAFTA award in 1964 for 'Best Cinematography'.

Media

LP

Soundtrack Recording London (US) M.76002 (8/63); Decca (UK) LK/SKL 4527 (5/63) [1. Train coming into Delhi/the astrologer predicts 2. Das warns Gandhi 3. Natu's father dies 4. Natu and Prahlad/Natu meets Rani 5. Wedding Dance 6. Rani's theme 7. Natu tells Rani of his oath 8. Indian Concert 9. Malabar Hill (Rani's theme)/Swiss Hotel (Natu and Rani) 10. Mourning Gandhi 11. The Fire 12. Indian Concert-Drums]; re-issued on CD – Artemis ART – F009; Vocalion CDLK 4371 [1. Original Main Title 2. Train Coming into Delhi/the Astrologer Predicts 3. Das Warns Gandhi 4. Natu's Father Dies 5. Parade Ground 6. Natu and Prahlad/Natu Meets Rani 7. Wedding Dance 8. Rani's Theme 9. Natu Tells Rani of his Oath 10. Indian Concert 11. Malabar Hill (Rani's Theme) - Swiss Hotel (Natu and Rani) *12. Assassination of Gandhi/Natu's Realisation/Mourning Gandhi 13. Nehru's Speech/End Titles 14. Closing Music.]

DVD EAN/UPC 8420266951595. 20th Century Fox. Spain. Region 2

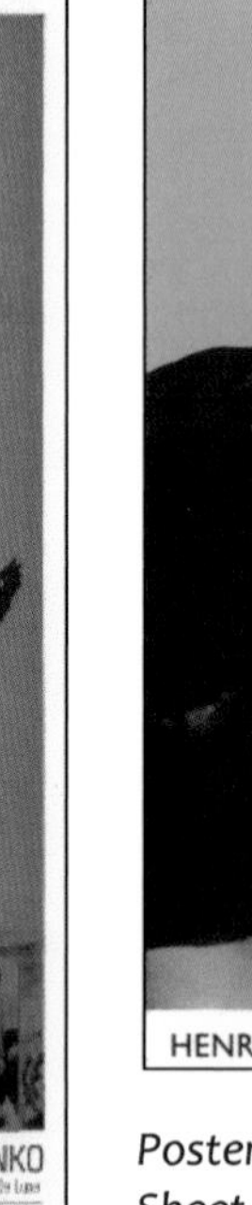

Poster

Sheet music

Book

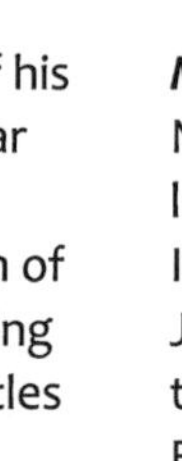

Music notes

Nine Hours to Rama – the nine hours leading up to the assassination of the Indian leader Mahatma Gandhi on 30 January 1948 and told largely from the viewpoint of the assassin (Horst Buchholz). The main titles, set dramatically against the inside of the assassin's watch-face, is scored for four players, each playing an Indian drum with its own individual shape and sound. From this moment Arnold supplies just the right amount of local colour in his score. Having spent a period of time in India studying the character and techniques of Indian music, he succeeds in making it sound right on the soundtrack, although only a connoisseur of Indian music could attest to its true authenticity. By using western orchestrations and assimilating them with Indian sitars and drums, a distinctly unsettling mood is created as the police realise that Gandhi's life is in imminent danger.

With the help of flashbacks, we learn much about the assassin's background. An earlier romance with a wealthy Indian woman Rani (Valerie Gearon) gives Arnold the chance of creating a lighter mood. With exquisite flute solo and supporting strings he creates a charming love theme for Rani and Natu (Horst Buchholz). It has a dreamlike, magical quality that is perfectly suited to what are memories in the mind of the troubled assassin. There are opportunities for some atmospheric source music. At a wedding there is rhythmic music for percussion and drums which is eventually transformed into a wedding dance sounding suitably authentic to western ears. At a concert the Indian drum sequence from the main titles is heard again played by the Vadya Vrinda Orchestra, an ensemble of four players.

As the climax approaches and many people gather at the prayer meeting, brass and drums that start as a background sound become louder and faster in tempo, drowning out all other sounds, thereby increasing the tension. Then a sudden stop and the moment of assassination. Indian voices and sitar come together in mourning and then the funeral procession for Gandhi begins. Arnold's music supports the occasion with a quiet dignity and finally sitar and drums bring in the end titles.

LP: London M.76002

LP: Decca LK/SKL 4527

Sheet music

Main theme arranged for piano solo

MAF performance

Title theme arranged for flute and piano by Alan Poulton: Ruth Morley (flute)/ Scott Mitchell (piano), 19 October 2014 (MAF 9)

Articles

(i) Review (M.D.), in New York Times, 20 August 2008

Notes

(i) Excerpts from the film were broadcast on 'Movie-Go Round' – BBC Light Programme, 24 March 1963.

Tamahine (1963)

Alt title **The Natives are Restless Tonight**

Production Seven Arts for Associated British Picture Corporation (1963)

Producer John Bryan

Director Philip Leacock

Stars Nancy Kwan, John Fraser, Dennis Price

Music played by Orchestra/Malcolm Arnold

Adapted screenplay

Dennis Cannan, from the novel by Thelma Nicklaus [*Publisher* Bodley Head, 1957; Four Square Books, 1959]

Locations

1. Bora Bora on the Leeward Islands, French Polynesia
2. Paris
3. Wellington College (a boy's boarding school) in Crowthorne, Berkshire

Release

UK premiere Empire, Leicester Square, London, 18 July 1963

US release date 3 May 1964

UK TV premiere BBC1 Television, 24 October 1972

Awards

Nominated for a BAFTA award in 1964 for 'Best British Cinematography'.

Media

DVD EAN/UPC 5027626432645. Network. UK. Region 2

Autograph score

Full score (in 29 sections); vocal score, voice and piano [1. Hallow School Song 2. Hallow Cricket Song 3. Never Forget, Boys]

Instrumentation 1 1 2+bcl 0 – 3 2 1 0 – gtr(2) +Hawaiian gtr perc(3) cel hp – str

and for the Concert Band sequence, including the 'Royal Fireworks Music': picc 1 3+ Eflat cl 2+cbsn – 4 2 3+euph 1 – perc

Currently at Eton College Library [MS 921 01 13]

Sheet music

Main theme arranged for piano, published by Harms Witmark; the three Hallow School Songs for unison voices and piano, though available in manuscript, were never published.

Poster

MAF performance
'Hallow School Song': Claire Thompson (soprano)/Scott Mitchell (piano), 19 October 2014 (MAF 9)
'Title theme' arranged for flute and piano by Alan Poulton: Alasdair Garrett (flute)/Jennifer Redmond (piano), 16 October 2016 (MAF 11)
'Hallow School Song', 'Hallow Cricket Song' and 'Never Forget, Boys': Claire Thompson (soprano)/Jennifer Redmond (piano), 16 October 2016 (MAF 11)
Concert arrangement
Royal Fireworks Music for wind band
First concert performance Royal Northern College of Music Wind Ensemble/ Clark Rundell – RNCM, Manchester, 3 November 1984 (BASWBE Conference)
Articles
(i) Review, in *The Times*, 18 July 1963
Notes
(i) Excerpts from the film were broadcast on 'Movie-Go-Round' – BBC Light Programme, 25 August 1963.

Book

TAMAHINE
by MALCOLM ARNOLD
ASSOCIATED BRITISH presents A JOHN BRYAN PHILIP LEACOCK production
Starring
NANCY KWAN
JOHN FRASER
DENNIS PRICE
in
TAMAHINE
Screenplay by DENNIS CANNON · Based on the novel by THELMA NIKLAUS · Produced by JOHN BRYAN · Directed by PHILIP LEACOCK
A CINEMASCOPE PICTURE IN TECHNICOLOR · Released through WARNER-PATHE
Piano Solo
HARMS WITMARK LTD., 25 Denmark Street, London, W.C.2. 2/6

Sheet music

The Chalk Garden (1964)

Production Quota Rentals/Ross Hunter Productions
Producer Ross Hunter
Director Ronald Neame
Stars Deborah Kerr, Hayley Mills, John Mills
Music played by Orchestra/Malcolm Arnold
Adapted screenplay
John Michael Hayes, from the 1953 play by Enid Bagnold. Acting edition: Samuel French, 1956.
Locations
1. Several shots on and around Beachy Head: Hayley Mills (Lauren) and Deborah Kerr (Miss Madrigal) in the 'sketching scene'
2. Preston Park Lawn Tennis Club, Brighton [A number of tennis players from the Club were recruited as 'background' in several shots]
3. Folkington near Polegate, East Sussex
4. The family house has been identified as Clapham House, Clapham Lane, Litlington, East Sussex [Despite being a Grade II listed building, it is understood that Clapham House has since been demolished]
5. MGM British Studios, Borehamwood, Herts

Release
UK premiere London, 2 April 1964
US premiere 21 May 1964

Poster; sheet music

European premiere Italy, 27 July 1964 (Taormina Film Festival)
South American release date Argentina, 3 March 1965
UK TV premiere BBC2 Television, 9 January 1971
Awards
(i) Edith Evans was nominated for an Oscar at the Academy Awards ceremony for 'Best Actress in a Supporting Role'.
(ii) Both Edith Evans and Deborah Kerr were nominated for BAFTAs in the 'Best British Actress' category.
(iii) Ross Hunter was nominated for 'Best Motion Picture' in the Golden Globes.
Media
7" vinyl
'Madrigal' [words: Mack David] (produced and arranged by Robert Mersey):
(i) Andy Williams (vocals) with an

The Chalk Garden: Malcolm Arnold's film score

Malcolm Arnold was immensely prolific, and wrote music for around 70 feature films and 50 documentaries. His music was tonal and he was a powerful communicator, a sort of British Shostakovich, and he wrote some amazing film scores; The Chalk Garden is a very good example of what he was doing.

It starts rather ingeniously with the main title music (Ex.1): the music echoes or articulates the main titles: we start off with a chord and then three notes – that's a nice jazzy chord anyway, a minor eleventh – and we see Deborah Kerr's name on the screen; then another chord, and Hayley Mills' name turns up; and then John Mills. So it's nice that he thinks of articulating even the main titles. He tries to catch as many things in the film as possible and he gives themes to individual characters – and this theme is really associated with Deborah Kerr's character.

The next theme (Ex.2) is associated with Hayley Mills' character, this rather troublesome delinquent girl called Laurel; she has this agitated little theme which is often accompanied by timpani which play what's known as an augmented fourth or a diminished fifth – a tritone, often associated with evil and people like Dracula, but here it is associated with a naughty girl. It's quite a good combination – very simple but very effective.

There are many little details that are quite fun in this kind of comedy-with-mystery-elements; for example, when John Mills' butler, Maitland, is interviewing, or arranging for the interview, of governesses for naughty Laurel, he says when he hears the summons, "The lions are calling for the Christian" and this doesn't please the two candidates, who are thinking "What the hell have I got myself into?" and a very simple little motif announces this moment of change and excitement.

The person who is going to interview Deborah Kerr's character is Dame Edith Evans, who plays Mrs St Maugham, and again a very simple little idea (Ex.3) announces this rather regal lady: just a B-flat major chord, but it's all you need – it says what you need to know: this is an important lady who has certain authority to her. She has her interview with the candidate in the little garden house, and then they walk out into the garden – the chalk garden of the title – and a recurrence of the main theme leads us out into the garden.

That theme recurs again when Miss Madrigal, Deborah Kerr's character, unpacks her suitcase in her bedroom, emphasizing that it's associated with her, and when Miss Madrigal and Laurel go out painting on the white cliffs of Dover (another chalky location). Then we cut to the night and go back inside, and this is articulated by a harp glissando, which is often used in films for scenes of transition. Then the main theme comes back again, but quietly on an oboe (Ex.4), so that it changes its mood and creates a sense of the night and tranquillity. So you can use the same theme, but depending how you orchestrate it and the dynamics, it changes its meaning or its effect.

Laurel is intrigued by seeing Miss Madrigal pacing around in her bedroom: what is she doing and why is she doing this? This is really rather mysterious. To create a sense of mystery we have a typical horror film effect of two notes clashing together, trilling – you hear that in horror films all the time. It's very quiet as well – it's rather worrying – and underneath it you have a musical pace, with the flute playing the tune (Ex.5). This shows how you can change what was originally quite upbeat and delightful into something rather sinister. This is the art of the film composer: not to be too complicated. It's much better if you can be simple but effective, and that's exactly what Malcolm Arnold was able to do.

Next we see Laurel taking out a doll and playing with it, and this tells us that Laurel isn't this delinquent; she's just very unhappy and feels neglected. She's actually a sweet girl underneath and when she plays with the doll, we see the real Laurel, as opposed to the troublesome child that

Music examples © Malcolm Arnold Estate

she's become because she's not being given any affection by Mrs St Maugham. Of course, the metaphor is that the lack of love is like the lack of nutrients in the chalk garden – nothing will grow – and Miss Madrigal is the person who's going to set all that right by loving Laurel. When she takes the doll out of the box, we hear the sound of the celesta, which is an instrument associated with childhood and innocence – it had been used by Tchaikovsky in the Dance of the Sugar Plum Fairy when the instrument was very new. So again, Arnold creates a sense of character by the association of a particular timbre – the childhood image of the celesta.

There's another rather comic moment when Maitland brings in the drinks and we see Mrs St Maugham in purple and looking very regal. There's a rather nice musical accompaniment to that: a little minuet (Ex.6), a stately dance, which is very appropriate for Dame Edith Evans in full sail. It's not too regal but it's dignified, and that's what you get from it. It's very simple – he doesn't elaborate too much – but it's highly effective.

There are also other little articulations of action which are quite fun to observe, for instance, when Miss Madrigal goes downstairs to get a book from the library; there she encounters Maitland and they have a chat. She opens the door and we have a little G major arpeggio on the harp which echoes the movement of the door. So often film music is about articulating or emphasising actions like that: you don't need very much – it's perfect.

However, we begin to realise that there's something strange about Miss Madrigal when she sees a photo of Felix Aylmer, who plays the judge who's invited to dinner later on. She sees the photo and she's worried by it; she seems to recognise it, so to create a sense of anticipation and anguish, we have vibraphones oscillating (Ex.7) – vibraphones are very good for moods of anguish and anticipation because the sound wobbles, so it's uncertain, and it reflects a sense of uncertainty emotionally as well. And then the flute comes in: Miss Madrigal's theme, played quite low down on the instrument, which is rather mysterious – a brilliant way of suggesting her emotion.

We hear that tritone associated with Laurel later on: she climbs a tree because she wants to get into Miss Madrigal's bedroom to snoop around and find out who she really is. To make this more interesting, Arnold creates a sort of mini piano concerto for the next little segment, while

Music examples © Malcolm Arnold Estate

Laurel is rooting around in Miss Madrigal's room; we get a lot of piano writing, which hasn't happened before. He takes part of Hayley Mills' theme – Laurel's theme – borrowing two notes from it, and exploits the percussive nature of the piano. It fits the scene rather well and could be taken out and developed into a concertante piece (like was done with *Stolen Face*).

Towards the end of the film there's a tennis match between Laurel and Miss Madrigal. How does Arnold accompany this? He takes the opening theme which introduced the various characters – Deborah Kerr has one, Hayley Mills has one – and he just speeds it up to suggest two people playing tennis (Ex.8a). It's really rather brilliant to hark back to the main title music to do that kind of thing, adding lots of brass to create a sense of excitement (Ex.8b).

Arnold does some rather avant-garde things like using tone clusters – notes crushed together – for the mysterious moments when the judge comes to dinner and Miss Madrigal explains that she was put in prison because she was like Laurel herself: she killed her own sister out of jealousy, and she's just got out of prison, and she wants to stop that happening again. Tone clusters are a good way of suggesting her dark past and her anxiety about meeting the man who put her in prison.

David Huckvale

This is a transcript of David's talk to camera included on the Blu-ray of the film. Used with kind permission.

Hayley Mills and Deborah Kerr

orchestra conducted by Robert Mersey – Columbia (USA) 4-43015; CBS AAG 192 (4/64)
(ii) Kellie Greene (piano) with orchestra – 20th Century Fox (USA) 492 (5/64); Stateside SS 303 (6/64)
(iii) The Wayfarers (instrumental) – Decca 45-F.12339 (2/66)

DVD EAN/UPC 5060082519383. Powerhouse UK. Region 2

Blu-ray EAN/UPC 9337369025315. Imprint. UK. Region B

Music notes

The score for this film is largely based on a gentle reflective theme for full orchestra with the strings in particular giving it a quiet, unassuming warmth. The theme is most closely associated with the governess Miss Madrigal (Deborah Kerr), a woman with a mysterious past who is devoted to her new charge, the troublesome Laurel (Hayley Mills). Tempo and orchestration depend largely on what is happening on screen to create a series of musical miniatures. The film and some of the acting is rather too theatrical in style and the scope for Arnold to develop his material is rather limited.

Sheet music

'Madrigal' theme published by Henrees Music: this haunting melody with words by Mack David was also published in France by Editions Feldman with the title 'Ton Souvenir' and French words by Hubert Ithier.

MAF performance

'Madrigal': theme song arranged for flute and piano by Alan Poulton: Ruth Morley (flute)/Scott Mitchell (piano), 19 October 2014 (MAF 9)

'Madrigal' (vocal version with flute obligato [words: Mack David]): Claire Thompson (soprano)/Alasdair Garrett (flute)/Jennifer Redmond (piano), 16 October 2016 (MAF 11)

Articles

(i) Movie Review (B.C.) in New York Times, 22 May 1964

(ii) See main article 'The Chalk Garden: Malcolm Arnold's film score' on page 97.

The Thin Red Line (1964)

Production A.C.E. Films/Security Productions

Producers Philip Jordan and Sidney Harmon

Director Andrew Marton

Stars Keir Dullea, Jack Warden, James Philbrook

Music played by Orchestra/Malcolm Arnold

Adapted screenplay

Bernard Gordon from the novel by James Jones [*Publisher* Charles Scribner, New York, 1962].
Film edition: Signet Books, 1964.

Locations

1. Madrid, Spain

Release

US release date 2 May 1964

Japanese release date 31 October 1964

Media

DVD EAN/UPC 8431797200540. Creative. Spain Region 2

Poster

Book

The Heroes of Telemark (1965)

***Alt title* The Unknown Battle**

Production Benton Film Productions

Producer Benjamin Fisz

Director Anthony Mann

Stars Kirk Douglas, Richard Harris, Ulla Jacobsson

Music played by Orchestra/Malcolm Arnold

Adapted Screenplay

Ivan Moffatt and Ben Barzman from the novel 'Skis Against the Atom' by Captain Knut Haukelid [*Publisher* William Kimber, 1954; revised edition, Fontana, 1973; reprinted North American Heritage Press, 1989].

Locations

1. Scenes early in the film when the main characters make their escape from occupied Norway were shot around Poole and Hamworthy in Dorset
2. The former Channel Islands ship TSS Roebuck (built in 1925) played the role of the hijacked steamer, and the SF Ammonia was used to represent the train ferry, the SF Hydro, in the final scene as it sinks to the bottom of the fjord
3. The three raids and the final attack on the heavy water plant in Rjuka in the Telemark District of Norway were filmed variously in Gausta, Oslo, Tinnsjo and Vermork
4. Pinewood Studios, Iver Heath, Bucks

Release

UK premiere London, 23 November 1965

UK release date 26 November 1965

European release date Norway, 12 December 1965

US release date 9 March 1966

UK TV premiere BBC1 Television, 30 August 1971

European TV premiere East Germany, 29 January 1985

Media

7" vinyl

Soundtrack excerpts [1. Main Title 2. German Army Band 3. Knute Skiing Away 4. Heroes of Telemark and End Titles]
Orchestra/Malcolm Arnold – Mainstream/Vogue INT.18 071

LP

Soundtrack recording. Mainstream (US) 56064/S6064 (5/66); Centipede Films LPCFLP019; later re-issued on CD – Intrada INTISC333 [1. Main Title 2. Stupid Fool 3. Must Get to England 4. German Army Band 5. Love Theme ('Anna') 6. Full Astern 7. Silent Night 8. Listen 9. Knute Skiing Away 10. Ferry Leaving Harbour 11. Destruction of Plant 12. Heroes of Telemark and End Titles]

DVD EAN/UPC 5037115055132. Carlton. UK. Region 2

Music notes

This Is the last of the Arnold war scores and alongside *Kwai* one of the very best. The main title music is Arnold at his most excitingly dramatic. Set against wintry Norwegian landscapes his music fits like a glove. The driving rhythms of the brass develop into expressively expansive string sections. It is a wonderful mixture of dramatic orchestral colour and majestic development of melodic line. Like the best of the Oscar-winning *Kwai* the music contains a marvellous onward-driven relentless feel about it, providing the necessary assertive quality to this true-life drama set in German-occupied Norway in 1942.

The use of authentic German military music gives the period feel as an army band plays in the main square of Oslo. Shortly after, it is heard again as a song sung by marching German troops. As Kirk Douglas and Richard Harris cross the North Sea by boat to England, there is an exciting sequence involving mines where Arnold uses his familiar device of ostinato to good dramatic effect. As they arrive in England the momentum of the story is picked up with an urgent rendition of the main theme with the strings prominent.

With Douglas and Harris back in Norway awaiting commando support there is a wonderful skiing sequence set against a darkening winter sky. Here Arnold introduces a glorious flowing melody which is developed from the love theme for Anna (Ulla Jacobsson), Douglas's ex-wife. Flute and harp solos supply a plaintive note as the two men

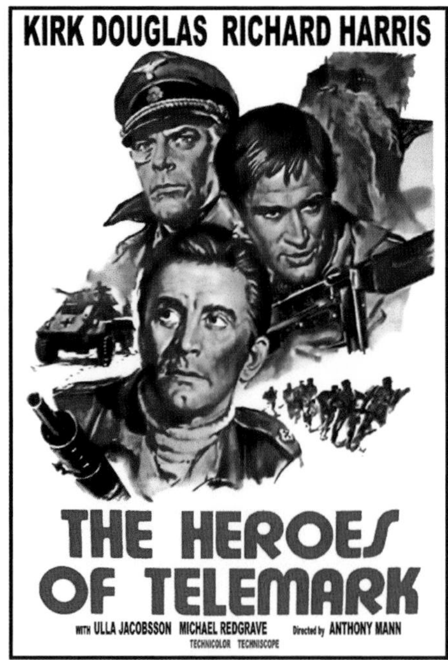

Poster

7" vinyl

arrive on skies at a remote outpost. A bittersweet version of Anna's theme underlines the failed marriage. There is more source music in the church at Rjukan where the congregation sing 'Silent Night' and on a remote snow-covered plateau a group of resistance fighters hum a patriotic song. A long sequence involving the commando raid on the 'heavy water' plant is unscored. Arnold and director Anthony Mann let the sights and sounds of snow-covered Telemark provide the necessary atmosphere.

One of the film's most memorable scenes is the ski chase where the music adds an extra dimension to the action; the pace is lifted and the drama heightened. The two-minute music cue is set off by gunfire with the busy strings being literally chased along by brass and drums. The speed of music and action is fast and furious. Skiers leap, the music leaps in unison. The orchestra drives on relentlessly as the pursuer chases his quarry. The cue ends on a gunshot.

Tremolo strings and ostinato support

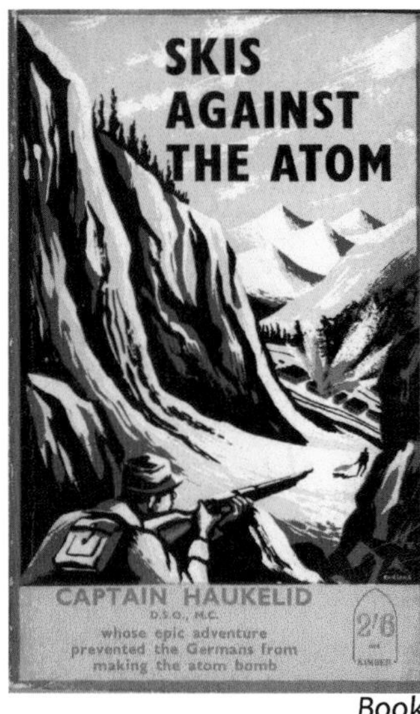

Book

Sheet music

LP: Mainstream 56064/S6064

from the brass lend dramatic weight in the final lead-up to the explosion on board the ferry. As Kirk Douglas and the survivors are picked up there is a note of quiet triumph in the music as the camera draws up and away giving a fine aerial shot of the fjord and an orchestral return of the main theme. The brief end titles are accompanied by Arnold's main theme as a quick march. The score for *The Heroes of* elemark makes as vivid and telling a contribution as the music did for *The Bridge n the River Kwai*. An Arnold gem.

heet music

Main title theme and **'Love Theme (Anna)'**, published by Columbia Pictures Music Corporation.

Concert arrangement

Suite from the film arranged for orchestra by John Gibbons (2017)

Duration c.10'

First performance Royal Philharmonic Orchestra/John Gibbons – Royal & Derngate, Northampton , 15 October 2017 (Twelfth Malcolm Arnold Festival)

Notes

(i) There is an account 'The Real Heroes of Telemark' by Ray Mears [*Publisher* Hodder & Stoughton, 2003, 2004].

ky West and Crooked (1966)

lt title **Bats with Baby Faces**

S title **Gypsy Girl**

roduction John Mills Productions

roducer Jack Hanbury

irector John Mills

tars Hayley Mills, Annette Crosbie, Laurence Naismith

usic played by Orchestra/Malcolm Arnold

dapted screenplay

Mary Hayley Bell and John Prebble, from an original story by Mary Hayley Bell (John Mills's wife and Hayley Mills's mother)

ocations

. Shot mainly in the south Gloucestershire village of Little Badminton

. Pinewood Studios, Iver Heath, Bucks

elease

K release date January 1966

outh American premiere Argentina, 7 March 1966 (Mar del Plata Film Festival)

outh African release date 24 June 1966

S release date July 1966

K TV premiere BBC2 Television, 22 August 1973

wards

Nominated for 'Best International Film' at the Mar del Plata Film Festival in March 1966.

Media

" vinyl

heme

The Wayfarers (instrumental) – Decca 45-F.12339 (2/66); Decca DFE 8655 [in] "Great Film Hits Vol.9" (2/66)

Gypsy Girl' [Words/Music: Anne and Milton Delugg]: Hayley Mills – Mainstream (USA) 656 (9/66)

DVD EAN/UPC 5027626316945. Network. UK. Region 2

Music notes

A rather curious tale this, about a young girl (Hayley Mills), slightly retarded due to a childhood accident, and her subsequently growing involvement with a

Poster

7" vinyl

young gypsy (Ian McShane). Director John Mills gets an interesting enough performance out of his daughter but is let down by the overall mood of the film which is distinctly melancholic. It is present in Arnold's title music; a light gentle melody and yet rather sad. The film seems unsure as to what direction to take and ultimately opts for the safe ground.

It is not difficult to see why the film and score have a pervading sense of sadness and melancholy: there are deaths, funerals, churchyards, a drunken mother and various rural eccentrics. Filmed in sunny Gloucestershire, Arnold's music is mostly of a light texture with frequent use of guitar, harp, chimes, strings and a gently-rocking rhythm section which gives it a suitable sixties slant. There are opportunities for some flute solos and good support from guitar and piano. The ending which brings the two lovers together is too abrupt and contrived and tacked on at the end a brief snatch of Hayley Mills singing 'I'm a Gypsy Girl' which would appear not to have been

Sheet music

written by Arnold. All in all rather a curiosity.

Sheet music

Main theme arranged for piano solo, published by Henrees Music.

Notes

(i) Interview with John Mills on 'Film Preview' – BBC1 Television, 21 January 1966.

The Great St Trinian's Train Robbery (1966)

Production Braywild
Producer Leslie Gilliat
Directors Frank Launder and Sidney Gilliat
Stars Frankie Howerd, Dora Bryan, George Cole
Music played by Orchestra/Malcolm Arnold

Original screenplay
Frank Launder and Ivor Herbert

Locations
1. Opening shot of Raymond Huntley (Sir Horace, Minister of Schools) at Palace Court, London, W2, on his way to meet Dora Bryan (Amber Spottiswoode), the headmistress, as she is driven away from Holloway Prison, Parkhurst Road, N7
2. The school is now relocated to 'Hammingwell Grange', filmed at Woking Public Library on Commercial Road, Woking, in Surrey and Littleton Park House in Shepperton
3. Other 'Hammingwell' location shots include The Barley Mow pub (still standing), Watersplash Road in Shepperton and London Street, Chertsey
4. 'Hammingwell Halt' is in reality Whitehill station on the Longmoor Military railway which closed in 1969. Both the fictional 'Fordingbridge' and 'Pudham' stations were filmed at LIss Station in Hampshire with Syers Road in the background. 'Nutcombe' station was filmed at Longmoor Downs Station (now itself buried underneath the main A3)
5. George Cole (Flash Harry) can be seen visiting The Rose and Crown pub on Sandhills Lane, Thorpe Green, near Virginia Water.
6. Shepperton Studios, Surrey

Release
UK release date 11 March 1966
South African release date Johannesburg, 2 September 1966
US release date Washington, 20 December 1967
UK TV premiere BBC1 Television, 23 December 1971

Awards
Won the NBR (National Board Review) Award for 'Top Foreign Film' in 1967.

Media
DVD EAN/UPC 5060034577782. Studio Canal. UK. Region 2
DVD EAN/UPC 5060034577560. Studio Canal. UK. Region 2 (Boxed set with Belles of St Trinian's / Pure Hell at St Trinian's / Blue Murder at St Trinian's)

Music notes
After a gap of six years those little monsters from St Trinian's are back and with their resident composer Arnold. Over the opening titles there is the 'Ballad of the Great Train Robbery' – bright and breezy with notable work for trumpet and percussion. However the overall effect is somewhat smothered by an overabundance of lyrics.

Another new headmistress (Dora Bryan) is appointed to St Trinian's and Arnold has plenty of fun with a 'rounding up of the teachers' sequence that involves a variety of short musical cues: a sedate St Trinian's tango, a French 'can-can' dance, a xylophone-piano rhythm accompaniment to striptease, a snatch of Flash Harry's theme, a glimpse of a calypso 'Rule Britannia' and a triumphant school song. In contrast, the gathering of the train robbers is unscored.

Throughout the film Arnold makes frequent reference to the title 'Ballad' with different tempos and ensemble. Other cues involve a piano-xylophone number for a gambling scene, a Spanish guitar with castanets and a St Trinian's tango and waltz. The rather over-extended chase up and down a nearby railway line is mainly scored with fragments of the title music and the school song. For the end titles Arnold signs off with a tango version of the St Trinian's school song. Despite valiant work from Frankie Howerd and Dora Bryan, one does miss Alastair Sim.

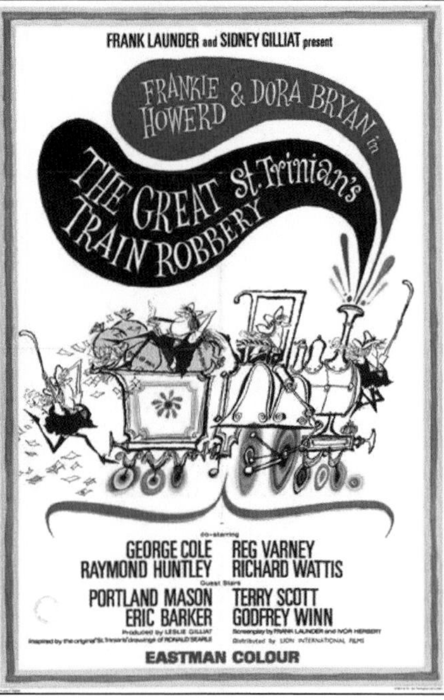

Poster

Sheet music
'Ballad of the Great Train Robbery'
(opening title sequence): although the vocal line was notated by the composer, it was never published as a separate item.

MAF performance
Opening Titles: The Ballad of the Great Train Robbery [words: Frank Launder and Sidney Gilliat], arranged for high voice and piano by Alan Poulton: Claire Thompson (soprano)/Jennifer Redmond (piano), 16 October 2016 (MAF 11)

Notes
(i) The girls used in the railway sequences were students from Alton Convent, which at the time was run by a French order of nuns known as the Sisters of Our Lady of Providence.
(ii) Excerpts from the film shown on 'Film Preview' – BBC 1 Television, 11 March 1966.

Africa: Texas Style (1967)

Production Vantors/Ivan Tors Films
Producers Andrew Marton and John Pellatt
Director Andrew Marton
Stars Hugh O'Brian, John Mills, Nigel Green
Music played by Orchestra/Malcolm Arnold
Original screenplay
Andy White
Locations
1. Kenya and Florida
Release
US release date May 1967
UK release date 8 June 1967
UK TV premiere BBC1 Television, 22 April 1972
Media
7" vinyl
'Swahili Serenade' [Words: Mack David] (produced and arranged by David Gates): Bobby Vee – Liberty (USA/Canada) F 55964 (6/67); Liberty (South Africa) LYS 104. [It was the B-side; the A-side was 'Come Back When You Grow Up', which reached No.3 in the US Billboard charts in 1967.]
DVD EAN/UPC 0628586322908 Cygnus. EU. Region 2
Music notes
Although a popular and exciting continent for filmmakers, Africa as a location does not contribute to many memorable films. This 1966 effort has the benefit of some authentic Kenyan footage but, as is often the case, it is defeated by a weak and ultimately dull script. Rancher John Mills employs American cowboys to rope and capture wild animals for game ranching and comes up against nasty cattle breeder Nigel Green.

For title music Arnold supplies a bold assertive theme for brass supported by rhythmic percussion which develops into a secondary theme of a gentler nature played almost as a slow fox-trot for woodwind, harp and timpani. This secondary theme becomes the love theme and is often carried gently by flute, guitar and harp. Many of the scenes involving the capture of the wild animals benefit from the energetic main theme, which gives some momentum to the dull plot.

Poster

Sheet music

Arnold also provides a motif for a little African boy with the help of xylophone and light percussion. The end title is given over to the secondary love theme played by guitar, harp and rhythm section with brass chords ending the film with a firm flourish.

Notes
(i) Excerpts from the film shown on 'Film Preview' – BBC1 Television, 23 June 1967.
(ii) The film was followed by a US television series *Cowboy in Africa* (1967).
(iii) Hayley Mills appears as the blonde girl at the airport in the first scene (uncredited).

The Battle of Britain (1969) [part/uncredited]

Production Spitfire Productions for United Artists
Producers Harry Saltzman and Benjamin Fisz
Director Guy Hamilton
Stars Michael Caine, Trevor Howard, Harry Andrews
Music played by Orchestra/Malcolm Arnold and William Walton (for the March)
Adapted screenplay
James Kennaway and Wilfred Greatorex, from the book 'The Narrow Margin' by Derek Ward and Derek Dempster [*Publisher* Pen & Sword, 2003].
Film edition: Arrow Books, 1969.

Locations
1. The French airfield scenes were filmed on the south side of RAF Duxford airfield in Cambridgeshire; much of this section has now been returned to farmland and the eastern side has now been bisected by the construction of the M11 motorway
2. Other airfield locations were at RAF Hawkinge, Folkestone, Kent (now the home of the Kent Battle of Britain Museum), RAF Bovingdon near Hemel Hempstead in Hertfordshire, and North Weald Airfield in Epping Forest, Essex, as well as RAF Bentley Priory near Stanmore, Middlesex [The use of RAF Hawkinge

Book

in the filming has been brought into question – see ukairfieldguide.net; RAF Bentley Priory was the Headquarters of Fighter Command during the Second World War and is now a Battle of Britain Museum]

3. The interception of the German Stukas by Spitfires was filmed above Beachy Head and Seven Sisters in East Sussex
4. The Jackdaw Inn, Denton, near Canterbury was used for shots of Christopher Plummer arriving in his open-top sports car, though the interior was actually filmed at The Hoops pub near Royston, Hertfordshire
5. The London blitz sequences were filmed at or near Weston Street, SE1, close to the New Kent Road flyover, others at Dragon Street in Camberwell and the old Aldwych Tube Station on the Strand (for both external and internal shots). Further blitz fires were filmed by the old warehouses near Tower Bridge (now occupied by the Tower Hotel)
6. Several locations in Andalucia (Spain) were used, including El Corpora and Tablada air bases in Sevilla and Huelva Beach in Huelva
7. Pinewood Studios, Iver Heath, Bucks

Release

UK premiere London, 15 September 1969

UK release date 16 September 1969

US premiere New York City, 20 October 1969

US release date 24 October 1969

UK TV premiere BBC1 Television, 15 September 1974

Awards

(i) Winner of the 1971 National Board Review award for 'Top Ten Films'.

(ii) Nominee at the 1970 BAFTAs for 'Best Soundtrack'.

Media

7" vinyl

Soundtrack excerpts [1. Theme 2. Battle in the Air 3. Aces High 4. Finale] Orchestra/Malcolm Arnold – United Artists (Spain) HU 067-152 (1969)

LP Soundtrack recording. United Artists (UK) UAS 29019 (9/69)/(US) UAS 5021 (1/70); Sunset (UK) SLS 50407 (10/77); later re-issued on CD – Varese Sarabande VSD 6578

DVD EAN/UPC 5039036030717. UK. Region 2 (Includes optional Walton / Arnold soundtrack)

Blu-ray EAN/UPC 5039036036856. DTS. UK. Region 2 (Ron Goodwin / Walton soundtrack only)

Sheet music

Main title theme (by Ron Goodwin), published by United Artists.

Articles

(i) Review, in *The Times*, 29 April 1971

(ii) Kögebehn, Günther: 'A Film score Odyssey' – *Beckus* 54, Autumn 2004

(iii) Kuykendall, Brooks: 'New evidence in the autograph manuscripts' – *Beckus* 114, Autumn 2109

Notes

(i) Arnold assisted in the orchestration of several sections and was responsible for re-scoring and expanding Walton's original soundtrack when more music was required by the film company – this included the famous 'Battle in the Air' sequence.

(ii) Interview with the director, Guy Hamilton, on 'Movie-Go-Round' – BBC Radio2, 15 September 1968.

(iii) Preview and excerpt from the film was shown on 'Film Night' – BBC2 Television, 24 August 1969.

(iv) Interviews on location, broadcast on 'Movie-Go-Round' – BBC Radio2, 14 September 1969.

(v) See main article 'The Battle of Britain: New evidence in the autograph manuscripts' on the next page.

Sheet music

LP: United Artists UAS 29019 (UK)/UAS 5021 (US)

The Battle of Britain: New evidence in the autograph manuscripts

William Walton's manuscripts are generally well-preserved and well-documented. Autograph material survives for half of his fourteen feature film projects.... Most surprisingly, the autographs reveal that the recent DVD release of *Battle of Britain* [1969 United Artists (UA)] which purportedly restores the discarded Walton score (actually written jointly with Malcolm Arnold) misplaces every cue.

Although Walton (in collaboration with his younger colleague Malcolm Arnold) composed a score for the film which was recorded for the soundtrack, it was subsequently rejected by the UA administration. It was replaced with a wholly new score by Ron Goodwin, and only due to the strenuous objections of Laurence Olivier (who threatened to remove his name from the picture) was even a small sequence of Walton's music retained.[18] Tapes of the soundtrack recording sessions of the Walton score were rediscovered and released on CD in 2000.[19] A new DVD of the film includes an optional audio track purporting to present "Original William Walton Score."[20]

Unfortunately, on this audio track the Walton/Arnold score was matched to the picture through overconfident guesswork.[21] This is a great pity, because almost all of the musical material survives—complete with detailed cue sheets—at the Beinecke Library. The correct synchronization for all of the surviving material could have been established with very little trouble. (The appendix details the correct placement of the Walton/Arnold score). Indeed, a comparison with the film as released suggests that the cue sheets provided to Goodwin were substantially the same as those provided to Walton.

It is instructive to note how often the music conceived for one scene can be convincing in another—but its effectiveness often wanes 20 or 30 seconds as the scenes diverge. For example, Walton's cue 6.M.1 was conceived for a scene of emergency recovery operations at a British air base that has just been bombed. The cue sheet indicates that Walton's cue is to begin in the very last seconds of the previous scene, as we see a British plane explode at the end of a dogfight. (This is at 0:50:27 on the DVD release.) In the ensuing scene, there are medical vehicles and firefighters combating the general chaos after the attack. A group of injured WAAF officers are getting on to the back of a truck; the section officer, Maggie Harvey, turns from the truck and sees a line of WAAF corpses. She walks closer to them. Obviously shaken, she reaches for a cigarette and begins to light it. The warrant officer yells, "Put that cigarette out! Can't you smell gas? The mains have gone." The camera zooms in on Harvey's face, increasingly stressed. She shouts, "Don't you yell at me, Officer Warwick!"

These details and more are listed on the cue sheet that is still affixed to this portion of the score. Walton's music starts with a generic mood of tension, but then (to accompany the poignant

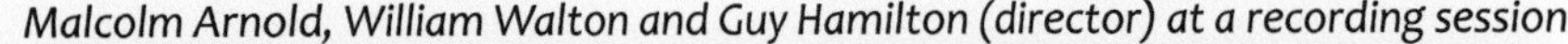

Malcolm Arnold, William Walton and Guy Hamilton (director) at a recording session

moment as Harvey surveys the corpses) a wistful cello solo—not unlike the first movement of Walton's Cello Concerto. This is interrupted by a burst of energetic music (as Warwick yells about the cigarette), a long-sustained tremolo and crescendo, and ends with a short, dissonant crash just before Harvey shouts back.[22] On the DVD release, this scene is given no music at all on the Walton audio-track. The correct music appears instead much later (1:10:58). It is prefixed there by an entirely separate cue which apparently preceded it on the recovered tapes. As the appendix shows, the same erroneous segues happened to six other cues—resulting in confusion which would certainly have added to the difficulty of locating the correct placement of the music.

This later (incorrectly matched) scene begins with another dogfight between the RAF and the Luftwaffe. While the generic tension which starts the 6.M.1 cue is plausible at the beginning of this scene, the transition to the cello solo does not match anything about the dogfight, nor (of course) the two plane explosions that seem so incongruously paired with the lyrical music. The energy of the music is renewed at just the wrong moment, and the editors fade out the dissonant crash that concludes Walton's cue because it does not make sense in this context. This apparently was not enough to demonstrate that the cue was misplaced.

Walton decided to use a motive based on Siegfried's horn call to characterize the German pilots, titling it "Young Siegfrieds". On the DVD release, these segments are comically out of place, with the Wagner motive associated with the RAF.[23] Aside from this egregious musical error, the cues are plausible in their wrong locations. A good example is Walton's 4.M.1. The music begins with a "sting" chord, which on the DVD becomes a reaction to the British ambassador's exclamation that time is "running out". There follows a scene of the RAF officers at leisure, wrongly accompanied by the Siegfried theme. A plane attempts to land without its landing gear down and the pilot is signalled by a flare. He makes a steep ascent, an impressive image on the screen that coincides with a grandioso gesture in the music (albeit still referencing Wagner). The cue ends as the plane has landed successfully.

To some extent it works, but the evidence of the autograph reveals that it is all wrong. Walton is not making an "ironic" use of the Wagner motive for

Battle of Britain: Original Soundtrack [1999]. The first 19 tracks are the OST, including Walton's 'Battle in the Air'; the final 8 tracks present Walton's original score

the RAF—although such a conclusion would be completely reasonable given the claims of the DVD. Instead the music is supposed to come later, depicting the Luftwaffe officers at their ease. The "sting" of the beginning is a brief shot of an RAF airman dead in the water. The German pilot that shot him down returns to his base for a bath. The increased grandeur of the score accompanies the arrival of a German officer. This—the correct scene for 4.M.1—is rather prosaic, and on the DVD release it appears without music on the Walton side of the audio track. Sadly, even after more than forty years, the *Battle of Britain* music remains unavailable in the form the composer intended, and the existence of the new DVD is likely to make any corrected version unmarketable for any time in the foreseeable future. Were the autographs not extant, however, there would be no way to know that the version presented under the authority of the film production company is not accurate.

Walton manuscript studies have hardly begun. A few scores are scattered among prominent archives (particularly the British Library, the Library of Congress, and the Harry Ransom Humanities Center at the University of Texas) or are held privately, and a few significant works are lost (the autograph full score of *Belshazzar's Feast*, for example, for which Oxford University Press offered a £1,000 reward in 1987). The depth and breadth of the Walton holdings at the Beinecke Library make it by far the most important repository, with a range of autograph materials for more than sixty works. The accessibility of materials from across Walton's career as a film composer offers a fascinating glimpse behind the

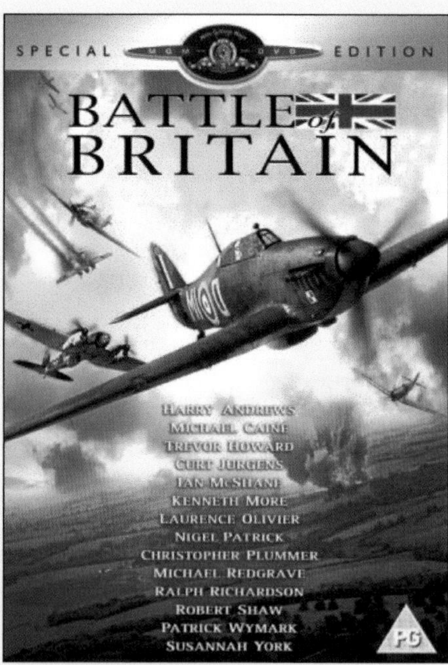

Battle of Britain: Special Edition 2-DVD set [2004]. You can choose whether to listen to the Ron Goodwin or William Walton soundtrack

scenes of mid-century British cinema production.

Footnotes

18. The story of this fiasco has been told many times. For recent summaries, see Martin Hunt, "Their Finest Hour?: The Scoring of *Battle of Britain*," *Film History* 14 (2002): 47–56; and Walton, *Film Suites*, ed. Kuykendall, xi–xiii.

19. *Battle of Britain: Original MGM Motion Picture Soundtrack* (Rykodisc RCD 10739 [2000]), CD.

20. U.K. release: *Battle of Britain: Special Edition* (MGM-DVD MZI 10001024 [2004]), 2 DVDs (region 2). U.S.A. release: *Battle of Britain: Collector's Edition* (Sony Pictures Home Entertainment 1008312 [2005]), 2 DVDs (region 1). In the U.K. it has subsequently been reissued as a "definitive" edition, although the Walton score remains erroneously synchronized.

21. A self-congratulatory account by those involved appears in Mark R. Hasan, "The Restoration of William Walton's *The Battle of Britain*", *Music from the Movies* 43 (2004): 64–66.

22. A photograph of the soundtrack recording session of this instant is reproduced in Cooke, *A History of Film Music*, 250.

23. A similar stylistic mismatch is the use of Walton's *nobilmente* English ceremonial march theme to accompany a triumphant Luftwaffe pass-in-review during the opening credits.

Appendix

Battle of Britain (1969): comparison of correct sequence of Walton/Arnold score with the DVD release

Ms. cue designation	correct placement in the film	comments	erroneous placement on DVD release	track title on CD release
2.M.2	0:12:56	wind band version of "Horst Wessel"	0:57:37	*Luftwaffe Victory* (00:00–00:14)
3.M.1	[0:26:03?]	Source music, not composed: WW indicates on the manuscript "Bagpipe music only going into highland lament"	[missing]	[missing]
3.M.2	[0:26:38?]	Slow waltz arrangement (for jazz band by Wally Stott) of "A nightingale sang in Berkeley Square"; a different arrangement (unnumbered) is also preserved among the Walton autograph materials, and was used in the film as released (0:26:38 and 1:15:55)	[missing]	[missing]
4.M.1	0:31:01	"Young Siegfrieds" scored by Walton	0:16:47	*The Young Siegfrieds*
5.M.1	0:42:12	"Young Siegfrieds" scored by Arnold	0:57:53	*Luftwaffe Victory* (at 00:15)
6.M.1	0:50:29		1:10:28	*The Few Fight Back* (00:00–00:28)
6.M.2	0:53:30	orchestral version of "Horst Wessel"	[missing]	[missing]
6.M.3	0:58:27		1:10:58	*The Few Fight Back* (at 00:28)
7.M.1	1:01:34		0:08:46	*Scramble! / Battle in The Air* (00:00–47)
8.M.1	?	WW's reference timing is 2'18"; autograph no longer extant— possibly never recorded	[missing]	[missing]
9.M.1	?	WW's reference timing is 54"; autograph no longer extant— possibly never recorded	[missing]	[missing]
9.M.2	1:20:23		1:21:10 (fades out prematurely)	*Scherzo: Gay Berlin*
10.M.1	1:32:03	Walton's reworking of 6.M.3 material	1:27:19	*Cat and Mouse* (00:00–01:17)
12.M.1	1:49:48?	Second version of 'Young Siegfrieds' music by Arnold; the only synchronization cue is 'INTERIOR HEINKEL / 1.5' at the end. The recording includes a lengthened introduction, adding about fifteen seconds to the cue."	1:42:05	*Dogfight*
13.M.1	1:58:32	"Battle in the Air"—used in the original release. Walton composed the first part of the cue (up to 2:00:33) and Arnold the second, but an internal repeat (at 2:01:22) complicates this.	[correct]	*Scramble! / Battle in The Air* (at 00:48)
14.M.1-2	near 2:07:20	Composed by Arnold; no cue sheets or synchronization captions.	1:28:39	*Cat and Mouse* (at 01:17)
14.M.3	2:09:00*	Introduction and march, scored by Arnold; synchronization captions indicate that this was intended to start at 2:09:00, but the cue is not long enough to last to the end of the credits.	0:09:53	*March Introduction & Battle of Britain March*
14.M.3A	[2:09:18?]	Alternative march introduction by Arnold, apparently to address the problem of 14.M.3	2:09:39	Finale: Battle of Britain March

Notes

Ms. cue designation: on the extant manuscripts and cue sheets, the sequence of the music cues is designated by reel of film. "2.M.2" indicates reel 2, music cue 2. The absence of a 2.M.1 is curious, but suggests merely that when the cue sheets were prepared music was intended for an earlier scene on that reel, but was subsequently cut—possibly even before music was composed for it. On the verso of cue sheet 2.M.2, Walton calculated the timings of a number of cues, including some for which manuscript materials are no longer extant (8.M.1 and 9.M.1), but 2.M.1 is not on this list.

Correct placement in the film: all placement timings are based on the U.S. DVD release, *Battle of Britain: Collector's Edition* (Sony Pictures Home Entertainment1008312 [2005]), 2 DVDs. Where it is possible, correct placement is determined by comparison of extant UA cue sheets affixed to the sections of the autograph. A question mark indicates that there is no evidence extant among the autograph materials to verify the precise synchronization.

Track title on CD release: given to facilitate comparison with the film. These listings correspond to *Battle of Britain: Original MGM Motion Picture Soundtrack* (Rykodisc RCD 10747 [2000]), CD.

James Brooks Kuykendall

Acknowledgment

Reproduced by kind permission from: James Brooks Kuykendall, 'William Walton's Film Scores: New Evidence in the Autograph Manuscripts', *Notes* 68, No. 1 (September 2011), pp.9-32. Published by Music Library Association. DOI: https://doi.org/10.1353/not.2011.0097. Further information: https://muse.jhu.edu/article/448059.

The Reckoning (1970)

***Alt title* A Matter of Honour**
Production Columbia Pictures Corporation
Producer Ronald Shedlo
Director Jack Gold
Stars Nicol Williamson, Ann Bell, Lilita De Barros
Music played by Orchestra/Malcolm Arnold

Adapted screenplay

John McGrath, from the novel 'The Harp That Once' by Patrick Hall [*Publisher* Heinemann, 1967].

Locations

1. Opening shots of the Rolls Building in New Fetter Lane, Farringdon, London
2. Williamson travels north to Merseyside: location shots filmed on Wheatland Lane in the Seacombe area of Liverpool; the parent's house was filmed in nearby Daisy Grove (now demolished) and Beaufort Road in the docks area of Birkenhead
3. Williamson is also seen crossing one of the Four Bridges connecting Birkenhead and Wallasey; he pulls into the King Street Service Station in Wallasey, travels near to 'The Shaggy Calf' pub in Liverpool (in reality Carlton Road in Slough); later we see 'The Firefly' pub in Wallasey (actually 'The Shepherd's Rest' in Union Street, Wallasey)
4. The churchyard scene is at St George's Church, Heyworth, in the Everton district of Liverpool, with the roof of the Everton Library clearly visible in the left background. Williamson glances down Havelock Street towards Seacombe Tower by the docks on the River Mersey.
5. There are several location shots in Virginia Water, Surrey: one is Pinewood Road where the road crosses the 18th fairway on Wentworth's West Course and another around the junction of Christchurch Road and Gorse Hill Lane.
6. Shepperton Studios, Surrey

Release

UK premiere London, 8 January 1970
Australian release date 9 July 1970
US premiere New York City, 9 January 1971
TV premiere West Germany, 24 September 1975

Media

DVD EAN/UPC 043396378445. Columbia. USA. Region 1
Blu-ray EAN/UPC 5037899071199. Indicator. USA. All regions

Music notes

For the first and only time in his film scoring, Arnold has to write title music while on-screen husband and wife (Williamson and Bell) make passionate love. Taking his 'cue' from the aggressive screen action, Arnold provides a suitably angry theme for brass, guitar and drum beat. There is a brief development into a more melodic theme before more driving brass and percussion complete this opening title sequence.

Poster

Book

Sheet music

Nicol Williamson, well cast as a rude ambitious sales executive, journeys to Liverpool to visit his ailing father who subsequently dies. Driving fast in his Jaguar, Williamson's moods are reflected in the music; the steady beat of the guitar, brass and drums, with guitar picking out the tune while the drums supply the beat. This is another example of Arnold preferring to work with a small ensemble. As Williamson arrives home in Liverpool there is a brief fragment of a tune perhaps associated with his childhood, for it is folk-like in character (Arnold made later use of it in his Eighth Symphony).

There are a couple of traditional Irish songs for solo male voice while discordant brass reflect Williamson's feelings of anger at the death of his father. When he does get the chance of revenge, the driving material from the title sequence returns. As he leaves Liverpool, woodwind and piano supply a final reminder of his roots and the gentle pastoral theme heard when he first arrived home.

In the final scene, having narrowly escaped crashing his car after going through a red light, Williamson with relief and a note of triumph in his voice says, 'If I can get away with that, I can get away with anything'. The end titles then give Arnold the chance to reprise his driving rhythmic main theme, the folk tune and a final dash of brass and drums. Arnold's music for *The Reckoning* reflects the changing society of the late 1960s. It is for the most part aggressive and hard-edged music for an angry, selfish man.

Sheet music

Selection of themes for piano (i) Title Theme; (ii) 'Believe me if all those endearing young charms' (traditional); (iii) Piano theme at party (Slow Foxtrot); (iv) March: Ireland's Enemy (a variant of the Title theme). Published by Screen Gems/Columbia Pictures Music Corporation. The title

Notes

(i) 'Michael Dean talks to Nicol Williamson' on 'Line-Up' – BBC2 Television, 15 January 1970.
(ii) The title theme was later incorporated in the first movement of Arnold's Eighth Symphony.

David Copperfield (1970)

Production Omnibus Productions
Producer Frederick Brogger
Director Delbert Mann
Stars Richard Attenborough, Cyril Cusack, Edith Evans
Music played by Orchestra/Malcolm Arnold

Adapted screenplay

Jack Pulman, based on the novel by Charles Dickens.
Film edition: Pan Books, 1970 (as 'Copperfield 70' edited by George Curry). The book includes a performance version of the screenplay, 16 pages of stills from the film, and an account of how Malcolm Arnold worked with the director and his team on laying down the soundtrack.

Locations

1. Opening shots of the 'White Swan Hotel', actually Little White (Cottage) Lodge, South Green, Southwold in Suffolk; later there are shots of Southwold Harbour and the Harbour Inn as well as the Promenade on Gunhill Cliff
2. Actual beach scenes believed to be the coastline at Easton (IMDb indicates Benacre Beach)
3. London locations:
   (i) in flashback Alistair Mackenzie (young David Copperfield) and Ralph Richardson emerge from the 'bottle-washing factory' located at St Katharine's West Dock, EC1 (the damaged warehouses near Tower Bridge are visible but now demolished)
   (ii) Robin Phillips bumps into Michael Redgrave outside The Lamb & Flag pub in Leicester Square and meets up with Susan Hampshire and Ron Moody in the lobby of the Covent Garden Opera House
   (iii) The drunken night out with friends was filmed on Kings Bench Walk, EC4; Corin Redgrave climbs up the nearest lamppost in Broad Court across Bow Street
   (iv) Phillips is later seen with Nicholas Pennell walking up Middle Temple Lane in Blackfriars to his accommodation in Hare Court
   (v) He meets Dora (Pamela Franklin) in the Inner Temple Gardens with Harcourt Building in the background [also identified as the Church of the Immaculate Conception, Mount Street Gardens, Mayfair] and returns to his accommodation at 4 Canonbury Place, off Alwyne Villas, Islington, N1 (after Dora's fall downstairs)
4. When Phillips visits the solicitors (Wickfield & Heap) in Canterbury, in reality it is 3 New Square in Lincoln's Inn, WC2
5. Later, St Katharine's Dock poses as Gravesend Docks in Kent
6. Twentieth Century Fox Television Studios, Pinewood, Iver Heath, Bucks

Poster

Book

LP: GRT Records 10008

Release

UK release date 15 March 1970
US release date 15 March 1970
UK television premiere 26 December 1975

Awards

(i) Nominated for 3 Emmy Awards in 1970 including one for 'Outstanding Dramatic Programme' for Frederick Brogger.
(ii) Nominated in 1971 for a Director's Guild of America Award for Delbert Mann in the category ' Outstanding Directorial Achievement in Television'.

Media

7" vinyl
Soundtrack excerpts [1. Main theme 2. David's Love for Agnes 3. End Title] Orchestra/Malcolm Arnold – GRT Records (Japan) UP-166-G (1970)
LP Soundtrack recording. GRT Records (US) 10008 (1970) [1. Main theme 2. The Child David 3. Stage to Yarmouth and theme for Agnes 4. Mr Micawber 5. The Affection of David for Agnes 6. Entr'acte: Reprise of Main theme 7. Love theme for Dora 8. 'Something of an extraordinary nature is about to turn up' 9. Agnes and David 10. The Search for Emily 11. 'Go to him...' 12. David's Love for Agnes and end title.]
DVD EAN/UPC 787364406098. Brentwood. USA. Region 1
DVD EAN/UPC 8436022321960. Spain. Region 2

Music notes
Arnold conjures up a haunting, beautiful melody carried by the strings and given a certain amount of support from the brass in his main title music for *David Copperfield* which was made for American television and shown in cinemas in this country. At well under two hours the film cannot do full justice to Charles Dickens' famous novel. Making the mistake of basing the screenplay on a series of flash-backs of David's life, the result is a rather superficial, fragmentary treatment where few of Dickens' marvellous characters are allowed a chance to make a real impact.

For Arnold at least it is an opportunity to complete his writing for films on a high. Horns and strings herald in the stagecoach to Yarmouth and there is a jaunty clarinet motif for Mr Micawber (Richardson) while Arnold's theme for Agnes (Susan Hampshire) has a poignant delicacy and fine shading from the woodwind and strings. It has a yearning quality that reflects an unspoken love.

Arnold, naturally enough, makes frequent use of his main theme, which is largely associated with David's sad, nostalgic memories of childhood and regrettable incidents in his past, including the deaths of his mother, his wife Dora, and his old school friend Steerforth. Much of this music is heard while David (Robin Phillips) walks slowly along the beach at Yarmouth, instigating many of the film's flashbacks. Gradually there is an almost invisible bringing together of the main theme with the secondary theme for Agnes which is given a shimmering delicate quality by the use of flute, harp and celesta. When David marries Dora (Pamela Franklin), the music is dominated by Agnes' theme as if we are seeing it through her eyes.

While there are discordant brass in the search for little Emily, there are optimistic brass fanfares for the departure of the emigrants Peggoty and Micawber. It is the brass that introduces the end title sequence and a final reprise of the David Copperfield theme for full orchestra. Recorded at Anvil Studios, Denham, this score neatly ends the year, the decade and the composing of film music for Malcolm Arnold.

Concert arrangement
Suite from the film
arranged for large orchestra by John Morgan [1. Main title 2. Return to Yarmouth 3. Visit to Aunt Betsy – Davy loves Emily 4. Agnes's Arrival – Mother's Funeral 5. Mr Micawber 6. Memories of Dora and Steerforth 7. Love for Dora 8. Mr Micawber Exposes Heep 9. Dora's Declaration 10. Agnes Leaves David 11. In Search of Emily 12. Emigration to Australia 13. David's Resolution and Finale]
Duration 30'
Recording Moscow Symphony Orchestra/ William Stromberg – Marco Polo 8.225167 (2001); Naxos 8.573366 (2015)
Suite from the film arranged by Philip Lane (1999) [1. Main Titles and Opening Scene 2. The Micawbers 3. Young Lovers 4. Finale]
Duration 11'
Instrumentation 2 2 2 2 – 4 2 3 1 – perc(2/3) cel hp – str
Publisher Novello
Recording BBC Philharmonic Orchestra/ Rumon Gamba – Chandos CHAN 9851 (The Film Music of Sir Malcolm Arnold, Vol.2); CHAN 241-12 (Main title only)

Notes
(i) Malcolm Arnold recorded the soundtrack at Anvil Studios, Denham in November 1969
(ii) 'Release' Arts magazine programme, on location in Suffolk – BBC2 Television, 24 May 1969.
(iii) Excerpts from the film broadcast on 'Movie-Go-Round' – BBC Radio2, 7 September 1969.
(iv) Highlights broadcast on 'Sound Screen 70' – BBC Radio2, 4 January 1970.

The Wildcats of St Trinian's (1980)

Production Wildcat Film Productions
Producer E M Smedley-Aston
Director Frank Launder
Stars Sheila Hancock, Michael Hordern, Joe Melia
Music played by Orchestra/Frank Barber
Original screenplay Frank Launder
Film edition: Armada (Fontana), 1980

Locations
1. Isle of Wight
2. Oakley Court, Windsor Road, Oakley Green, Berkshire
3. Bray Studios, Down Place, Oakley Green, Berkshire

Release
UK release date early 1980
Australian release date 21 August 1980

Media
DVD EAN/UPC 644827984725. UK. Region 2.

Notes
(i) The film uses some of the music which Malcolm Arnold had composed for earlier St Trinian's films [1. School song 2. The Charge of the Fourth Form 3. End Titles 4. St Trinian's March]. The rest of the soundtrack was written by James Kenelm Clarke.
(ii) This was the last time any of Arnold's music was used in a St Trinian's film. The latest series of St Trinian's films ('St Trinian's', 2007; 'St Trinian's 2: The Legend of Fritton's Gold', 2009; 'St Trinian's 3: Battle of the Sexes', in development, possibly cancelled) employs a new team of writers, editors and composers to gratify the current generation of cinema-goers who are totally alien to the 'innocent' world of the 1950s.

Book

List of documentaries

Film/television archives

The following abbreviations indicate the archives where the documentaries are held:

BFI	British Film Institute	www.bfi.org.uk
BrP	British Pathe	www.britishpathe.tv
BPFA	British Petroleum Film Archive (BP Video Library)	www.bpvideolibrary.com
CFA	Colonial Film Archive	www.colonialfilm.org.uk
CW	Cine Wessex	
FI	Film Images	
HFA	Huntley Film Archive	www.huntleyarchives.com
IWM	Imperial War Museum	www.iwm.org.uk/collections/film
LAC	Library and Archives Canada	www.bac-lac.gc.ca
RAFM	Royal Air Force Museum	
SFA	Shell Film Archive	
SSA	Scottish Screen Archive (Moving Image Archive)	movingimage.nls.uk

In most cases you can view the archives' catalogues and many of the documentaries on line; documentaries may also be available on YouTube (www.youtube.com).

Note. Not all these titles held in archives will necessarily be viewing copies (some rarer material will be classified as preservation copies) and researchers should check this out with the relevant archivist before they arrive.

Avalanche Patrol (1947)

***Alt title* Swiss Avalanche Patrol**
Production Universal Pictures (USA) for the Swiss Avalanche Patrol
Duration 24' (music: 14')
Synopsis The life and work of the men who form the Avalanche Patrol
Director Jack Swain
Music played by London Symphony Orchestra/John Hollingsworth
First [televised] transmission BBC Television, 16 August 1962 (repeated 27 September 1963)
Notes See main article 'Avalanche Patrol: Arnold's first commission' on the next page.

Accident Prevention Concerns You (1948)

A series of nine flashes ('shorts')
Production Crown Film Unit for the Royal Air Force
Archive RAFM
Duration approx. 2–3' each
Synopsis A series of safety education films: 1. Refuelling Procedures 2. Pre-flight Checks 3. Care with Improvisation 4. Flight Authorisation Book 5. Switching-off Procedures 6. Oxygen Mask Care 7. Escape Hatch Security 8. Ground Crew Vigilance 9. Slipstream Dangers.
Music played by [London Symphony] Orchestra/John Hollingsworth
Notes
(i) Listed erroneously in the 1986 Faber catalogue as 'Two RAF Flashes' and 'Seven RAF Flashes'
(ii) The complete series was filmed at RAF Grimston during the summer of 1948

Charting the Seas (1948)

Production Realist Film Unit for the Central Office of Information/Admiralty
Archive BFI/IWM
Duration 23'
Synopsis The work of Britain's Admiralty Hydrographic Department.
Director Harold Lowenstein
Music played by [London Symphony] Orchestra/John Hollingsworth

Gates of Power (1948)

***Alt title* Stairway to the Sea**
Production Anglo-Scottish Films for the Central Office of Information/Board of Trade/GFD
Archive BFI
Duration 19' (music: 11')
Synopsis British achievements in hydro-electric power projects in Britain and New Zealand.
Director Anthony Squire
Narrator Robert Harris
Music played by London Symphony Orchestra/John Hollingsworth

Report on Steel (1948)

Production Data Film Productions for the Central Office of Information/Ministry of Supply
Archive BFI
Duration 10'
Synopsis The process of steel-making and how maximum output is being obtained.
Director and Editor Michael Orrom
Music played by [London Symphony] Orchestra]/John Hollingsworth
Notes In 1951 Arnold re-worked the music into his Symphonic Study 'Machines' for brass, percussion and strings Op.30

Mining Review (series) (1948)

Production Data Film Unit for the Central Office of Information and the National Coal Board
Archive BFI
Synopsis A series which covered the drive for increased pit production and mechanisation as well as social activities for miners and the need for health centres.
Director Michael Orrom
Music played by Orchestra/Malcolm Arnold
Notes We have not been able to ascertain whether Malcolm Arnold provided the title music for this long-running series, which ran from 1947 to the demise of the National Coal Board Film Unit in 1984 (after 420 editions), or whether he provided the soundtrack only to the 1948 series of monthly programmes. At its height the series was watched by 12 million people and distributed to over 700 cinemas nationwide, mostly in mining areas. The series producer was Donald Alexander.

Avalanche Patrol: Arnold's first commission

We owe it to Sidney Twinn, a violinist in the wartime LPO, for badgering the young Malcolm Arnold to send off a score or two to the Denham Film Studios. Apparently Muir Mathieson's assistant at Denham, John Hollingsworth, had been present at London's Royal Albert Hall in October 1943 for a Committee (later Society) for the Promotion of New Music concert at which Arnold had conducted his own Delian symphonic poem Larch Trees. Realising the strong cinematic language of this music, Hollingsworth suggested that Arnold should send some scores to Mathieson. In any event, it was a further three years or so before Arnold finally succumbed to Twinn's persistence and sent the score of Beckus the Dandipratt to the studio. The result was almost immediate: the first commission from the film studio to provide the musical soundtrack for the documentary film Avalanche Patrol.

In an article in *Movie Collector*, Vol. 1 Issue 5, April 1994, Arnold recalled: "I became involved in film scoring through John [Jack] Swain who was a very close friend[1]. Dear John [Hollingsworth] got me *Avalanche Patrol*, a film made by [this] one man, Jack Swain, a photographer who did his own editing – there's music all the way through ... no dialogue [either]. All it used to say on the poster was 'A Film by Jack Swain and Malcolm Arnold'. I thought I was made. I used to take my whole family and in-laws to see this film. It played to packed houses and it has to be the only documentary that made money apart from Auden's *Night Mail.*[2]"

A contemporary report of the film's release in 1948 (see right) reveals that Jack Swain was Producer and Director as well as Photographer, and that the 24-minute documentary had a soundtrack played by the London Symphony Orchestra conducted by John Hollingsworth. It was a considerable coup to engage the services of a major British orchestra and conductor to record the music for a documentary 'short' produced by a couple of relative unknowns in their mid-twenties. Swain, as Producer, would also have secured the services of Hugo Lehner[3] in the starring role of the Swiss mountain guide; in addition, Swain would probably have written the background commentary spoken by Howard [H.E.] Marion-Crawford.

UK distribution

The immediate popularity of the Swain/Arnold film following its release in early 1948 is borne out by a random survey within the columns of regional newspapers where they publicised the weekly programmes at their local cinemas. (During the post-war boom it was not unusual for each town to have two or more separate picture houses.)

For instance, in July 1948, the Radio Centre Cinema in East Grinstead, Sussex, announced the screening of the feature film *Mine Own Executioner*[4] with *Avalanche Patrol* as the 'supporting act'. The *Whitstable Times and Herne Bay Herald* of Saturday 13 November 1948 announced the presence of the 'star' performer "Hugo Lehner in *Avalanche Patrol*" beneath a poster of the Warner Bros production *Life with Father* starring Irene Dunne and William Powell. The *Leamington Spa Courier* of 11 February 1949 reviewing "the magnificent epic" *Caesar and Cleopatra* being screened at the Scala concluded with the news that the supporting film *Avalanche Patrol* is "a short which will appeal to all lovers of mountain scenery and sport".

1 Jack Swain (born John Earl Swain) cut his cinematic teeth while working as an (uncredited) film technician on the Orson Welles movie *Citizen Kane* in 1941. He later worked as a cinematographer and Director of Photography on many blockbuster TV series in the sixties, seventies and eighties, including *Rawhide*, *Cannon* and *T. J. Hooker*. Fess Parker of *Davy Crockett* fame remembers working with Jack Swain in the sixties on the NBC series *Daniel Boone*, describing him as "the best of cameramen". Swain was born in New York in August 1922 and died in California in July 1987, aged 64.

2 With music by Benjamin Britten.

3 Hugo Lehner (1900-1952) was a fine skier and won a bronze medal at the 1928 Winter Olympics in St Moritz as a member of the Swiss Biathlon team. Lehner also appeared as an actor in several famous mountaineering movies such as *Struggle for the Matterhorn* (1928) and *Mountains on Fire* (1931).

4 Music by Benjamin Frankel. In a lecture given in January 1962 Arnold made particular reference to this "heavily dramatic score" as being very good "even though I don't really enjoy writing harrowing things like this".

The KInema at St Leonard's, Hastings, :creened *Avalanche Patrol* for three days uring March 1949 as the supporting lm to Somerset Maughan's *The Moon nd Sixpence*. The following June at the incoln Savoy, *Avalanche Patrol* was aired somewhat incongruously with n Esther Williams/Peter Lawford musi-al (set in a swimming pool!) entitled *An land with You*; the local paper described ie supporting 'short' as showing "the ien who maintain the constant battle to ontrol avalanches in the Swiss Alps". If iat wasn't incentive enough, the article oncluded with the exciting news that iey would also be showing the film of ie Mills-Woodock fight!

The Swain/Arnold documentary had significant billing increase (bigger ont size!) when it was screened at the nperial Cinema, Newton Abbott, Devon, i November 1949, as the support film o *The Winslow Boy*; later in the same ionth at the Derby Cosmo ("The Cosy inema") the film had acquired a new ub-title 'Epic of the Snows'. Later, at he Oxted Plaza, Surrey, in May 1950, it ot only supported the Trevor Howard pic *Golden Salamander* (see below), but vas preceded by another documentary short' *Shadow of the Ruhr*, part of the :onic series 'This Modern Age', directed y Sergei Nolbandov.

Arnold himself contributed music to everal of these shorts including *Women i Our Time*, which was screened at the ellshill Picture, Motherwell, at the end f November 1949. In the meantime *valanche Patrol* was still doing the ounds in Festival of Britain year: for in-tance, the Falkirk Scientific Film Society resented a Charity Show in aid of oc H at the Regal Cinema on Sunday 23 eptember 1951. In addition to *Avalanche Patrol*, other documentaries presented vere *Killers of the Sea* and *Running Vild*. Reviews talked of the "outstand-ng" Arnold/Swain documentary which 'showed the important and exciting vork of the Avalanche patrol in the Alps" nd "thrilled the audience".

rom skiing to cricket

s a result of his earnings with *Avalanche atrol*, we know that Arnold and his vife were able to take a short holiday o Yugoslavia in the summer of 1948[5]. low with an increased confidence in his bility to produce a film score on demand nd on time, Arnold was soon offered is first feature film *Badger's Green*; the soundtrack was again performed by the London Symphony Orchestra conducted by John Hollingsworth. A second feature, *Britannia Mews*, followed shortly after-wards. Coincidentally, these two feature films were programmed together at the Scala, Leeds, as early as March 1949. Arnold's long journey as a film composer was now gathering pace and would span another two decades.

AVALANCHE PATROL

G.B. 1948. 35mm and 16mm. 24 mins.

Producer .... Jack Swain
Director .... Jack Swain
Photography by .... Jack Swain
Music composed by .... Malcolm Arnold
Played by the London Symphony Orchestra
conducted by John Hollingsworth.
Commentator .... H.E.Marion-Crawford
The Guide .... Hugo Lehner

A straightforward documentary on the work of the Swiss Avalanche Patrol during the great spring thaw, when the avalanches have to be broken up before they reach dangerous proportions, trains have to be averted from impending disaster, overhanging cornices of ice and snow dispersed by explosives, trapped people rescued. The treatment is competent, the background photogenic.

A contemporary record of the film

The search for *Avalanche Patrol*

Unfortunately, the British Film Institute does not hold a copy of the film, and the archives of the London Symphony Orchestra have nothing pertaining to their recording of the soundtrack in 1947 or, indeed, any orchestral parts/scores. Other avenues I have pursued to no avail over the last ten years or so have includ-ed the Swiss Film Archives in Lausanne and the Motion Picture National Archives in Maryland, USA. A contact at NBC/ Universal advised: "We do not show this title in any of our rights or archive data-bases ... maybe Universal only distributed it and did not own it." This would seem to be correct, as Jack Swain was, as we have determined earlier, both the film's Producer and Director – the creative force behind the film. With the excep-tion of the musical soundtrack, it was Swain's film from start to finish. We can only hope that this unique piece of cinematic history will turn up one day on eBay or Amazon in either 16mm or 35mm format; it would be fascinating to hear Arnold's 24-minute score played by a full orchestra. In the meantime I am pursu-ing another line of enquiry through the archives of John Hollingsworth, who died in 1963.

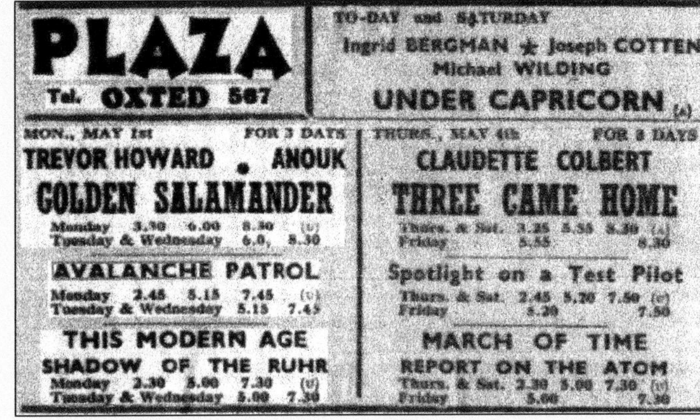

Postscript

Just as I was putting this article to bed I discovered through the BBC's Genome Project that *Avalanche Patrol* had made two appearances on BBC Television! The first transmission was on 16 August 1962 and it was repeated on 27 September 1963.

The synopsis in *Radio Times* read: "A film from France (sic) on the part played by a famous guide in saving lives threatened by avalanches in the Alps – commentary spoken by Howard Marion-Crawford." It is possible therefore that a tape of either transmission still exists; however I must point out that the BBC were quick to 'wipe' tapes once used or to record another programme over the original; this is one reason why we are not able to view the original performanc-es of Arnold's *The Open Window*, *Parasol* or *The Turtle Drum*, all commissioned by BBC Television and transmitted in the sixties!

ALAN POULTON

; Paul Harris and Anthony Meredith, *ogue Genius*.

Every Drop to Drink (1948)

***Alt title* Hydrography**
Production World Wide Pictures for Metropolitan Water Board/ British Lion
Archive BFI
Duration 20' (music: 7')
Synopsis The story of London's water supply.
Director Mary Francis
Narrator Frederick Allan
Music played by [London Symphony] Orchestra/John Hollingsworth

Queen o' the Border (1948)

***Alt title* Hawick Weaving**
Production Crown Film Unit for the Central Office of Information/Board of Trade/Hawick Hosiery Manufacturers Association
Archive BFI/SSA
Duration 10' (music: 7')
Synopsis Report on the town of Hawick and its weaving industry.
Director Martin Wilson
Music played by [London Symphony] Orchestra/John Hollingsworth

Women in Our Time (1948)

'This Modern Age' series No.22
Production J. Arthur Rank Organisation
Archive HFA
Duration 20' (music: 19')
Synopsis The role of women in Britain – their achievements and activities since their emancipation, their role in World War II and the struggle for equal pay.
Series Producer Sergei Nolbandov
Series Associate Producer and Literary Editor James L Hodson
Music played by London Symphony Orchestra/Muir Mathieson (?)
Notes
(i) The John Huntley Film Archive have the soundtrack on 78 rpm discs only
(ii) First televised transmission: 18 February 1949 (a BBC Sound Archive Recording)

Lancashire's Time for Adventure (1948)

'This Modern Age' series No.23
***Alt title* Cotton**
Production J. Arthur Rank Organisation
Archive BFI
Duration 20' (music: 20')
Synopsis The cotton industry in Britain, its present state, the reasons for its decline and possible ways of improving it.

Charting the Seas (1948)

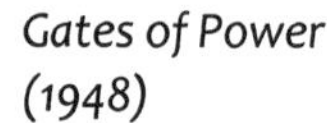

Gates of Power (1948)

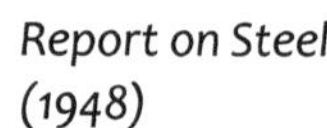

Report on Steel (1948)

John Hollingsworth

John Hollingsworth (1916-1963) [see photo page 10], was a prominent conductor in the concert hall, the ballet and opera theatre, and the film studio. He was Sir Malcolm Sargent's assistant conductor at the Proms, where he conducted over 60 times.

He did much to encourage Arnold to write for film, and conducted many of Arnold's film scores, including his first documentary *Avalanche Patrol* (1947) and his first feature film *Badger's Green* (1948). He also made one of the first recordings of Arnold's *Tam O'Shanter* Overture [with the Royal Philharmonic Orchestra (EP) Philips NBE 11038 (9/56); (LP) Philips NBL 5021 (1958)].

He died suddenly of pneumonia in London in 1963, aged only 47.

The Struggle for Oil (1949)

'This Modern Age' series No.25
Production J. Arthur Rank Organisation
Archive BFI
Duration 20' (music:20')
Synopsis The importance of oil and the history of its use in the modern world, showing the Middle-East oil companies and their development.
Music played by London Symphony Orchestra/Muir Mathieson

European Volunteer Workers (EVWs) (1949)

***Alt title* Code Name: Westward Ho!**
Production Data Film Unit for the Central Office of Information/Ministry of Labour (1949)
Duration 30'
Synopsis Two volunteer workers arrive in Britain and settle down as a miner and a cotton worker.
Director Mary Beales
Music played by [London Symphony] Orchestra/John Hollingsworth
First televised transmission BBC Television 1 September 1949 (repeated 25 October 1949)

This Farming Business (1949)

Production Greenpark Productions for the Central Office of Information
Archive BFI
Synopsis The story of an unsuccessful farmer who seeks help and advice from the National Agricultural Advisory Office.
Music played by [London Symphony] Orchestra/John Hollingsworth

The Frasers of Cabot Cove (1949)

***Alt title* An Island Story**
Production Greenpark Productions for the Central Office of Information/ Commonwealth Relations Office
Archive LAC
Duration 38'
Synopsis The love story of Mary Fraser of Cabot Cove grafted on to a realistic picture of daily and seasonal life in Newfoundland.
Director Humphrey Swingler
Editor John Trumper
Commentary writer John Sommerfeld, from his own story 'An Island Story'
Music played by [London Symphony] Orchestra/John Hollingsworth
Notes
(i) The roles of Mary and Tom Fraser were played by Eileen Shea and Tony Grace
(ii) The film was reviewed in 'Kine', 25 August 1949

Drums for a Holiday (1949)

Production Anglo-Scottish Films/British Lion for Cadbury and the Gold Coast Cocoa Bean Industry
Archive BFI
Duration 36'
Synopsis A film set on the Gold Coast (Ghana), including a record of the 1946 Ashanti Durbar at Kumase.
Director A R Taylor
Music played by Orchestra/James Walker

Magic Electrons: Terra Incognita (1949)

Production Verity Films
Archive BFI
Duration 28'
Synopsis How the electron microscope works and its application in various fields.
Music played by Orchestra/Malcolm Arnold

The Fair County of Ayr (1949)

***Alt title* The Beautiful County of Ayr**
Production Anglo-Scottish Films/British Lion
Archive SSA
Duration 33' (music: 17')
Synopsis General views of the County of Ayr including its farming and fisheries industries as well as a look at Burns country with its leisure activities.
Director Charles Heath
Commentary writer James Burke
Narrator James McKechnie
Music played by Philharmonia Orchestra/ James Walker
Notes
(i) Some of the music was later incorporated into the second movement of the Four Scottish Dances Op.59
(ii) See main article 'The Fair County of Ayr: the Scottish music sources' on the next page.

Dollars and Sense (1949)

Production Crown Film Unit for the Central Office of Information and the Economic Information Unit
Archive BFI
Duration 11' (music: 7')
Director Diana Pine
Synopsis An explanation as to what is involved in the devaluation of sterling.
Music played by [London Symphony] Orchestra/John Hollingsworth

Fight for a Fuller Life (1949)

'This Modern Age' series No.30
Production J. Arthur Rank Organisation
Archive BFI
Duration 20' (music: 20')
Synopsis The facilities available in Britain for further education, the variety of trades taught, and the problems raised by the greatly increased demand.

Trieste: Problem City (1949)

'This Modern Age' series No.32
Production J. Arthur Rank Organisation
Archive BFI
Duration 20' (music: 20')
Synopsis Report on the state of Trieste and the surrounding free territory, and the three alternative forms of government which might enhance her future prosperity.

When you went away (1949)

'This Modern Age' series No.33
Production J. Arthur Rank Organisation
Archive BFI/HFA
Duration 20' (music: 17')
Synopsis The increased tendency of the British population towards longer holidays and its consequent effect on post-war leisure patterns.

The Riddle of Japan (1949)

'This Modern Age' series No.35
Production J. Arthur Rank Organisation
Archive BFI/IWM
Duration 20' (music: 20')
Synopsis Post-war industrial development in Japan and the attempts by the occupying American forces to establish a democratic political system.

Where Britain Stands (1950)

'This Modern Age' series No.36
Production J. Arthur Rank Organisation
Archive BFI
Duration 20' (music: 20')
Synopsis Economic and social achievement in post-war Britain as the April 1950 general election approached.

The Fair County of Ayr: the Scottish music sources

The *Scotsman* of 12 July 1949 announced an ambitious exhibition representing "the past, present and future planning of Ayrshire [which] will be housed in the County Hall and two committee rooms... The special section for visitors will deal with Burns interests, the domestic architecture of the county, ancient monuments, scenic beauty and famous people... A special feature on the opening day will be a film 'The Fair County of Ayr' made by Anglo-Scottish Pictures Ltd, London, whose general manager Mr Eugene Andrews was the producer. Mr Andrews belongs to Girvan and was thus dealing with his native shire. The script was written by James Barke, the novelist, whose home is at Pinwherry in South Ayrshire, and the music has been arranged from old Scottish airs by a young composer, Malcolm Arnold. The commentary will be spoken by James McKechnie, the radio and film actor. The exhibition will cost £1,200 and the film £400. By these outlays it is hoped to draw attention to Ayrshire's tourist and industrial attractions, and to stimulate interest in planning among the people at home."

The intriguing reference to Arnold's arrangements of "old Scottish airs" was finally solved following a recent visit to the Eton College Library. Among the miscellaneous manuscripts were several A3 pages of numbered sketches consisting of a single line of music; these were not in Arnold's hand but had written notes above and below each tune. A quick glance through revealed that these sketches were the blueprint for the documentary film 'The Fair County of Ayr'.

The first of these sketches [*Andante*, Ex.1] was marked "suggest for Mains [title] that the 'snap' be removed – the count[r]y shots are smooth and a long line will give the right feeling". The second, marked "Brisk" [Ex.2] has the suggestion "can be used in variations for Trout fishing and most scenery"; there is an even more detailed description of the second half of the tune: "one sheep running about" (for which it is indeed used in the film!). The third sketch, again marked "Brisk" [Ex.3], was immediately more familiar: this was the tune Arnold recycled in the second movement of his Four Scottish Dances Op.59 and was a 1796 tune (to words by Robert Burns) entitled 'We'll Gang Nae Mair to Yon Town'. Described on the manuscript as

rather a cod this" and with the sugges-
on that the tune might be used for shots
f a "housing scheme", it did eventually
ppear (albeit briefly) in a cattle market
cene! Finally, there is a fourth tune,
lively Jig [Ex.4] for which "Industrial
nots" are suggested: "[These] can be
orked up as shots intensify" (as they
id, most effectively, on the soundtrack).
wo other suggested tunes were written
ut, one of which was 'Sweet Afton', but
either was used in the final cut.

So who was Arnold's provider of
nese Ayrshire tunes and written instruc-
ons as to their use? I believe that the
nost likely person was the conductor of
ne film's soundtrack, James Walker, per-
aps with a contribution from the film's
roducer, Eugene Andrews, as to context
an example, rare in Arnold's film career,
f the adage "He who pays the piper calls
ne tune". Not that this prevented Arnold
om contributing his own stamp on the
oundtrack: the very opening of the film
and several other occasions too) is domi-
ated by a brief fanfare-like motif played
n trumpets and trombones [Ex.5]. At
rst hearing, this motif appears to be un-
elated to any of the tunes suggested by
ames Walker, but closer examination of
ars 10-11 of the *Andante* tune in Example
reveals its possible source. Later on,
uring some shots of a housing scheme,
he motif is slowed down and extended
nto an Elgarian march [Ex.6] reminiscent
f the one Arnold wrote for the scene
utside the Houses of Parliament in his
961 film score for 'No Love for Johnnie'
listen out too for the brassy horse-racing
nusic which Arnold would reuse seven
ears later in the film 'Trapeze').

The *Scotsman* of 1 August 1949
reviewed the film, which was shown on
aturday 30 July:

"The film deals competently with the
ounty's varied assets – historical and
cenic, food producing and manufactur-
ng. The famous dairy breed of cattle ... is
iven its due place but it is fishing which
teals the film ... the majesty of Ailsa
raig is seen in several close-ups. The
ommentary, by James Barke, is perhaps
ver-romantic. It might occasionally be, if
ot factual, at least more matter-of-fact
but] it is excellently spoken by James
AcKechnie. The music by Malcolm Arnold
nd including arrangements of Ayrshire
unes is outstandingly good. It fits the
nood and theme throughout and car-
ies the interest where the camera has
agged. It is hoped that the film, which
as been accepted for viewing at the
nternational Film Festival in Edinburgh,

Music examples © Malcolm Arnold Estate

will be shown abroad."

The film was shown again on the opening day of the Exhibition (3 August 1949) in the presence of the Under-Secretary of State for Scotland, Mr J J Robertson.

The *Scotsman* of 19 August 1949 reported: "Scotland's representation [at the International Film Festival] is disappointingly small. 'Queen of the Border', a ten-minute sketch of Hawick [music also composed by Malcolm Arnold], 'Harnessing the Hills', an interim report on the work of the North of Scotland Hydro-Electricity Board, and 'The Fair County of Ayr' are, however, to be included on one of the morning programmes at the Monseigneur News Theatre."

After its showing on 30 August 1949, the reporter in the *Scotsman* suggested: "The best thing about 'The Fair County of Ayr' – apart from the subject – is the musical accompaniment, witty and appropriate and a pleasure to listen to."

The following month the *Falkirk Herald* reported: "In another edition of the Scottish radio film magazine 'Screentime' to be broadcast on 28 September 1949, the music feature this month will be centred on the film 'The Fair County of Ayr', which was produced by the Ayr Borough Council for their recent exhibition, the music to which created a most favourable impression on the critics."

Clearly the Ayrshire film was to make quite an impact. Under the headline 'Following Ayr's Example' the *Scotsman* of 18 January 1950 announced:

"Since the making of 'The Fair County of Ayr' … shown at the Edinburgh Festival, a number of county councils in Scotland have been toying with the idea of following Ayr's example. It was thanks to the vision of the Ayr County Council that the film – which was trade shown here last week and is being distributed commercially shortly – was made. A representative of the Anglo-Scottish Documentary Unit has been in Scotland to discuss with various civic authorities the possibility of making further films of that nature … what is making the prospect more attractive is the recent decision of the 1951 Festival of Britain authorities to include in their own 'film festival' a number of films from Local Authorities … depicting the British way of life. Many of these will be shown at the Festival's cinema on the South Bank site and a showing there would be an ideal way of displaying Scotland's tourist attractions."

One of the first to take up the challenge was Perth. Under the headline 'Perth Seeks Screen Fame', the *Dundee Evening Telegraph* of 7 June 1950 reported: "The Council have discussed the question of producing a propaganda film of the city and shire to encourage the tourist trade. Recently they saw a film entitled 'The Fair County of Ayr'. Now the matter has been taken up with the Scottish Tourist Board … and it is expected that the Lord Provost of Edinburgh will call a meeting of local authorities to discuss filming possibilities."

In the meantime, Ayr's film went on nationwide distribution as the 'documentary interest' before the main feature in such far-flung places as Sevenoaks (August 1950), Gosport (September 1950), Edinburgh (December 1950) and Birmingham (January 1951) (see right).

ALAN POULTON

Music examples prepared by Franck Leprince; and reproduced with the kind permission of Katherine Arnold and the Malcolm Arnold Estate and the Provost and Fellows of Eton College.

Thurs., Aug. 24, for 3 days
Robert Donat in
CURE FOR LOVE
Thurs. and Sat. 3.24, 5.54, 8.26
Fri. 5.54, 8.26 (U)
Documentary Interest
THE FAIR COUNTY OF AYR
Thurs. & Sat. 2.30, 5.0, 7.32 (U)
Fri. 5.0, 7.32

[illegible]
DOUGLAS FAIRBANKS Jnr., GLENIS JOHNS—in
STATE SECRET
[illegible] — also
FAIR COUNTY OF AYR (u).
LAST COMPLETE SHOW AT — [illegible]

REGAL (A.B.C.) Open 12.30.
STERLING HAYDEN, LOUIS CALHERN, JEAN HAGEN, in "THE ASPHALT JUNGLE" (A.) At 2.10, 5.25, and 8.45 p.m.
HEDY LAMARR, JOHN HODIAK, JAMES CRAIG, in "A LADY WITHOUT PASSPORT" (A.) At 2.45, 3.55, and 7.10 p.m.
And PATHE NEWS.
Café Open 10.30 a.m. till 9.0 p.m.

THE NEW, 56 PRINCES STREET.
Open 1.30 p.m.
Joseph Cotten, Linda Darnell, Jeff Chandler, Cornel Wilde, "TWO FLAGS WEST" (U.)
1.55, 4.15, 6.40, 9.05.
"FAIR COUNTY OF AYR" (U.)
Outstanding Interest.

CINEMAS

SCALA—TODAY: Jennifer Jones. David Farrar in "GONE TO EARTH" (A) in Technicolor. Also "FAIR COUNTY OF AYR" (U).

ODEON, New Street—Cont. 10 a.m. Clifton Webb, "FOR HEAVEN'S SAKE" (a); "I Killed Geronimo" (u); This Modern Age — Fight in Malaya (u)

Science in the Orchestra (1950)

A series of three film 'shorts'
Production Realist Film Unit for the Central Office of Information/Ministry of Education
Archive BFI/HFA
Duration 12' each
Synopsis Designed as the scientific counterpart of the 1946 film 'Instruments of the Orchestra' where the music was provided by Benjamin Britten. The titles of the three films are: 1. Hearing the Orchestra 2. Exploring the Instruments 3. Looking at Sounds.
Director Alex Strasser
Editor Gwen Baillie
Music played by London Symphony Orchestra/Muir Mathieson
Notes
(i) This series of three films won First Prize in the Music Section of the Venice International Film Festival in 1951.
(ii) It was repeated several times on BBC Television between 1951 and 1953 as part of an Educational Newsreel 'For the Children'; the first transmission was on 24 January 1951.

'Oil Review' series: No.5 (1950)

Production Greenpark Productions
Archive BFI
Duration 9' each
Music played by [London Symphony] Orchestra/John Hollingsworth
Notes A total of eighteen 'Oil Reviews' were issued between 1950 and 1953.

Ideas at Work (1950)

***Alt title* ECA Productivity Team**
Production Crown Film Unit for the Economic Co-operation Administration (USA)
Synopsis Illustrations on how ideas are being applied in British industry.

Fifty Acres (1950)

Production Greenpark Productions for the British Electrical Development Association
Archive BFI
Duration 18'
Synopsis Dramatised account of the beneficial effects of electrical machinery on the farm.
Director Peter Plaskitt
Editor Joe Mendoza
Commentary writer Joe Black

Music played by Orchestra/John Hollingsworth
Notes See *Beckus* No.37 for a fuller account of Joe Mendoza's association with Malcolm Arnold during the early fifties.

Airways (series Nos. 1-3) (1950)

Production John Marvel Productions
Archive BFI
Synopsis A series of three training 'shorts' for the Aviation industry; the titles of the three films are: 1. Standard Beam Approach 2. Airport Control 3. Area Control.
Music played by [London Symphony] Orchestra/John Hollingsworth

This is Britain (series) (1950)

Production Crown Film Unit/Merlin Films for the Central Office of Information/ Board of Trade
Archive BFI
Duration approx. 9–11' each
Music played by [London Symphony] Orchestra/John Hollingsworth
Notes A series of documentaries about Britain in the 1940s and 1950s for which Arnold may well have provided the title music – the series producer was Michael Hankinson.

Alien Orders (1950)

***Alt title* Malaya**
Production Crown Film Unit for the Central Office of Information/Foreign Office and Commonwealth Relations Office
Archive BFI/CFA
Duration 11'
Synopsis The film's summariser explains: "The scene of the film is Malaya at a key point in the struggle in the East for which Britain is, of course, primarily responsible."
Music played by [London Symphony] Orchestra/John Hollingsworth
Notes There is an extensive analysis of this film by Tom Rice (February 2010) on the Colonial Film Archives website.

Power for All (1950)

'The Changing Face of Europe' series No.1

Production Wessex Film Productions for the Economic Co-Operation Administration (USA)
Archive BFI/IWM
Duration 20' (music: 20')
Synopsis the building of hydro-electric power schemes in Italy and Austria as well as other forms of power generation in other European nations.
Directors Anthony Squire and Graham Wallace
Narrators Leo Genn and Jacques Brunius
Music played by Orchestra/Malcolm Arnold
Note The six-part series had an alternative title 'Grand Design Progress Report from Europe' – the Series Producer was Ian Dalrymple

Men and Machines (1950)

'The Changing Face of Europe' series No.4

***Alt title* Industry**
Production Wessex Films for the Economic Co-Operation Administration
Archive IWM
Duration approx. 20'
Synopsis Comprehensive study of industry from individual craft skills to mass production in the machine age.
Director Diana Pine
Narrators Leo Genn and Jacques Brunius
Music played by Orchestra/Malcolm Arnold

Farming Review No.1 (1950)

Production Greenpark Productions/Film Producer's Guild for Harry Ferguson
Archive BFI
Synopsis Examples of mechanisation aiding modern agriculture compared with primitive methods still used in South East China.
Director Joe Mendoza
Notes Mendoza recalls Arnold's 'March of the Little Tin Tractors' in an article in *Beckus* No.37. The detailed synopsis of this documentary also happens to mention "a Staffordshire farmer with 400 acres [who] works them with four tractors".

Antony and Cleopatra (1951)

Parthian Productions/Young America Films
Duration 33'
Music played by Philharmonia Orchestra/ Malcolm Arnold
Notes See also 'Julius Caesar' below.

Julius Caesar (1951)

Parthian Productions/Young America Films
Duration 33'
Music played by Philharmonia Orchestra/ Malcolm Arnold
Note The two drama-documentaries 'Antony and Cleopatra' and 'Julius Caesar' were adapted (condensed) from the original Shakespeare plays and were aimed at high school students in America as a supplement to a study of Shakespearean plays in theatre and drama classes. [The sale price of the film in 1951 was $117.50.] A narrator was used to supply the transitions of time and place which aided the interpretation of the important scenes; these starred Pauline Letts and Robert Speaight, as well as Cecil Trouncer (in 'Julius Caesar').

Local Newspaper (1952)

Production Crown Film Unit for Central Office of Information/ Foreign, Commonwealth Relations and Colonial Offices
Archive BFI/FI/IWM
Duration 17' (music: 6')
Synopsis The story of the *Newbury Weekly News* and the work undertaken by its reporter and editor, its printing and distribution.
Music played by [London Symphony] Orchestra/John Hollingsworth

Channel Islands (1952)

Production British Transport Films for British Transport Commission
Archive BFI/HFA
Duration 20' (music: 14')
Synopsis A look at the various places and activities of the Channel Islands.

This British Transport Films/BFI DVD includes 'Channel islands' (1952)

Director Michael Orrom
Music played by Orchestra/Malcolm Arnold
Notes DVD available from British Transport Films or BFI.

The Island (1952)

***Alt title* Kent Oil Refinery**
Production Data Film Productions for the Anglo-Iranian Oil Company
Archive BFI
Duration 25' (music: 7')
Synopsis The construction of the BP oil refinery and port on the Isle of Grain in Kent.
Directors and commentary writers Peter Pickering and John Ingram
Music played by [London Symphony] Orchestra/John Hollingsworth

Copenhagen, City of Towers (1952)

Production Seven League Productions (Loew's Incorporated/MGM) for Fitzpatrick Traveltalk
Duration 9' (music: 9')
Synopsis The beauty of Copenhagen, including the fish market and the Tivoli Gardens.
Director Hans M. Nieter
Narrator Richard Ainley
Notes Music of various composers arranged by Malcolm Arnold.

Warm Welcome (1952)

Production Greenpark Productions for Anglo-Iranian Oil Company/Film Producers Guild
Duration 10'
Synopsis A report on the American liner *United States* docking at Southampton after securing the Blue Riband for the fastest trans-Atlantic crossing.
Director Joe Mendoza
Producer Humphrey Swingler
Notes According to Joe Mendoza, he is convinced that Malcolm Arnold provided the soundtrack to this documentary.

Man of Africa (1953)

***Original title* Soil Erosion**
***Alt title* Kigezi Story**
Production Group Three/British Lion
Archive BFI/CFA
Duration 84'
Synopsis The dramatisation of the Bakiga people's migration to cultivate the Kigezi District of Uganda and their encounter and relations with the Pygmies they found there.
Director Cyril Frankel
Commentary writer Montagu Slater, with Anthony Steven, from an original story by Cyril Frankel.
Editor Alvin Bailey
Narrator Gordon Heath
Music played by Orchestra/Malcolm Arnold
Notes
(i) In the 1980s the BFI invited Cyril Frankel for a Q&A after its screening as part of a series entitled 'Projecting the Archive'.
(ii) It was also a featured film in the 30th Regus London Film Festival during November-December 1986.
(iii) In this drama-documentary the part of Jonathan was played by Frederick Bijurenda and that of his girlfriend Violet by Violet Mukabureza.
(iv) There is an extensive analysis of the film by Tom Rice (October 2009) on the Colonial Films Archive website.

Powered Flight: the Story of the Century (1953)

Production Shell Film Unit for Shell Petroleum and the Royal Aeronautical Society
Archive BFI/HFA/IWM
Duration 54'
Synopsis A review of progress in powered flight; the pioneers and their classic flights and Britain's contribution to their development.
Director Stuart Legg
Editor Ralph Sheldon
Music played by Orchestra/Malcolm Arnold
Notes Documentary based on original research for the Royal Aeronautical Society by Adrian de Potier; the film was first televised on BBC2, 23 March 1972.

Major Farming (1953)

Production Verity Films/Film Producers Guild for the Ford Motor Company
Archive BFI
Director Joe Mendoza
Notes We have not been able to verify that Malcolm Arnold was the composer of the soundtrack.

This Pathe DVD includes 'Welcome the Queen!' (1954)

Royal Tour – New Zealand (1954)

'The Royal Tour' series No.3

Production Pathe Documentary Unit for Associated British Pathé
Archive BrP
Duration 29' (music: 25')
Synopsis Highlights of the Royal Tour in New Zealand.
Series Producer Howard Thomas
Editor Lionel Hoare
Commentary writer John Pudney
Narrator Edward Ward
Music played by Orchestra/Muir Mathieson

Welcome the Queen! (1954)

Production Pathe Documentary Unit for Associated British Pathé
Archive BFI/BrP
Duration 46' (music: 21')
Synopsis A lengthy report on the newly-crowned Queen Elizabeth II on her tour of the Commonwealth States including Jamaica, Fiji, Australia, Sri Lanka and Uganda.
Producer Thomas Howard
Editor Lionel Hoare
Commentary writer John Pudney
Narrator Edward Ward
Music played by Orchestra/Muir Mathieson
Notes Written in conjunction with Sir Arthur Bliss who composed the title music, the March 'Welcome the Queen!'.

Var in the Air

ee under 'Arnold on the Small Screen' next page).

.et Go For'ard! (1955)

roduction Esso Film Unit for Esso Petroleum
rchive BFI/CW
uration 20' (music: 20')
ynopsis The search for oil reserves and the way of life of those who worked on the tankers during the hey-day of the oil industry's expansion, pre-North Sea oil.
irector Geoffrey Gurrin
Ausic played by Orchestra/Malcolm Arnold

Roses Tattoo (1956)

roduction Anglo-Scottish Pictures for Cadbury
rchive BFI
Ausic played by Orchestra/James Walker
Notes
i) Not be confused with the contemporary feature film 'The Rose Tattoo' starring Burt Lancaster and Anna Magnani with music by Alex North.
ii) It is probable that the correct title for this documentary is in fact 'Roses All the Way', an advertisement for Cadbury's chocolate and produced by Anglo-Scottish Pictures. The latter had been responsible, along with Malcolm Arnold who wrote the music and James Walker who was the conductor, for providing the soundtrack to another Cadbury film in 1949 'Drums for a Holiday' (qv).

Coupe des Alpes (1958)

Production Shell Film Unit for Shell Petroleum
Archive BFI/HFA/SFA
Duration 36'
Synopsis The story of the 1958 Alpine Cup competed for by the world's greatest rally car drivers including Pat Moss, the sister of Stirling Moss, and her co-driver Ann Wisdom, the winners of the Ladies' competition. In all, 56 production cars from eight countries struggled to maintain a set average speed over the 2,400-mile course – only seven finished.
Director John Armstrong
Music played by Orchestra/Malcolm Arnold
Notes Also used as a BBC2 Trade Test Film in the sixties – it was first shown on 5 November 1962 and finally on 7 November 1968. It was one of the longest trade test films at 36 minutes duration.

North Sea Strike (1968)

Production Gerald Holdsworth Productions for the Esso Petroleum Company
Archive BFI/CW
Duration 20' (music: 15')
Synopsis A retrospective survey of North Sea gas and oil exploration as seen from the viewpoint of one of the participating oil groups.
Director Don Kelly
Music played by Orchestra/Malcolm Arnold
Notes The film was updated and reissued with the same title in 1972.

Divertimento (1968)

Divertimento (1968)

***Alt title* Oil under the Microscope**
Production Verity Films/Film Producers Guild for the British Petroleum Company
Archive BPFA
Duration 7' (music: 7')
Synopsis Filming oil through a microscope and other optical devices: the weird and colourful world revealed is set to the music of Arnold's 1952 Divertimento for flute, oboe and clarinet Op.37.
Series *Producer* Seafield Head
Director David Cons
Notes The film was one of a series of 20 from BP used on BBC2 Television as a trade test colour film. It was first shown on 29 December 1969 and finally on 20 August 1973.
The film is available to view at the BP Video Library www.bpvideolibrary.com/record/446

NEL Offshore News (1975)

Production National Engineering Laboratory for the Central Office of Information/Department of Industry
Synopsis A magazine programme illustrating how the National Engineering Laboratory is assisting the Offshore Industry in problem solving.
Series *Producer* Howard Thomas
Director K. R. Offord
Script Robin Crichton
Notes Frank Chacksfield composed part of the soundtrack.

Arnold on the small screen

This list includes the music Arnold wrote for the small screen (television documentaries and various television series/dramas) as well as his occasional personal appearances in several 'tribute' programmes celebrating the lives of, among others, Gerard Hoffnung, Margot Fonteyn, Constant Lambert – and himself.

The film and television archives which hold these titles are shown as follows:
BFI British Film Institute
IWM Imperial War Museum

The Dancing Master (1952)

One-act opera for Granada Television (Op.34)

The original intention was for the opera's first performance to be televised by Granada. The commissioning producer was Denis Foreman, who also financed the cost of the composer producing a vocal score.

There is evidence that a 39-page mock-up storyboard with graphics and a 58-page camera script was created by Joe Mendoza as well as a demo tape featuring six soloists from Sadler's Wells Opera with piano accompaniment, conducted by Marcus Dods. However, the project fell through, because the opera was felt to be "too bawdy for family audiences".[1]

Libretto Joe Mendoza after the play by William Wycherley
Duration 65'
Instrumentation 1+picc./2/2/2 - 4/3/3/1 - timp.perc.cel.hp.str.
First staged performance (with piano) Barnes Music Club, March 1962.
First broadcast performance (concert performance) soloists/BBC National Orchestra of Wales/James Holmes, Broadcasting House, BBC Wales, Cardiff, 25-26 May 2006 (for broadcast on BBC Radio 3's *Composer of the Week*, 16-20 October 2006)
First public performance (semi-staged) soloists/Ealing Symphony Orchestra/ John Gibbons, Royal & Derngate, Northampton, 20 October 2012 (Seventh Malcolm Arnold Festival)
First public performance (fully-staged) soloists/Orchestra of Guildhall School of Music and Drama/Dominic Wheeler, Silk Street Theatre, Barbican Centre, London, 2-9 March 2015
First recording soloists/BBC Concert Orchestra/John Andrews. Resonus Music RES 10269 (2020).

1 See also *Maestro* No.1, p.15 ('Malcolm Arnold and me' by Joe Mendoza); *Beckus* No.101, p.8 ('Up at the Villa – Appendix 1. The four Arnold operas').

War in the Air (1954-55)

BBC Television Service with the Air Ministry

There were a total of 15 films in this series which ran from November 1954 to February 1955. The Series Director was Philip Doreté (then Head of Television Films at the BBC), who, writing an explanatory note to Squadron Leader Gerald Bowman's book 'War in the Air' (Pub: Evans Brothers Ltd, London), tells us that the series was commissioned as a result of the success of the United States Navy Department/Admiralty with their series of films 'Victory at Sea': "They generously invited the BBC to televise them and the public clamoured for a British television film series 'Victory in the Air'. With government support the production was launched: this took almost two years and nearly 12 million feet of Allied and enemy film were viewed to illustrate the story." Doreté concludes with the news: "The film series had been shown three times by the BBC [as well as] in Canada, Belgium and Switzerland and that it will shortly appear on the American Television screens."

The episodes (with transmission dates) scored by Malcolm Arnold were:
No.1. The Fated Sky (8 November 1954)
No.4. Maximum Effort (29 November 1954)
No.10. Operation Overlord (10 January 1955)

Instrumentation (for 'The Fated Sky') 2/1/2/1 - 4/3/3/1 - timp. perc. str.
Director and commentary writer John Elliot
Series advisor Air Chief Marshal Sir Philip Joubert
Music played by London Symphony Orchestra/Muir Mathieson
Archive IWM
Notes
(i) The full score of 'The Fated Sky' is held by the BBC Music Library (MS 1383)
(ii) The complete series is available on DVD EAN 5019322327264 (UK)

Right: the 1956 book by Gerald Bowman produced by arrangement with the BBC; the DVD; a letter from film editor Jim Pople to Malcolm Arnold, 8 December 1996.

Fanfare for ABC Television (1956)

Written for the launch of the ABC Television Network in 1956

Duration 30"
Music played by Orchestra/Muir Mathieson
Notes See *Beckus* No.96 for more details about this Fanfare.

'What the Papers Say' (1956)

Granada Television series

Presenter Brian Inglis (though Kingsley Martin also presented the programme in the early stages of the format)
First transmission ITV, London and the North West, 5 November 1956
Notes
(i) The original music was 'The Procession of the Sardar' by Mikhail Ippolitov-Ivanov, but it was replaced by Arnold's **English Dance No.5** (No.1 from his Second Set of English Dances Op.33).
(ii) Arnold's music was retained despite a later switch of the format to BBC2 in May 1990 and its eventual revival (after being dropped from the BBC's schedules in 2008) on BBC Radio 4 in April 2010, where it continued until 27 March 2016

The Open Window (1956)

One-act opera for BBC Television (Op.56)

Libretto Sidney Gilliat after a short story by Saki (H. H. Munro)
Duration 21'30"
Instrumentation Fl.Cl.Bsn.Hn.2Vn.Va.Vc. Db.Perc.Hp.
Director George Fox
Designer Richard Wilmot
First transmission English Opera Group Orchestra/Lionel Salter, BBC Television, 14 December 1956 (Principals: Ethel Lyon, John Carolan, June Bronhill, Flora Nielsen, Niven Miller and David Oddie)
Publisher Novello (vocal and full scores)

Notes The opera has received two separate performances at the Third (2008) and Ninth (2014) Arnold Festivals

Kneller Hall Centenary Concert (1957)

BBC Television

An Open Air Concert given at Kneller Hall, Twickenham, Middlesex, as part of the school's Centenary celebrations and transmitted live from the event. The concert included the first performance of Arnold's **March: The Duke of Cambridge** Op.60, specially written for the occasion and played by the Band of the Royal Military School of Music conducted by Lt. Col. David McBain.

Introduced by Franklin Engelmann
First transmission BBC Television, 26 May 1957

Royal Prologue: Crown and Commonwealth (1957)

BBC Television Christmas special

Commissioned by the BBC
Written by Christopher Hassall.
Producer Rex Moorfoot
Duration 31'
Instrumentation 1/1/2/0 - 1/2/1/0 - timp. perc. hp. pno. str.
Music played by Trumpeters of the Royal Military School of Music*/Royal Philharmonic Orchestra/Malcolm Arnold, with Sir William McKie (Organ) and Sir Laurence Olivier (Narrator). (*in the first performance of **'A Richmond Fanfare'** conducted by Lt Col David McBain)
First transmission BBC Television, 25 December 1957

The National Youth Orchestra of Great Britain in Concert (1958)

ITV

A concert given in Birmingham Town Hall by the National Youth Orchestra of Great Britain conducted by Malcolm Arnold on 4 January 1958. The concert included Bach's Double Violin Concerto and Tchaikovsky's 'Romeo and Juliet', as well as Arnold's **Second Symphony** – see *Beckus* No.110, pp 10-14.

First transmission ITV, 5 January 1958 (and later broadcast on the BBC Home Service, 13 January 1958 in their 'Music to Remember' series)

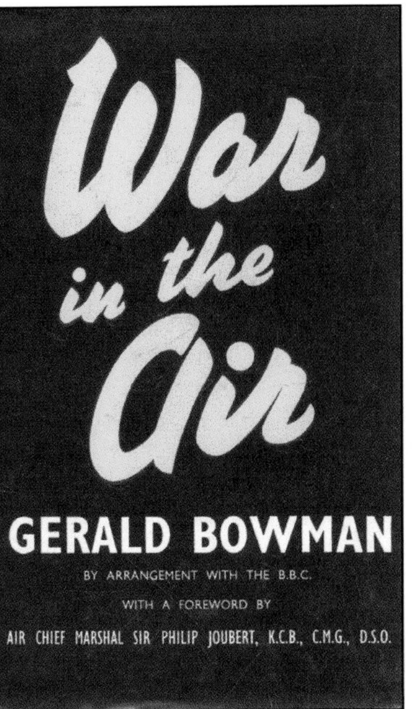

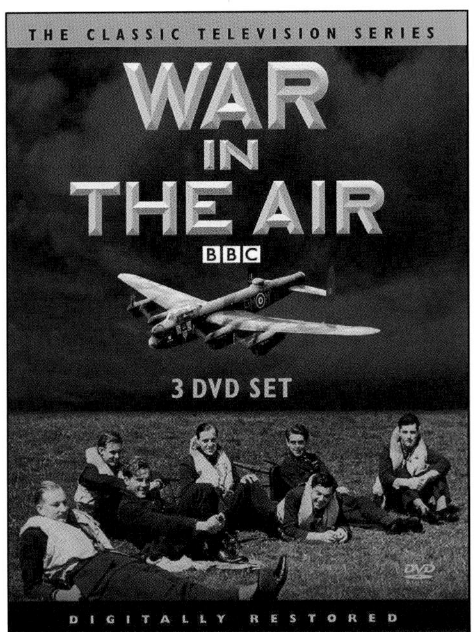

"Lyme House"
Pound Street
Lyme Regis
DORSET DT7 3JA
Tel:01297 444746

Sir Malcolm Arnold
c/o Conifer Records Ltd:
Horton Road,
WEST DRAYTON,
Middx: UB7 8JL.

Dear Sir Malcolm

You may have long forgotten 1954 and the BBC series "War In The Air"

I was the film editor on Films One and Four and so we met preparing Shot Lists for Bar Sheets- long before the days of time coded VHS cassettes!

One of my last tasks in 1955 before "defecting" to ITV was to "break down" the 35mm: magnetic tracks to salvage the "white spacing" in between 1M1 and 1M2 etc: I thought it would be a pity to lose all of this forever and so I put together much of the music from all 15 films into an 80 minute compilation, for my own pleasure and had a ¼" tape copy made. I subsequently learned that even those original reels that I left behind were later junked at the BBC.

I have recently found this tape again, 42 years on, and although the quality is not perfect, I have taken the opportunity of copying what remains of your music for Films 1,4 and 10 on to the enclosed cassette.

I suspect that this may now be the only surviving "clean" record of all that music. Antony Hopkins, John Veale, William Alwyn, Roberto Gerhard, Clifton Parker and, of course, yourself.

I have always enjoyed your music from those days onward, and having a fair amount on disc, I reckon that I am always able to recognise those brass chords!

Anyhow, I hope this will be of interest and may I add my own congratulations for your 75th: Anniversary.

Yours most sincerely,

Jim Pople

J.C.S.POPLE 8th: December 1996.

Concert Piece for percussion (3 players) (1958)

BBC Television

Originally written for BBC Television; the score is dated 1 June 1958
Duration 4'
Instrumentation Pno.Timp.Perc.(3 players)
Publisher Faber, 1984
Notes
(i) The original title of this piece is open to question as it is now clear that James Blades did not take part in the television première! It is possible that the piece was included in a series of programmes for schools entitled 'Music Makers', No.6 Percussion, first transmitted on 28 October 1960, but I have not been able to verify this. The presenter was Richard Evans and the producer John Hosier, with two (of the three) percussionists named as Patricia Brady and David Johnson.
(ii) James Blades did however re-arrange the piece (with some cuts to the score) the following year so that he might include the work as part of his lecture tours and gave it the title: **'Concert Piece for percussion and piano'** (1961). It was later dedicated to James Blades by the composer.
Duration 4'15"
Instrumentation Pno.Timp. Perc. (1 or 2 players)
First performance James Blades (Perc.)/ Joan Goossens (Pno.), Grendon Hall, Northants, 6 December 1961 (another source cites an earlier date of 17 December 1959 but this would predate the BBC Television series above)
First broadcast performance Above artists, BBC Music Programme, 30 December 1966
First recording Above artists, Discourses ABK 13
Publisher Faber, 1984
Notes See *Beckus* No.110, pp 8-10, for an article on James Blades and an essay on the Concert Piece written by Evelyn Glennie.

A-Z: Letter 'A' (1958)

BBC Television series

The first in a series of weekly programmes taking in the world of entertainment presented by Alan Melville and based on an idea by Wolf Mankowitz. Among the participants were Eamonn Andrews, Adrianne Allen and Larry Adler, with Gerald Moore representing accompanists and Malcolm Arnold*, composers.

Producer Bryan Sears
Designer Tony Abbott
Choreography Beryl Kaye
Music played by Studio Orchestra/Eric Robinson
First transmission BBC Television, 15 October 1958
*Notes** Arnold's recording of his **English Dance No.5** (No.1 from Set 2 Op.33) with the Philharmonia Orchestra was played 'live' in the studio (and probably danced to the choreography of 'Solitaire').

Music for You (1958)

Signature tune for BBC Television series

Duration 2'30"
Instrumentation 2 + picc./2/2/2 + cbsn. - 4/3/3/1 - timp. perc. hp. str.
First transmission Eric Robinson Orchestra/ Eric Robinson, BBC Television, 22 March 1959 (first transmission using Arnold's tune)

The Ivor Novello Awards (1959)

BBC Television special

Live broadcast of the 1958 Ivor Novello Awards held at the BBC Television Theatre and introduced by Christopher Hassall. The Song Writers Guild of Great Britain awarded Malcolm Arnold for his film score to **'The Inn of the Sixth Happiness'**. The composer conducted the BBC Concert Orchestra in a performance of the film's main theme during the ceremony.

Producer Francis Essex
First transmission BBC Television, 25 May 1959
Notes This concert was later given a radio broadcast on the General Overseas Service on 15 February 1960 and repeated on the Home Service on 25 March 1963.

Parasol (1960)

BBC Television musical

Commissioned for BBC Television by Eric Maschwitz, Head of Television Light Entertainment. Book and lyrics were by Caryl Brahms and Ned Sherrin, based on the 'Anatol' dialogues by Arthur Schnitzler. The musical numbers include: 1. Only a Parasol 2. The Face of Love 3. A Woman would be lost without a Man 3. Goodbye Champagne 4. Sleep 5. Who do I love? 6. The Other One? 7. Don't think it hasn't been fun.

Duration 75'
Producer Ned Sherrin
Designer Clifford Hatts
Costumes Angela Flanders
Principals William Hutt, Hy Hazell, Pip Hinton, Peter Sallis, Irene Hamilton, Moira Redmond
Music played by Eric Robinson Orchestra/ Marcus Dods
Musical numbers staged by Alfred Rodrigues
First transmission 20 March 1960 (pre-recorded 18 March 1960)
Publisher B. Feldman & Co, 1961 (vocal selections)
Notes
(i) See the articles in *Beckus* Nos.104 and 105 for a full account of the musical, and again in *Beckus* No.106 for an article on the first concert performance given at Wymondham College conducted by Ian Hytch in May 1987. Excerpts from the rehearsal and subsequent performance were filmed for later transmission on BBC2.
(ii) The full autograph score is untraced but the piano reduction and some orchestral parts are held by the BBC Music Library. The complete score wa restored by Ian Hytch for the first con cert performance, under the guidance of the composer.

Music for Films: 1. Music and Atmosphere (1962

BBC Television series

First in a three-part series of Schools Programmes on the important contribution of music to heighten the atmosphere and action in a film. The music examples played were from Virgil Thomson's 'Louisiana Story' and Aaron Copland's 'The Red Pony', as well as from Arnold's **'Sound Barrier' Rhapsody** (Columbia EP SED 5542) and the Opening Sequence to the film **'Hobson's Choice'**.

Producers John Hosier and Margaret Ross Williamson
Introduced by John Huntley (of the British Film Institute)
First transmission BBC Television, 2 and 3 May 1962 (pre-recorded on 29 March 1962

Music for Films: 2. Music and Action (1962)

BBC Television series

Second in the three-part series, in which John Huntley shows how Sir William Walton's music to the battle charge in nry V' was built up. Then Malcolm old, in conversation with Huntley, ws how he sets about planning his film res – this was illustrated with specially rranged music (for chamber quintet) sequence from **'Hobson's Choice'** and ne footage from the original film. The gramme concluded with a brief extract m the soundtrack to **'The Bridge on the er Kwai'** (Philips BBE 12194).

t transmission BBC Television, 9 and 10 May 1962 (pre-recorded 2 April and 8 May 1962)

sic for Films: The Film Composer at Work 62)

C Television series

he third part of this series, Malcolm old, with a chamber orchestra in studio, shows how he fits the music the picture in a recording session. chamber orchestra of ten players s conducted by Malcolm Arnold in Opening Sequence from **'Hobson's oice'** in an arrangement made specially the programme by the composer. er, in conversation with John Huntley, discusses the music he has written for t films including **'The Bridge on the er Kwai'**. Footage from other Arnold ns include **'The Angry Silence'**, **'Whistle wn the Wind'** and **'The Inspector'**, and rief sequence of Malcolm Arnold at the no talking about 'Colonel Bogey' and own 'River Kwai' March. The pro- mme concluded with an extract from Wayfarers' recording of the theme m 'Whistle Down the Wind' (Decca 370).

st transmission BBC Television 16 and 17 May 1962 (pre-recorded 3 April and 15 May 1962)

t Ahead (1962)

eme for the BBC Television series

ducer Innes Lloyd
tings Lionel Radford
itor Peter Pierce
senter Peter West
tes
The final was relayed from the Carlton Rooms, Maida Vale, London, on 24 May 1962
The signature tune (theme) was Arnold's **English Dance No.4** from the first set of English Dances Op.27

Monitor No.103 (1962)

BBC Television series

A fortnightly magazine arts programme with its distinctive signature tune the opening of Dag Wiren's 'Serenade for strings'. The opening item in this programme was an interview/discussion conducted by Malcolm Arnold with François Baschet of Les Structures Sonores (a group of five players). In the Transmitted Programme as Broadcast summary kindly provided by the archivist at BBC Caversham we are told: "This group plays unique instruments made from metal sheets, glass rods, plastic balloons etc. The interview was all about these instruments and the music they produce, and illustrations were played."

Editor Humphrey Burton
Producers Nancy Thomas and David Jones
Introduced by Huw Weldon
First transmission BBC Television, 23 December 1962
Notes
(i) In a review of the programme in the 'Show Gossip' columns of the *Newcastle Evening Chronicle*, 29 December 1962, they reported: "'Monitor' presented a fascinating musical programme by a French group of musicians who performed on instruments that look like something from an exhibition of abstract art. Stroking glass rods produced what Malcolm Arnold described as 'a marvellous noise'. I liked his left-handed compliment when he said, 'You can play tunes,' and to prove it the group played a Bach minuet which Arnold enthusiastically said had a Gothic sound 'like a baroque organ in a large cathedral'. I couldn't help feeling that the conventional instruments produce equally good music with less distraction on the eye. But I'm all for the experimental and I enjoyed the programme, but I wonder what the purist and the stern music critic thought of it."
(ii) The programme also included a performance of 'A Child's Christmas in Wales' by Dylan Thomas, a film shot from still photographs about Christmas in a Welsh village in which Thomas himself reads the poem and a caption sequence depicting Giotto's frescoes in the Arena Chapel in Padua with narration, based on the Golden Legend, read by Anthony Jacobs.

Espionage on DVD

Espionage (1963)

ATV series

Arnold contributed music to 14 episodes as well as the title/end music of this series which was first transmitted on 2 October 1963:

- Main Title, Bumper and End Title [1'40"]
- Covenant with Death (recorded 29 August 1963) [13']
- The Weakling [music: 20']
- The Gentle Spies [5']
- He Rises on Sunday and We on Monday [17']
- The Dragon Slayer [10']
- To the Very End [15'30"]
- The Light of a Friendly Star (recorded 24 October 1963) [15']
- A Tiny Drop of Poison [17']
- Festival of Pawns [19']
- Never Turn your Back on a Friend [13'30"]
- Medal for a Turned Coat [10']
- Final Decision [original title: Sentence of Death]
- Do you Remember Leo Winters? [5']
- A Camel to Ride (recorded 24 October 1963) [16']

Music played by Studio Orchestra/Malcolm Arnold
Executive Producer Herbert Hirschman
Notes The complete series is available on DVD EAN 5027626279745 (UK)

Gala Performance: Richard Attenborough, Julian Bream and Malcolm Arnold

Gala Performance (1963)

Opening and closing titles for BBC Television series

Duration 1'30"
Instrumentation 2/2/2/2 - 4/2/3/1 - timp. perc.(2) hp. gtr. str.
Producer Patricia Foy
Designer Clifford Hatts
Presenter Richard Attenborough
First transmission Philharmonia Orchestra/ Malcolm Arnold, BBC Television, 19 November 1963 (pre-recorded 27 October 1963)
Notes
(i) The concert included a performance of the final movement from Arnold's **Guitar Concerto** played by Julian Bream, excerpts from Tchaikovsky's 'Swan Lake' and Khachaturian's 'Gayaneh' ballets, and operatic arias performed by Joan Sutherland and Geraint Evans.
(ii) Arnold also conducted the Philharmonia Orchestra in a subsequent edition of the programme, televised on 10 December 1963, in which Julian Bream played an excerpt from Rodrigo's 'Concerto de Aranjuez'.
(iii) A revised version of the Opening and Closing titles was recorded on 2 October 1964 and transmitted for the first time on 23 October 1964.

The Royal Ballet in Rehearsal: Electra (1963)

A 'behind-the-scenes' film of the dress rehearsal of Arnold's complete ballet **'Electra'** plus some sections repeated in medium shot.

Choreographer Robert Helpmann
Scenery and costumes Arthur Boyd
Music played by Orchestra of the Royal Opera House, Covent Garden/John Lanchberry
Principals Nadia Nerina, David Blair, Monica Mason, Derek Rencher
Archive BFI

Monitor: The New Generation 1964 (1964)

BBC Television series

An outside broadcast from the Whitechapel Art Gallery, illustrated with excerpts from Arnold's **Guitar Concerto** and introduced by Huw Wheldon.
First transmission BBC1, 26 April 1964

Workshop: In Search of Constant Lambert (1965)

BBC Television

A portrait of Constant Lambert and his music by his friends and colleagues, researched by Rhona Shaw. Arnold appeared in the programme alongside, among others, Michael Ayrton and Frederick Ashton.

Executive producer Humphrey Burton
Writer and Director Barrie Gavin
Narrator and Interviewer Francis Coleman
First transmission BBC2 Television, 26 July 1965 (repeated 15 October 1967; the programme was again repeated on 5 September 1976 to mark the 25th anniversary of Lambert's death)
Archive BFI

Theme for 'Players' (1965)

Written for John Player Tobacco as a TV advertising theme – it was not used.

Duration 45"
Notes Later revised by Alan Poulton (in conjunction with the composer) for whistler and piano as: **'Thème pour mon Amis'** (1984) at the request of John Amis (hence the punning title) for performance on the BBC Televisio programme 'My Music'.
Duration 70"
First performance John Amis (whistler)/ Steve Race (Pno.), BBC2 Television, 19 December 1985 ('My Music' Christmas programme)
First recording John Amis (whistler)/ Penelope Thwaites (Pno.), Nimbus NI 5342 (CD)

Music on Two: The New York Brass Quintet (1966)

BBC Television series

A programme about the New York Brass Quintet's revival of brass music and new commissions. It concluded with a perform ance of two movements from Arnold's **Brass Quintet** Op.73 (a work they had premièred in New York some five years earlier).
First transmission BBC2 , 17 January 1966

The Turtle Drum (1967)

A children's play for BBC Television (Op.92

Commissioned by BBC Television for their opening programme of the series 'Makin Music'. Libretto by Ian Serrailleu: 1.The Turtle Drum 2. Go Back Where You Belong 3. Round of Welcome 4. Divertissement o the Deep 5. The Four Seasons 6. Sayonara Song.

Alt title Kaisoo the Fisher Boy
Duration 50'
Instrumentation Fl/Picc. Tpt. Gtr.(s) Perc. Db.
First performance Chamber Ensemble (pupils of the David Livingstone Primary School Thornton Heath, Surrey) with James Blades (percussion), BBC Television, 26 April 1967
Series Producer John Hosier
Director Moyra Gambleton
Publisher OUP, 1968; Faber Music, 1986
Notes Manuscript held by the BBC Music Library (MS 11595)

Chuck Connors and Tom Nardini in 'Cowboy in Africa' (1967)

owboy in Africa (1967-68)

eme music for the American TV series

e success of the feature film **'Africa: xas Style!'** (1967) (qv), led to this spin-f TV series starring Chuck Connors, plus m Nardini, Ronald Howard and Gerald lwards (all of whom appeared in all episodes between 1967-68). Arnold's eme was derived from the music he rote for 'Africa, Texas Style!' entitled wahili Serenade' and was used for the st 16 episodes. The musical soundtrack as composed by George Bruns (10 epi-des) and Harry Sukman (6 episodes).

ries producer Ralph Helfer (whose ranch at Soledad Canyon Road, Acton, in California was used as the filming location)
ecutive producers/writers Andy White and Ivan Tors (both of whom had been involved in the earlier feature film as Screenplay Writer and Producer respectively)
rector Andrew Marton (first 4 episodes)
rst transmission 11 September 1967 (USA) and 22 June 1971 (West Germany)

.U.C. 1868-1968 (1968)

BC Television

concert from the Royal Festival Hall, ondon, to mark the centenary of the ades Union Congress. Among those king part were Yehudi Menuhin (in the ruch Violin Concerto), Sir Adrian Boult, tanley Pope and Malcolm Arnold, the st conducting the Royal Philharmonic rchestra in the first performance of s specially commissioned overture **'eterloo'** Op.97, on the theme of the great working-class demonstration in St Peter's Field, Manchester, on 16 August 1819.

Director Brian Large
Introduced by Richard Baker
First transmission BBC1, 9 June 1968 (a recording of the concert held on 7 June 1968)

The First Lady (1968)

Opening and closing titles for BBC Television series

This mini-series created by Philip Levene consisted of 39 episodes in two parts. It starred Thora Hird as a crusading local councillor in the fictional borough of Furness in Lancashire and explored the inner workings of local government.

Duration 2'
Instrumentation 0/0/0/0 - 0/3/3/1 - perc.(2) cel. hp.(2) + SATB chorus
Series Producer David E. Rose
Directors David Sullivan Proudfoot and Brian Parker
Series written by Alan Plater, Cyril Abraham and Robert Storey
First transmission 7 April 1968 (the last episode was televised on 17 July 1969)
Music played by Studio Orchestra/conductor not traced (probably Marcus Dods)
Notes
(i) At the end of the series Arnold's theme was used in an arrangement for brass band by Ronnie Hazlehurst
(ii) Arnold's original score is held by the BBC Music Library (MS 8675)
(iii) The original master tapes were wiped, so only one episode is available. The hunt is on: see the website tvbrain.info

Omnibus: Malcolm Arnold (1969)

BBC Television series

Filmed on the northern coast of Cornwall in and around Padstow, where John Amis talks to Malcolm Arnold about his life and music. Among the excerpts were several film soundtracks as well as concert works such as the **Four Cornish Dances, Peterloo, Tam o'Shanter**, the **Guitar Concerto** (with Julian Bream) and the **Padstow Lifeboat March**. It also included a rare televised excerpt from the Truro Cathedral concert 'A Salute to Thomas Merritt' held on 16 March 1968.

Producer Herbert Chappell
First transmission BBC1, 2 March 1969

Omnibus: Margot Fonteyn: Birthday of a Ballerina (1969)

BBC Television series

A 50th birthday tribute to the great ballerina including excerpts from many of the ballets which made her famous. Among the conductors were John Lanchbery, Marcus Dods and Malcolm Arnold (probably in an extract from his Coronation ballet of 1953 **'Homage to the Queen'**).

Introduced by James Mossman
Producer Patricia Foy
First transmission BBC Television, 18 May 1969

The Public Purse: 8. A Penny for Your Arts (1970)

BBC Television series

A series focussing on the Government's spending plans. This programme asked the question: "If the government did not subsidise the arts, most of them would vanish and we would be reduced to a state of barbarism. But is this a good enough reason to expect government subsidy? If so, who gets the money and who benefits as a result?" Among those taking part were the Rt Hon Jennie Lee (Minister for the Arts), Hardie Ratcliffe (General Secretary of the Musicians' Union) and Malcolm Arnold.

Series Advisor Samuel Brittan
Producer Richard Hooper
Director Joy Curtiss
Presenter Alan Peacock
First transmission BBC2, 3 March 1970

Best of Both Worlds: Jon Lord's Concerto for Group and Orchestra (1970)

BBC Television series

Director Andy Finney
First transmission Deep Purple/Royal Philharmonic Orchestra/Malcolm Arnold, BBC Television, 4 April 1970 (a concert recorded at the Royal Albert Hall, London on 24 September 1969)
Notes
(i) This performance is available on DVD EAN 0724349294196 (US)
(ii) An excerpt from this performance was included on the soundtrack to the 1973 French film 'The Mother and the Whore' directed by Jean Eustache.
(iii) The first half of the concert included a performance of Arnold's Sixth

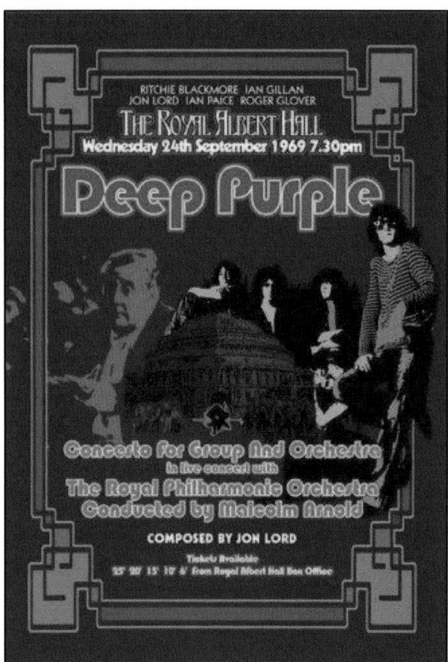

Best of Both Worlds: The first performance of Jon Lord's Concerto for Group and Orchestra

Symphony, the RPO conducted by the composer.

Music Now: Arnold's Viola Concerto (1972)

BBC Television series

A programme in which John Amis visits the Northern Sinfonia, in Carlisle and Newcastle-upon-Tyne, with Malcolm Arnold directing and rehearsing the orchestra in the première of his **Viola Concerto** Op.108 with Roger Best as soloist.

Directors Roy Tipping and Denis Moriarty
Introduced by John Amis
First transmission BBC2, 9 January 1972

William Walton Seventieth Birthday Concert (1972)

BBC Television

Arnold's contribution was **'Popular Birthday'**, a one minute tribute dedicated to Walton "with homage and every expression of friendship" – it quotes Walton's own 'Popular Song' from 'Façade'.

Instrumentation 1+2 picc./2/2/2 - 4/3/3/1 - timp. perc.(2) hp.str.
First transmission London Symphony Orchestra/Malcolm Arnold, BBC 1, 28 March 1972 (simultaneous broadcast on Radio 3 direct from the Royal Festival Hall, London)
Notes Other tributes were composed by Richard Rodney Bennett, Thea Musgrave, Robert Simpson, Peter Maxwell Davies and Nicholas Maw.

Walton at 70 (1972)

BBC Television

An affectionate tribute to Sir William Walton on his 70th birthday with excerpts from 'Façade' and the Guitar Bagatelles played by Julian Bream. Among the other composers who contributed were Hans Werner Henze, André Previn and Malcolm Williamson. Arnold rearranged his orchestral tribute **'Popular Birthday'** for a chamber group of eight players* which was played live on the programme.

Director Roy Tipping
Introduced by John Amis
First transmission Nash Ensemble/Marcus Dods – BBC 2, 29 March 1972
Notes *Flute, Piano, String Quartet and 2 Percussion.

Election Forum (1974)

Theme music for the BBC Television series

Producer Christopher Capon
Director Mike Catherwood
Presenter Ludovic Kennedy
First transmission probably October 1974 (in advance of the General Election held on 10 October 1974)
Archive BFI
Notes
(i) Among the interviewees were Harold Wilson and Edward Heath.
(ii) An extract from Arnold's **Brass Quintet No.1** was used as the programme's theme music.

Omnibus: Two Lives in Music (1976)

BBC Television series

1. 'The first 70 years are the worst, or what it takes to be a composer' – a portrait of Elisabeth Lutyens
2. Horn Player – a profile of Barry Tuckwell

Executive producer Barrie Gavin
Directors Peter West [1] and Rodney Greenberg [2]
First transmission BBC1 Television, 9 December 1976
Archive BFI
Notes The Barry Tuckwell Quintet played part of Arnold's **Brass Quintet No.1**

The Lively Arts in Performance: Hear Hear, Hoffnung (1976)

BBC Television series

In this portrait of Gerard Hoffnung the BBC Concert Orchestra is conducted by, among others, Lawrence Leonard, Simon Rattle and Malcolm Arnold. This was part of a recording of a Hoffnung Concert given in the Royal Albert Hall, London, in December 1976.

Director Ian Englemann
Introduced by Robin Ray
First transmission BBC1 Television, 18 December 1976
Archive BFI
Notes Probably the earliest BBC televised performance of an Arnold work was from the Hoffnung Festival of 1956, namely, the première of his **'Grand, Grand Overture'** Op.57 with Dennis Brain (organ) and the Morley College Symphony Orchestra conducted by the composer at the Royal Festival Hall, London, on 13 November 1956.

Hard Times (1977)

Theme music for the ITV series

A mini-series in 4 episodes, based on the novel by Charles Dickens, adapted for television by Arthur Hopcraft. The series, which starred Patrick Allen, Timothy West, Edward Fox and Rosalie Crutchley, won three awards at the 1978 BAFTAs.

Instrumentation 3 Fl. Ca. 2 Hn. 3 Tpt. 3 Tbn. Timp. Perc.
Producer Peter Eckersley
Director John Irvin
Music played by Ensemble/Marcus Dods
First transmission Granada Television, 25 October 1977 (later transmitted on WNET Channel 13 in New York)
Notes
(i) The theme is an arrangement by Marcus Dods of the 'Cavatina' from the **Little Suite for Brass Band** Op.93
(ii) The series is available on DVD EAN 5027626303440 (UK)

Roots of England (1978-81)

BBC Television series

A series of 12 documentary films, in two series of six, "in which English families and their communities still look remarkably different from each other".
Series 1 (September–October 1978):
1. Whitby, North Yorkshire 2. The Black Country 3. Houghton, Lancashire

Hard Times on DVD

ʾortland, Dorset 5. Washington, rthumberland 6. Kersey, Suffolk; ies 2 (September 1980–March 1981): ɛoman Road, Bow 2. Saddleworth 3. St t-in-Penwith, Cornwall 4. Hull 5. Guiting wer, Glos. 6. Cambridge.

ector John C. Miller
senter Brian Trueman
:hive BFI
tes
Arnold's **Cornish Dance No.1** was used in Series 2 No.3. The synopsis reads: "Streams of summer visitors come to this Western tip of England but few linger in the collection of granite mining villages where the firm local view is that 'this is Cornwall, not England'. Brian Trueman discovers that optimism about the tin mine is tempered by memories of a harsh past and by a fierce debate about the area's priorities for the future."
A piano solo transcription of the Cornish Dance No.1 was later published by Chester Music (the arranger was not credited).

A. in Music: 4. Classical Music 982)

C Television series

is was an innovative magazine proamme where B.A. Robertson, the ottish singer/songwriter, introduced "a e night show with conversation and mu". The second item in this particular proamme was a short interview "with Dr alcolm Arnold CBE and B.A. Robertson cussing his oscar (sic) awards for comsing for films and a short biography of his composing career".

Producer Frances Whitaker
Director Philip Chilvers
First transmission BBC1, 9 August 1982
Notes Other items in the programme included B.A. Robertson playing Chopin's Prelude No.4 in E minor and an interview with Christopher Warren-Green, the newly appointed leader of the Philharmonia Orchestra, as well as a spoof performance of the song 'Bang-Bang' in the style of Gilbert and Sullivan performed by B.A. Robertson and members of the D'Oyly Carte.

Sheridan Morley Meets ... Malcolm Arnold (1984)

BBC (East) Television series

"An interview with the Northampton-born composer and Oscar winner (who) wrote the music for 'The Bridge on the River Kwai' in ten days. Filmed on location in Norfolk around Oulton Water and the Parish Church where Arnold's great-grand-father is buried."

Producer Mike Purton
Editor Karen Heward (the daughter of the conductor Leslie Heward who was much admired by Malcolm Arnold)
First transmission BBC2, 6 December 1984 (recorded 20-22 February 1984)

Spitting Image (1984-85)

BBC Television series

Arnold's **English Dance No.5** (No.1 from Set 2 Op.33) was used in three episodes: 1 April and 15 April 1984 (from Series 1) and 24 February 1985 (from Series 2).

Folio (1986)

Anglia Television arts programme

This programme featured excerpts from a 65th Birthday Concert for Malcolm Arnold held at the Blackfriars Hall, Norwich, on 9 November 1986. It included Arnold conducted a rare performance of his **'Song of Freedom'** Op.109. Taking part were the Norwich Brewery Youth Brass Band and the Hewett Junior School Choir.

First transmission Anglia Television, 24 November 1986

An Act of Friendship (1989)

Central Television, 'Contrasts' series

A programme about the commissioning, rehearsal and first performance of the **Brass Quintet No.2** Op.132 given by the Fine Arts Brass Ensemble at the Cheltenham Festival in July 1988.

Director Terry Bryan
First transmission 7 February 1989
Note I had first spoken to Fine Arts Brass about a second Brass Quintet as long ago as May 1984 when they played the first Quintet at a Wigmore Hall concert in the presence of the composer and members of his family. – AP

Live from the Proms (1989)

BBC Television

A concert from the Royal Albert Hall, London, commemorating the 50th Anniversary of the outbreak of the Second World War and featuring works by Britten (Sinfonia da Requiem Op.20) and Mahler (Symphony No.7), the City of Birmingham Symphony Orchestra conducted by Simon Rattle. During the interval, John Tusa interviewed key eye-witnesses – Malcolm Arnold, Moura Lympany, Steve Race and Dame Eva Turner – who recounted their individual struggles to maintain a public musical life, despite the bombs which had destroyed the Queen's Hall and forced the BBC Symphony Orchestra to evacuate to Bristol.

Executive Producer Kenneth Corden
Directors Barrie Gavin (Concert) and David Stevens (Interval Talk)
Introduced by John Tusa
First transmission BBC2, 3 September 1989 (in a simultaneous broadcast with Radio 3)

Notes from Norfolk: A Portrait of Malcolm Arnold (1990)

Anglia Television, 'Folio' series

Duration 25'
Director Richard Fawkes
Interviewer Anne Gregg
Notes A copy of the interview is likely to be held in the East Anglian Film Archives at the University of East Anglia, Norwich.

Rick Stein's Taste of the Sea on VHS

Omnibus: Arnold at 70 (1991)

BBC Television series

This 70th birthday tribute included an excerpt from the closing pages of Arnold's Ninth Symphony conducted by the composer.

Producer Kriss Rusmanis
Editor Andrew Snell
First transmission 11 October 1991
Notes Kriss Rusmanis gave a talk on Arnold's music and, in particular, his 'Omnibus' film at the Eleventh (2016) Arnold Festival.

He Just Writes the Music (?) (c.1992-3)

BBC East (?) production

Narrator Sheridan Morley (?)
Notes The programme ends with the closing pages of the **Ninth Symphony**, possibly taken from the 'Omnibus' recording of October 1991.

Rick Stein's Taste of the Sea (1995)

Theme music for the BBC [Bristol] Television series

A series of six 30-minute programmes in which seafood chef Rick Stein shared some of his culinary secrets.

Director David Pritchard
Presenter Rick Stein
First transmission BBC2 Television, 12 September 1995
Notes
(i) Rick Stein chose Arnold's **Cornish Dance No.1** for his theme music; he had known Arnold when he lived near Padstow.
(ii) The series was available on VHS tape.

Simon Rattle (1998)

BBC Television

Duration 2'
First transmission BBC News, 23 February 1998 (and repeated in a BBC Arts programme on 6 February 2015)
Note Report of a successful 'record-breaking' attempt by Simon Rattle at a 'Music for Youth' concert in Symphony Hall, Birmingham, during which he rehearsed and conducted 3,503 schoolchildren in a performance of Arnold's **Little Suite No.2**, with the composer in the audience.
An earlier attempt by Simon Rattle on the BBC's 'Record Breakers' programme on 21 October 1996 (Arnold's 75th birthday) had been disallowed by the organisers of the *Guinness Book of Records* as the piece of music chosen was too short – under 5 minutes in duration – because the orchestra had played it too fast!
There is a BBC Arts video clip at www.bbc.co.uk/programmes/p02jc0hr

'Toward the Unknown Region' on DVD

The South Bank Show: Toward the Unknown Region: Malcolm Arnold – A Story of Survival (2004)

Documentary for London Weekend Television

Commissioned by Melvyn Bragg and the South Bank Show in a co-promotion with Isolde Films and RTE, this two-part film on the life and music of Malcolm Arnold includes extracts from some of his many films and concert works plus an interview with the 83-year-old composer himself.

Co-producer Simon van der Borgh
Director Tony Palmer
Introduced by Melvyn Bragg
First transmission London Weekend Television, 26 September (Part 1) and 3 October 2004 (Part 2)
Notes A DVD was released in January 2010: EAN 9781844497966 (UK)

Malcolm Arnold (c.2005-06)

Spanish Television production

A programme featuring short excerpts from the films of Malcolm Arnold interspersed with pithy comments from the composer himself. According to Anthony Day, it was the last TV interview Arnold ever did.

Alphabetical lists

List of feature films

1984 (1956)

Africa: Texas Style (1967)
A Hill in Korea (1956)
Albert R.N. (1953)
A Prize of Gold (1955)

Badger's Green (1949)
Beautiful Stranger (1954)
Blue Murder at St Trinian's (1957)
Britannia Mews (1949)

Curtain Up (1952)

David Copperfield (1970)
Devil on Horseback (1954)
Dunkirk (1958)

Four Sided Triangle (1953)

Hobson's Choice (1954)
Home at Seven (1952)
Home to Danger (1951)
I am a Camera (1955)
Invitation to the Dance (1956) [rejected]
Island in the Sun (1957)
It Started in Paradise (1952)

Nine Hours to Rama (1963)
No Highway (1951)
No Love for Johnnie (1961)

On the Fiddle (1961)

Port Afrique (1956)

Sky West and Crooked (1966)
Solomon and Sheba (1959) [part/uncredited]
Stolen Face (1952)
Suddenly Last Summer (1959) [part]

Tamahine (1963)
The Angry Silence (1960)
The Astonished Heart (1950) [arranger/uncredited]
The Barretts of Wimpole Street (1957) [rejected]
The Battle of Britain (1969) [part/uncredited]
The Belles of St Trinian's (1954)
The Boy and the Bridge (1959)
The Bridge on the River Kwai (1957)
The Captain's Paradise (1953)
The Chalk Garden (1964)
The Constant Husband (1955)
The Deep Blue Sea (1955)
The Great St Trinian's Train Robbery (1966)
The Heroes of Telemark (1965)
The Holly and the Ivy (1952)
The Inn of the Sixth Happiness (1958)
The Inspector (1962)
The Key (1958)
The Lion (1962)
The Night My Number Came Up (1955)
The Pure Hell of St Trinian's (1960)
The Reckoning (1970)
The Ringer (1952)
The Roots of Heaven (1958)
The Sea Shall Not Have Them (1954)
The Sleeping Tiger (1954)
The Sound Barrier (1952)
The Story of Gilbert and Sullivan (1953) [arranger/uncredited]
The Thin Red Line (1964)
The Wildcats of St Trinian's (1980)
The Woman for Joe (1955)
Tiger in the Smoke (1956)
Trapeze (1956)
Tunes of Glory (1960)

Up for the Cup (1950) [part/uncredited]

Value for Money (1955)

Whistle down the Wind (1961)
Wicked as They Come (1956)
Wings of Danger (1952)

You Know What Sailors Are (1954)
Your Witness (1950)

List of documentaries

Accident Prevention Concerns You (1948)
Airways (series Nos. 1-3) (1950)
Alien Orders (1950)
Antony and Cleopatra (1951)
Avalanche Patrol (1947)

Channel Islands (1952)
Charting the Seas (1948)
Copenhagen, City of Towers (1952)
Coupe des Alpes (1958)

Divertimento (1968)
Dollars and Sense (1949)
Drums for a Holiday (1949)

European Volunteer Workers (EVWs) (1949)
Every Drop to Drink (1948)

Farming Review No.1 (1950)
Fifty Acres (1950)
Fight for a Fuller Life (1949)

Gates of Power (1948)

Ideas at Work (1950)

Julius Caesar (1951)

Lancashire's Time for Adventure (1948)
Let Go For'ard! (1955)
Local Newspaper (1952)

Magic Electrons: Terra Incognita (1949)
Major Farming (1953)
Man of Africa (1953)
Men and Machines (1950)
Mining Review (series) (1948)

NEL Offshore News (1975)
North Sea Strike (1968)

'Oil Review' series: No.5 (1950)

Powered Flight: the Story of the Century (1953)
Power for All (1950)

Queen o' the Border (1948)

Report on Steel (1948)
Roses Tattoo (1956)
Royal Tour – New Zealand (1954)

Science in the Orchestra (1950)

The Fair County of Ayr (1949)
The Frasers of Cabot Cove (1949)
The Island (1952)
The Riddle of Japan (1949)
The Struggle for Oil (1949)
This Farming Business (1949)
This is Britain (series) (1950)
Trieste: Problem City (1949)

Warm Welcome (1952)
Welcome the Queen! (1954)
When you went away (1949)
Where Britain Stands (1950)
Women in Our Time (1948)

Index of titles

This index contains films, documentaries and TV programmes, including alternative and US titles. Numbers in **bold** indicate main articles (for films).

Printed in Great Britain
by Amazon